Unmarried Couples

A Guide to Your Legal Rights
and Obligations

Unmarried Couples

A Guide to Your Legal Rights and Obligations

Elliot D. Samuelson, J.D.

With a Foreword by
Raoul Lionel Felder, Esq.

INSIGHT BOOKS

Plenum Press • New York and London

Library of Congress Cataloging-in-Publication Data

Samuelson, Elliot D.
    Unmarried couples : a guide to your legal rights and obligations /
  Elliot D. Samuelson ; with a foreword by Raoul Lionel Felder.
      p.   cm.
    Includes bibliographical references (p.   ) and index.
    ISBN 0-306-44322-8
    1. Unmarried couples--Legal status, laws, etc.--United States.
  I. Title.
  KF538.S26   1992
  346.7301'6--dc20
  [347.30616]   92-17045
                                                             CIP

ISBN 0-306-44322-8

© 1992 Plenum Press, New York
A Division of Plenum Publishing Corporation
233 Spring Street, New York, N.Y. 10013

An Insight Book

Printed in the United States of America

To Bea,

My living-together partner of thirty years

Acknowledgments

I wish to acknowledge the editorial assistance of Evelyn Rubin and Mitchell Kulick, who helped to make this work possible.

Foreword

Anyone in today's society who decides to live together with another person in a shared residence, with or without children, owes it to himself or herself to read this book to learn of the legal entanglements that may be caused by such a relationship. *Unmarried Couples* is perhaps the first book of its kind to explain to the public, in a clear, cogent, and readable manner, the risks that may be encountered and the corresponding financial rights that one may receive from this more and more commonly accepted lifestyle.

I have not read a more informative book that treats such a broad group of personal relationships, including never married and divorced persons, senior citizens, and gay and lesbian couples. Written by one of this country's most respected matrimonial lawyers, Elliot Samuelson's *Unmarried Couples* is chock full of practical advice for such persons (referred to by the author as *domestic partners*). He delves into issues that uniquely affect their lives, including living-together and prenuptial agreements; estate, pension, and inheritance rights and planning; rights and obligations stemming from common-law marriages; housing and employment discrimination; adoption, custody, and visitation of children; and the corresponding legal obligation to support a child not legally adopted.

Special attention is given to each group. For example, the

book contains a recommended living-together agreement to protect domestic partners against both unwanted support obligations and lost property rights. Senior citizens who must sometimes choose, for financial reasons, to live together without getting married often encounter the problem of caring for their partner when he or she later becomes seriously ill. The author discusses the use of living wills, health care proxies and durable powers of attorney, and the legal difficulties of gays and lesbians and their battles with sexual discrimination concerning their own lifestyle, as well as their need to adopt children or obtain custody or visitation rights. The subjects are fully reviewed and tastefully treated.

Elliot Samuelson has managed to produce a singularly authoritative book that is easily read and understood by any person without any legal background. At the same time, *Unmarried Couples* ought to be required reading for any lawyer unfamiliar with the legal needs of domestic partners. Mr. Samuelson writes with depth, sensitivity, and understanding. He has called upon his thirty-one years of extensive experience as a prominent, nationally recognized legal authority in the field of domestic relations to produce a book that is destined to become a classic for anyone who must consider legal rights or obligations before moving in or out of a shared residence with a "significant other."

RAOUL LIONEL FELDER

Contents

Explores the emotional trauma encountered by
persons recently single because of death or
divorce, their fears, loneliness, and abilities to
cope with their new life relationships.

With the mourning period concluded, the
recently single person begins to reaccept the
challenges of business and family and to
resume financial, cultural, and social activities.

The legal rights and obligations that can be
imputed to the living-together couple are
discussed. Ability to enter into written or oral
agreements that can avoid unwanted legal
implications. Negotiating tips and suggestions
for contents of agreements.

Discusses the ways legal rights can be enforced by the spurned spouse or lover and the need to obtain psychological support to withstand the disruption caused by an unwanted separation. Ways by which to sustain, as well as break, written agreements are examined. Courtroom procedures, witness preparation, and attorney contact are also reviewed.

Methods to employ in order to ensure the selection of a skilled attorney or health care professional. Things to look for when interviewing a lawyer or psychiatrist.

A detailed listing of organizations to aid the living-together couple or newly single persons.

APPENDIXES

Introduction

As the rate of divorce and the likelihood of remarriage increases, most people will at some time in their adult lives be faced with the moral and legal dilemmas of living together with another person without benefit of marriage. Still others will be widowed, adding to the growing number of single persons within the United States who may enter into informal living-together arrangements.

The unwary may be thrust into a legal relationship with a live-in companion and incur legal obligations or entitlements that they never dreamt possible.

The law governing the relationship of couples living together without formal marriage vows is in its infancy but is rapidly developing. The mores of our society now readily accept divorce and nonmarital living arrangements. Who would have thought some years ago that divorce would become socially acceptable or that a president of the United States could attain such office with a previously severed marriage? Because the pool of single persons within our country continues to swell each year due to divorce or death, it is more than likely that most every adult, regardless of his or her sexual preference, will one day be forced to deal with the legal and psychological implications of living together.

In many instances the problems that arise between partners contemplating a later marriage and partners who do not may be similar to each other, but the laws governing premarital agree-

1

ments are more defined and have been chiseled into society over a far greater period of time. The laws of most states permit parties to marry or remarry and contract with each other as to how they will distribute their property in the event of death. It was usually possible for one or both spouses to waive their inheritance rights or to elect a spousal share against a will provision, whether there was a provision in the will for the spouse or not. This is true since in almost all states in the absence of agreement it is not possible to disinherit your spouse. However, until most recently, it was generally impossible to contract for the waiver of alimony, support, or the distribution of property in the event of divorce. Now, with the advent of both community property and equitable distribution laws, all this has changed, and parties may freely opt out of state divorce laws, forge legal agreements that may vary existing rules, or ignore such laws regarding property and support divisions between spouses. Whether couples who live together can enter into similar agreements uniformly throughout the United States remains to be seen, but recent developments in the law appear to portend such rights.

Couples who live together in one of the 13 common-law states or the District of Columbia (see Appendix A) may, under certain circumstances, be considered legally married as though they had obtained a marriage license and participated in a formal ceremony. Moreover, even couples who reside in states that do not recognize common-law marriages may incur the legal obligations of marriage by visiting a common-law state and holding themselves out as husband and wife. The more difficult question to answer is whether couples who live together for many years and have had children and then separate will be accorded the same benefits as married couples if they have no written agreements between them.

When children are born or brought into a living-together relationship, there are additional legal concerns. In a *New York Times* article (July 23, 1991) entitled "Children of Divorce: Steps to Help Can Hurt," the emotional trauma to children caused by the conflicts between their parents was studied. The article noted that one-half of the marriages contracted in the 1970s will end in divorce and that although society has reduced the scorn and shame associated with such separation, there appear to be no signs of alleviating the anguish of children of separating parents. Referring to a study of 110 American families, the article pointed out that during the years immediately preceding divorce or separation, the children may show the same developmental disturbances that are typical of children of divorce. The article concluded that when divorced parents remarry, there is greater stress introduced into the lives of the children than they experienced even during the divorce. When parents remarry, the children undergo radical changes in personality and may experience great hostility to their parents, no matter how hard the stepparent seeks to establish a warm and caring interaction with the child. These problems, as well as the financial and legal obligations of support, are dealt with in this book.

There may be circumstances where the law will compel a person to support a child whom he or she has lived with, even though the person is not the child's natural or adoptive parent. This book will also examine the doctrine of implied adoption and the obligations to support children, including assuming the costs of advanced education, that are based upon the past conduct of the person from whom support is sought.

One of the most fascinating and potentially explosive areas of emerging law in this country is the adjustment of legal rights of domestic partners. The courts presently are wrestling with these problems and attempting to achieve a balance between public policy that does not desire to recognize out-of-wedlock relationships and the need to protect individuals who live together against injustices, particularly with respect to their property rights and support obligations. Whether justice and fairness to cohabitants will be uniformly obtained remains an open question.

Armed with this knowledge, readers can readily understand that it is important to consider the following issues when contemplating a first, second, or later marriage or simply an informal living-together relationship: what the legal and psychological ramifications of such an arrangement might be; how to preserve previously owned property as well as the enhanced value of property that may accrue during the relationship; and what obligations to pay or rights to receive support or property in the event of death or separation.

Although at first blush most single persons entering into an informal living-together relationship may feel that they will not have to address such concerns unless they legally marry, this instinctive belief is not necessarily so; such individuals may incur legal obligations or obtain legal rights without actually intending to do so.

It is these potential entanglements that are thoroughly treated throughout this book, which, it is hoped, will transpose the unwary into knowing and informed persons, fully recognizing the risks, obligations, and potential benefits that can accrue to the unmarried couple. Similarly, through the use of illustrations and easily understood fact patterns, readers will become fully informed of the rights and obligations a legal marriage will provide so that they can intelligently participate, along with their attorney, in the successful negotiation of a pre- or postmarital agreement that will be enforced in the courts in the event of a later legal attack. In the appendices are sample agreements that can be adapted to both circumstances (but, of course, cannot be used indiscriminately by the reader without regard to his or her particular situation and financial circumstances). While it is always best to consult with an attorney when dealing with complex legal issues, the knowledge to be garnered within these pages will certainly enable readers to gauge the exposure and potential risks that may arise between the time they find themselves single and the time they begin a new relationship or once again say, "I do."

Other areas discussed in this book include the legal and psychological impact upon gay couples and seniors who decide to live together without marriage. The term *domestic partnership* has evolved to refer to either straight or gay couples who live together and share housing and financial responsibilities. A growing number of public and private employers are now extending equal benefits to domestic partners. For example, municipal employees in cities such as Seattle, Berkeley, and Madison, Wisconsin, enjoy recently enacted laws that entitle domestic partners to receive the same death benefits, pensions, and the like as married partners. Some universities and colleges throughout the country, as well as some nonprofit organizations such as the American Psychological Association, the Metropolitan Museum of Art in New York City, and the American Friends Service Committee, have already provided benefits for domestic partners that were formerly accorded only to married partners. Recently, the highest court in New York State recognized the right of a gay man's surviving life partner to take over his interest in a rent-controlled apartment,[1] deciding that the survivor was part of the decedent's family within the meaning of the law. However, although these recent developments appear to be according equal benefits to cohabiting couples, there are still many employers who do not recognize couples living together who have adopted what they consider an unpopular lifestyle.

According to the United States Chamber of Commerce, up to 40% of a worker's remuneration comes in the form of fringe benefits. There are many who believe that a policy that uses marital status or sexual orientation as the basis for determining who receives these benefits is grossly unfair and contrary to the equal protection clause of the Constitution. Nonetheless, discrimination based upon lack of marital status continues to be pervasive, despite opinion polls taken by *Time* magazine and the Cable News Network that found that 54% of the adults surveyed believed significant job-related benefits should be extended to unmarried partners, whether gay or heterosexual.

Determining whether domestic partners should fit into the definition of a family was explored by the American Home Economic Association, which adopted a definition of a family unit as "two or more persons who share resources, share responsibilities for decisions, share values and goals, and have a commitment to one another over time . . . regardless of blood, legal ties, adoption or marriage."

Currently, the cities of San Francisco, Seattle, and Madison, Wisconsin, have adopted domestic partnership laws that enable heterosexual or gay couples to register their relationships at City Hall. The law is largely symbolic. It does not accord to such domestic partners the benefits that married couples receive, but it allows them to declare that they have lived together for at least six months and to certify their promise to share living expenses together. It appears that the public recognition of the relationship was the matter of importance to such couples, among whom, of course, are homosexual partners. It has been predicted that these new registration laws will provide the basis for living-together couples to contest issues like employee benefits, insurance coverage, and division of property.

Senior citizens who decide to live together are also a subject addressed in this book. Whether to marry or not may depend upon what loss of social security benefits may occur if marital vows are taken. In addition, a senior citizen must be especially cautious entering into such a relationship because of the likelihood of illness accompanying advanced years. When illness strikes a senior citizen, his or her partner, whether married or not, may very well incur substantial financial obligations for medical treatment, hospitalization, nursing, and nursing-home expenses. Dealing with a terminal illness and drawing a health care proxy, living will, or durable power of attorney, together with their legal distinctions, are all explained in detail in Chapter 11.

All of these topics are explored at length within the pages of this book. Living together without benefit of marriage may become a recognized lifestyle, but it has yet to be accorded equal legal status by the courts and our state legislators. It seems unwise, if not potentially catastrophic, for a person today to consider a relationship with a significant other without knowing what the legal and psychological implications of such a relationship may lead to. It is for this reason that this book has been written.

Note

1. *Braschi v. Stahl Assoc. Co.*, 74 N.Y.2d 201, 543 N.E.2d 49, 544 N.Y.S.2d 784 (1989).

Chapter 1

Uncoupling

The Initial Shock

You have just lost your spouse to a protracted illness spanning many months. The previous years of companionship, commitment, and childrearing, the day-to-day joys and challenges of marriage are now but a distant memory. The bonds that have provided security and emotional stability are now shattered. No longer will there be a friend to share life's problems and vicissitudes. No longer can you experience the touch of a familiar hand, an understanding glance, the security of a warm and loving home. Tears now replace laughter, and there is a sense of desperation and fear for what life will now bring forth. Sadness, loneliness, depression, anger, and hopelessness are all emotional elements of the mourning process that now besets you and assails your former positive disposition and optimistic outlook on life. For many, the emotional trauma caused by the death of one's spouse will cast an indelible pall over the future and their ability to enter into a meaningful relationship with another person for many years. For others, the mourning period will be of shorter duration but by no means less devastating or emotionally draining.

The loss of a spouse because of divorce or separation evokes similar emotional responses and is not at all dissimilar to the mourning period experienced by a person whose loved one has

7

died. In fact, many persons going through a divorce proceeding have expressed the view that the process is akin to the prolonged illness and death of their partner. In truth, the experiences can be quite similar. Persons who have experienced separation from their spouse by either death or divorce must now begin the difficult process of learning to cope in the single world. They enter a period of self-evaluation, and some must deal with a self-imposed and unfounded guilt for causing the divorce, death, or illness.[1] It is not unusual for self-recriminations to flow: "If only I had insisted that she go to another doctor"; "If only I had not caused him so much anxiety"; "If only I had been more attentive during the illness"; "It was my fault that he left; I was spending too much"; "I did not do enough to understand her needs"; "I did not try hard enough to make the marriage work." All such statements of remorse are spoken over and over again by individuals who find themselves alone and in a process of self-assessment, one that, hopefully, will lead to rehabilitation, renewed self-esteem, and an ability to go on with life and enter into new and meaningful relationships. One fact is clear: there must be an acceptance of the loss and its impact before the healing process can begin.

The First Step toward Recovery

Several days or perhaps a week after the funeral or the granting of a formal divorce judgment, people must return to the point where life seemed to halt. Those who were employed will return to work; others must return to the demanding duties of running a home and rearing children. All now sense the real effect of the severance of the relationship. There is no one to come home to, there is no one who will be coming home. All decisions now must be made alone, without counsel or guidance from your spouse or companion. The problems with the children can no longer be shared. There is no one to talk with before falling asleep, no one with whom to share the intimacy of marriage, its challenges, pains, and exhilarations. In a word, you are alone, and the loneliness will be the greatest difficulty to overcome or accept.

However, the acceptance of the separation from the partner may ultimately be the catalyst for finding the strength and will to seek a new companion. If acceptance is delayed, loneliness can lead to a depression that is far more perverse and debilitating. It may be so stifling that friends and family cannot offer sufficient solace, and the individual may need to seek the advice of a psychiatric social worker, a psychologist, or a psychiatrist. Once the problem is recognized and professional help sought, the loneliness and depression, as well as other emotional difficulties, can then be explored and treated, with a view to helping the sufferer resume an active and fulfilling life and enter into new social relationships.

In addition to access to individual psychotherapy, most communities throughout the country have churches, synagogues, or other houses of worship that maintain group counseling services for their parishioners. There are also group therapy programs sponsored by local hospitals, schools, universities, and self-help or civic groups such as Parents Without Partners and the National Organization for Women. The recognition that one cannot cope with the difficulties following the loss of a spouse should be made at the earliest possible moment, before symptoms produce clinical depression, which may require the ongoing care of a physician, medication, and/or hospitalization, a result to assiduously resist and avoid.

There have been many books written on the subject of coping with the emotional impact of death or divorce, any one of which may prove helpful to the individual who has been able to handle the adjustment period with a minimum of difficulty.[2]

The important point to ponder is whether you are able to get your life in order by yourself, aided by family or friends, or whether this goal is unattainable without professional counseling. The longer you defer the decision to get such counseling, the more intense the problems may become, with the course of treatment being prolonged and the potential for even deeper trauma and emotional illness becoming greater. This self-assessment may be extremely difficult to make; you must listen carefully to those with whom you have frequent contact and who can consider your mental state from an objective viewpoint. Listen to others who care about you and who recognize that you are not adjusting capably within a reasonable period following the loss. We all have a tendency to deny an emotional problem, fearing that it will be regarded as a social stigma or a sign of weakness. But such denial is an invitation to disaster and almost a confirmation of the emotional difficulties. By acknowledging your need for counseling you are taking the first step toward returning to emotional health and your position as a well-adjusted member of society. You, your children, and the people around you whom you care about and love deserve no less.

The Woman's Dilemma

The vicissitudes of separation from your partner include still other considerations. Women who have not previously been in the work force or handled financial matters are now thrust headlong into the problem of securing employment to supplement the support they may be receiving or the money they may have inherited, at the same time that they may be continuing to fulfill the responsibility of raising a family. "What skills do I have?"; "Am I employable if I have not worked since before the marriage?"; and "How will I be able to tend to the children and at the same time pursue a career?" are all meaningful questions that require careful thought, exploration, and analysis.

The initial reaction to these and other similar questions may, understandably, be fear and despair. Yet women must find comfort in the fact that they are not alone and that many other women have dealt with these very problems and have satisfactorily resolved what may appear at first to be an insurmountable problem. The comfort a woman may draw from this fact, together with determination, can lessen the impact of these serious concerns, enabling her to deal with them effectively. Franklin D. Roosevelt once remarked, in the depths of American despair during World War II as Japanese bombs destroyed Pearl Harbor, "There is nothing to fear but fear itself." These eloquent words are no less meaningful to the separating spouse who must do battle with life's cruelest pronouncements. Again, the sense of desperation experienced in 1941 by the British people while they huddled together in underground compartments in fear for their lives because of Nazi air strikes is akin to the helplessness experienced by the woman who is suddenly thrust into the situation in which she alone, though ill-equipped and unprepared to accept such responsibilities, must support and guide the family.

A long journey must begin by a single step. That step is taken when there is a realization that accepting the challenge is the beginning of the walk on the path to recovery and a return to the status of a well-adjusted adult who is able to function effectively and enjoy the pleasures of life. The ways in which this rehabilitation can occur, enabling you to return to vocational, family, financial, cultural, and social activities, is discussed in subsequent chapters.

The Man's Dilemma

The plight of a man faced with the loss of a spouse through death or divorce may be somewhat different, but no less severe than the woman's. When children are involved, he too is faced with new concerns: "How will I be able to cope with getting the children off to school and being at home for them before my work is ended?"; "If I obtain a housekeeper, how can I be sure she will be good with the kids?" And he too fears the future and suffers from self-recrimination: "How will I be able to adjust to being single again?"; "The marriage failed because I am a failure"; "If I had been more caring and concerned, this would never have happened." Thus, although dealing with financial problems and engaging in meaningful employment may not be concerns for a man, the fear of being alone and rearing children present serious challenges. When a divorce does not result in a father receiving custody of a child, visitation problems often take on serious proportions. "Will the divorce interfere with my relationship with the children?" is perhaps the most frequent question. A father worries that the animosity engendered between him and his wife during the divorcing process may spill over and affect his relationship with his children. Being an absentee father is a totally foreign experience and presents challenges that will require great sensitivity and empathy for the needs of the children, and perhaps even professional consultation. Organizations exist nationally, such as Parents Without Partners, that address these concerns, conduct group therapy or rap sessions, and are able to make referrals to health care professionals when the need exists.

The emotional concerns of men are no different from those of women, discussed earlier in this chapter. The sense of loneliness and frustration and the fear and uncertainty of what the future may bring are indeed gender-neutral and are shared by everyone who has endured the hardships of separation caused by death or divorce. Men, as well as women, are well advised to seek professional counseling when a reasonable period of time has passed and they are unable to "get hold of" themselves and return to their previous pursuits without feelings of deep depression. Often, loss of appetite and lack of interest in one's job or social activities portend serious problems and may be telltale symptoms of clinical depression. Being able to recognize these signs is a first step toward eliminating them. Men may also exhibit symptoms of sexual dysfunction, as well as a loss of interest in sexual activities (as may women), symptoms that more often follow death of the partner than loss through divorce. The path to effective coping with such common reactions is the recognition that a problem exists, coupled with the desire to effect a change. When a man cannot accomplish this by himself, professional treatment is indicated and necessary.

Many young people in today's society choose to live together without thought of, or perhaps as a prelude to, marriage. Their separations can cause profound emotional upheaval, not dissimilar to what divorcing couples experience. Still others have chosen to live together, rather than marry, following an earlier divorce. As will be observed later in this book, their legal, social, and emotional relationships and their abilities to cope with them will be vastly similar to older people who live together because of a death or divorce.

Notes

1. See, for example, Patrick Mullahay, *Oedipus Myth and Complex: A Review of Psychoanalytic Theory* (New York: Hermitage House, 1953).
2. See, for example, Lily Pincus, *Death and the Family: The Importance of Mourning* (New York: Pantheon Books, 1974); Therese A. Rando, *Grieving: How to Go on Living When Someone You Love Dies* (Lexington, MA: Lexington Books, 1988); Judy Blume, *It's Not the End of the World* (Toronto: Bantam Books, 1972); and William Josiah Goode, *After Divorce* (Glencoe, IL: Free Press, 1956).

Chapter 2

Rebirth and New Beginnings

The mourning period has at last come to an end. The period of rebirth has begun. New friends, new responsibilities, new challenges have become realities. The air smells fresher. It is easier to get up in the morning and easier to fall asleep at night. The children seem to have adjusted to their new situation, going to work again becomes a joy, and dating is no longer the frightening enterprise it was perceived to be following the loss of the partner. *New beginnings* is a phrase commonly spoken, but reaching this point is not easy or free of pain; it requires much effort and involves, at times, deprivation and apprehension. How does one reach this point in life and leave behind the tumultuous past? Only through hard work, a desire to overcome adversity, and the adoption of achievable and realistic goals for change.

When does the healing process begin that will enable you to accept anew the challenges of family and work and to participate once again in diverse cultural and social activities? The answer will depend upon your emotional stability, the bond that existed between you and your former partner, and the degree to which you are prepared to face the realities of your circumstances and accept the fact that dwelling on the past is not only counterproductive but an incubator for mental distress that will prolong the pain

15

and exacerbate any mental afflictions that may have been caused by the loss of the partner. Whether this juncture is reached with or without the aid of a mental health professional is of less importance than achieving this end. Because of the support received by a dedicated friend or member of the family, some people will traverse this path at a quick pace, others will do so with less rapidity, and still others will experience the therapist's couch in their quest for rebirth, but all share the achievement of healing and recovery.

Coping in the Single World: The Children

After healing occurs, attention must be directed toward integrating into the single world and meeting its demands. For both newly single men and women the first concern is the care of their children when they return to work (or, in the case of homemakers, enter the work force for the first time). Where finances are sufficient, the selection of a housekeeper, as opposed to seeking out a competent child care center, may be the first important decision to be made. As with most other selections regarding personal service, a word of mouth recommendation is probably more reliable than the results of placing an ad in a local newspaper or scanning the situations-wanted columns. Asking around the office or consulting with other persons who have lost a spouse is so obvious that it might be overlooked as a viable method to find a competent housekeeper who is good with children. Employment agencies abound that specialize in domestic help and may be well worth the fee charged since they will screen all applicants and carefully check their references. However, even when working with a reputable agency, it is essential to conduct an in-depth personal interview in your home, so that the candidate will be familiar with your home environment and can meet the children and you can assess their reactions to each other. The personal interview is your opportunity to let your prospective employee know what will be expected of her and to discuss any difficulties she may encounter in your home. Someone who does not have prior extensive experience in caring for children in a single-parent home should be immediately excluded. Where a pet is an integral part of the family, the candidate must be free of allergies and have no fear of animals. The ability to independently prepare appetizing and nutritious meals is another important consideration to discuss with the applicant. Days off, vacation time, and every duty she will be asked to perform must be disclosed before, not after, the job begins. By doing so you can avoid the complaint "You never told me I would have to do that." Nothing should be left for future discussion or negotiation. Any potential problems should be fully explored since it may be especially harmful and disruptive to the children if it becomes necessary to seek a new housekeeper even before they have adjusted to the loss of the other parent.

If it is possible, a trial weekend in the home may prove to be the best test of whether the person selected will blend into the routines of the family and is a competent and caring individual. The way in which she speaks and reacts to the children, her degree of tolerance for stressful situations, and her ability to cope with the demands of your particular home life can only be determined under actual live-in conditions. By exercising these cautions, hiring the wrong person, with its own attendant trauma and disappointments, can be avoided.

When family finances do not permit the employment of a caretaker for the children who will also act as a housekeeper in the home, several alternatives must be explored. The first choice would be a willing relative, friend, or neighbor who may be able to keep an eye on school-age children for a few hours between the time school is concluded and the time you arrive home from your job. The demands are not great, and you may be surprised to learn that one or more persons are willing to lend a hand to enable you to enter or return to the work force.

Of course, preschool children require far more time and attention from a caretaker, and your search for help will necessarily lead you to determine the child care facilities available in your community. There will be many to choose from in cities with sizable populations. Churches and synagogues offer these services to their congregations and, at times, to the community at large. Governmental units such as states, cities, towns, and villages may also sponsor child care centers. Again, the recommendation by a parent whose child already attends the child care program will prove invaluable to a satisfactory placement. There are a variety of private organizations such as Kinder Care; Children's Discovery Centers of America; Children's World Learning Centers; and Rocking Horse Child Care Centers of America that may provide acceptable care, and the availability of these private services in your community should be examined.

Coping in the Single World: Finances

For many women or men who have not been involved in the financial matters of the home, the separation from a partner presents serious problems. Coping with personal finances, which includes paying the bills and budgeting expenses, as well as adopting a prudent investment plan, can be a difficult adjustment. For some, obtaining a competent accountant and/or investment adviser is of prime importance. A skilled certified public accountant can assist with budgets and payment schedules in addition to rendering tax advice and tax planning. Some may be willing to assist and offer advice with respect to investment options while others will refuse to do so and may refer you to a seasoned investment planner. An officer of a local bank might also be a source of information on local investment opportunities. Numerous books have been written on the subject, and local adult education programs offer a myriad of courses in these fields. There is no such thing as too much knowledge; the more sources of information you look into, the more conversant with the subject you will become, enabling you to ask cogent questions that will provide you with the answers you seek. It would be unwise to accept recommendations from salespeople before acquiring a general working knowledge of investment opportunities: mutual fund salesmen, life insurance agents, and investment brokers all have a singular point of view and may exert pressure upon you to make quick decisions. Resist the temptation to do so, and instead give yourself a chance to seriously reflect upon the recommendation and to discuss it with an accountant, attorney, or a personal investment adviser. There are few investment opportunities that will disappear within 24 hours, so the need to respond immediately should not be taken seriously.

Once a person has reasonably solved the problems of child care and finances, the social challenges of the single world will become a priority.

Coping in the Single World: The Singles Scene

Social activities for singles abound. Some have made a substantial living catering to the needs of singles for social intercourse. One need only peruse the personal want ads of local newspapers and regional magazines to realize that the quest for a mate today includes the utilization of mass media. Local civic, religious, and governmental agencies run a plethora of programs that appeal to singles and encourage new relationships. Organizations such as Parents Without Partners, National Organization for Women, and Single Gourmet abound. Local branches of the YMCA or YMHA conduct additional social and educational activities, classes, and programs. Even the local phone directory will provide information on other organizations existing within your community. To your delight, you will even learn that your coworkers, friends, and relatives are eager for you to meet a "friend" who has also entered the single world. With your first social contact, regardless of how it was arranged, your mourning period will have come to an end and your new life begins.

Few of us will by choice live alone. The warmth, companionship, and love of another individual is sought by all of us. Young singles search out the singles scene searching for mates. Divorced or widowed individuals are more likely to remarry than their never-married age peers. All share the common quest for companionship, and all will necessarily incur the same legal involvements. To the uninformed, these legal implications can have an unwanted but profound effect upon their lives. Let us now explore these awesome legal rights and obligations.

Chapter 3

The New Relationship
Its Legal Impact

A companion that you feel you are about to enter a meaningful relationship with has at last been found. Behind you are the singles bars, the clubs joined, and the casual obligatory dates. Not sure enough of the relationship to allow yourself to contemplate marriage yet, you now consider whether to suggest to the person in your life that you live together. Furthest from your mind is the thought of entering into a relationship that can impose upon you legal obligations of support or of division of any property you may acquire during this time that you will be living together. In fact, few people are even aware that the law can impose unwanted legal obligations as well as impute the state of matrimony itself. To the unwary, the obligation to pay alimony and child support or to divide property may soon become a shocking reality. This chapter deals exclusively with the contractual relationships, either expressed or implied, that can result from cohabitation, while later ones will explore common-law marriages and the obligations to support children born of the relationship or brought into it by either party.

One might ask how there can be any legal obligations associated with living together when the state of your residence does not recognize common-law marriages—and you never even travel to a common-law state during your relationship. At first blush it might be reasonable to conclude that none exists, but recent developing case law throughout the United States renders such a conclusion not only inaccurate but extremely dangerous. The fact is that contractual obligation, known to the law since biblical times, is being applied with increasing frequency to couples who have decided not to enter into formal marriage but nevertheless conduct themselves in a fashion similar to that of married persons.

Nature of the Contract

How can a contract be implied in law? Through a variety of ways and circumstances. To understand the theory, consider the following illustration. You have arrived at a busy airport and have some time to kill. You spy a bootblack chair and decide to have your shoes shined. Climbing the steep step, you seat yourself and place one shoe on the metal stirrup. The bootblack picks up a large brush and begins to briskly rub the surface of your black loafer. Neither you nor the bootblack has uttered one word to the other, yet a contract between you has been made that is no less binding than a formal written agreement that has been negotiated and signed. This is an example of a contract that has been made by *implication of law*.

Contracts may take two forms. They may be written or oral (except when prohibited by an express state law—known sometimes as a *statute of frauds*—that requires a contract to be in writing in order for it to be legal and binding). For example, contracts to sell real estate are, for the most part, required to be in writing in most states. They may also be expressed in words or implied (that is, no words are spoken but the conduct of the parties is sufficient to warrant the imposition of contractual obligations between them). Our bootblack and customer exchanged no words, yet their implied contract would have been no stronger if it had had all the formal trappings of a written agreement replete with frequent *whereas* and *wherefore* flourishes.

Contracts are made when one person makes an offer to another person who, in turn, accepts the offer in the identical terms made. If the acceptance is conditional or sets forth new terms, it is deemed to be a new offer or, as the law calls it, a counteroffer, which will require an acceptance from the person who made the original offer in order for a contract to be formed. The other formal requirement contained in the law books, in addition to the offer and acceptance, is that there be "a good and valuable consideration" to support the offer and acceptance.

What does this language mean? Is consideration some deep and esoteric concept that only lawyers and judges can understand? Absolutely not. The term simply requires that something of value pass hands or that there be an act performed, or the forbearance of an act (discussed in the next paragraph), that is consistent with the offer and acceptance.

These concepts can best be understood by returning to our bootblack–customer illustration. Already discussed was the offer and acceptance. What was the consideration? The mutuality of consideration that the law requires was the completion of the shoe shine by the bootblack and the payment of the fee by the customer. In most circumstances, it is the performance of a service or the transfer of goods, coupled with the payment of money, that forms the necessary consideration that the law requires. Purchasing food at the supermarket, bringing clothing to the dry cleaner, and eating at a restaurant are all contractual relationships that occur without any writing and are completed by the payment of money and the receipt of the goods or services from the selling party. Sometimes, the forbearance or withholding of an act or certain conduct may form a sufficient consideration. For example, when a person buys a business, the purchaser is usually concerned that the seller may open in the same area a competing business similar to the one sold and thereby materially reduce the volume of business or customers that existed when the business was purchased. This is a major concern of any prospective purchaser of a business. In order to eliminate this threat, the purchaser frequently requires that the seller refrain from competing with the purchaser in a similar business within a prescribed geographic location for a specified period of time. In short, the seller has agreed to refrain (forbear) from some conduct he is free to pursue, a concession that constitutes the consideration necessary to support the contract. The seller may expect an additional payment from the purchaser for such forbearance, and an additional sum of money to be paid by the purchaser is, in fact, normally negotiated.

When does a failure of consideration occur that will prevent a contract from being formed or will cause it to be considered illegal? Had the bootblack failed to finish shining your shoes, through no fault of your own, there would have been a failure of consideration; despite the fact that an offer and acceptance had taken place, there would be no obligation for you to pay for the incompleted shoe shine. Sometimes, consideration is deemed illegal, such as, in some states, providing gambling services or the attempt to transfer illicit goods or services. Far more relevant to the matters discussed in this book are contracts to provide sexual services, which are frequently regarded as illegal consideration. Depending upon the state in which you reside, this very concept, as will be seen later in this chapter, may determine whether the living-together couple can be held to have entered into a binding contract. However, it is sufficient to note at this juncture that the mere fact that a sexual relationship exists, among the myriad other activities of persons living in the same household, will not prevent a contract from being formed in many states.

Why is it important for you to understand these basic concepts affecting contractual relationships? Once understood, will they enable you to prevent unwanted liability? The answer is decidedly yes, since legal liability is incurred whenever a contract, either written or oral, express or implied, has been made by parties because of their conduct or because of what was said by them before or during their living-together relationship. Once you understand these principles, it may be possible for you to take steps to avoid a liability that might otherwise occur, to avoid a consequence you were not even aware could follow from what you deemed to be such innocent behavior. Forewarned means being forearmed.

In recent years more and more couples contemplating marriage or remarriage are considering, and in some instances insisting upon, a prenuptial agreement in order to prevent property acquired before marriage from being distributed by a divorce court. There is also concern for the right of the surviving spouse to inherit the partner's property despite the existence of a will. (This is frequently referred to as the right of election of a surviving spouse; in most states one cannot disinherit a surviving spouse in the absence of waiver contained in a written agreement.) Today, the prenuptial agreement may even contain binding provisions for the amount of alimony ("maintenance," in some states) that need be paid following divorce or for a division of property acquired during marriage that can differ from state law directives. Some jurisdictions refer to these contracts as "opting out."[1] Despite the different names, they are all agreements entered before marriage that control the legal obligations acquired during the marriage in the event of death, divorce, or separation; such agreements will be discussed at length in chapter 10. Whether an agreement by those who live together but never marry will be recognized in the state in which they reside depends on a number of factors, unless in that particular state such agreements are specifically excluded since they are held to be contracts solely for the performance of sexual favors (and thereby considered void). You are strongly advised to consult an attorney if any doubt exists as to the rules that apply in your home state. Certainly, even in states that presently prohibit contracts for sexual favors or in states that hold that living-together couples do so solely because of this reason, the law frequently can change rapidly; what was once unacceptable conduct can become an accepted practice.

Setting Up House

You have made a commitment to live together. It is not a decision that has been lightly made. The many nights engaged in conversation until the early morning hours, the moments of indecision, the fear and anxiety of entering such an intimate relationship—all that is behind you, and there is a sense of guarded anticipation for better things to come. Or are better things to come? Will each of you be free at any time to call it quits and simply walk away? Of course, one cannot ever do so without emotional distress. Leaving a person with whom you have shared for a protracted period a home and companionship, the problems and rewards of life, is at best an unsettling experience. When you are left by the other person, it can present even greater trauma. The trauma associated with the legal obligations that may possibly flow to the former partner will certainly be equal to, if not far greater than, that experienced prior to and at the time of separation. These possible legal obligations are addressed in the following paragraphs.

Accentuate the Negative and Eliminate the Positive

The single best way to attempt to eliminate legal entanglement is to keep one's mouth shut concerning support or the sharing of property and avoid making the following statements: "We'll be partners and share things equally"; "I will always provide for you"; "Anything that we acquire will be ours"; and "As long as you take care of me, I will always be there for you." All such phrases are to be avoided since they impart an implied, if not an express, promise of support and an understanding that there will be some kind of a division of property or support in the event of separation. If you are totally unwilling to accept such obligations, there must be an affirmative declaration on your part not to do so. Clearly advise your mate that there are to be no financial commitments, using language such as the following:

> I can make you no promises as to the future; as long as we live together, I will share our expenses.

> There can be no expectation that we will divide any property purchased or acquired during our relationship, nor will I agree to ever do so. While I will pay for some expenses as

long as we live together, I will not do so when we decide to
part.

These words impart a present intention not to become obligated
for any support or division of property when a breakup occurs,
although they can never be a guarantee that a court, because of the
conduct exhibited during the relationship, will not find to the
contrary. On balance, there is far greater likelihood that a court
will conclude "no liability" following such a declaration to avoid
financial commitment than following promises to take care of the
person you plan to live with. Words alone might be used as a
shield, but they simply do not provide total protection.

Sometimes the length of the relationship coupled with the
rearing of children born out of the relationship can lead a court to
simply disregard the express language uttered and determine that
there must be an equitable financial adjustment made between the
parties. There are few absolutes in the law when it adjusts the lives
of marital partners or others who have lived together in a long-
term relationship. It would appear that the sympathies of the court
are more and more frequently accorded to persons living together,
especially in a long-term partnership, as society begins to recognize that such persons represent a substantial percentage of the
adult population. Regardless of the ultimate direction of the law,
one would do well to avoid positive pronouncements of financial
commitment and underscore the negative ones. The old Johnny
Mercer lyric to "accentuate the positive, eliminate the negative,
and don't mess with mister in-between" should be altered in your
mind to "accentuate the negative, eliminate the positive, and
certainly don't mess with mister in-between."

Getting It in Writing: Absolving Your Liability

While words alone are no assurance of eliminating legal
entanglements, they certainly cannot hurt. Lawyers refer to this
phenomenon as the "chicken soup approach." There is undoubt-

edly a better way to do things than to let a court interpret what your intentions really were, and that is to enter into a formal written agreement that will preserve your thoughts and goals and present far greater difficulty for a court to ignore.

A written agreement must be carefully drawn to avoid the conclusion by a judge that it lacks the necessary legal elements of a contract and is, therefore, unenforceable. It must clearly outline the scope and limits of your relationship. It must be unambiguous; there can be no dual interpretation of the intent of the parties in entering the agreement. It must be written in clear, concise, and intelligent language. It must meet the stringent requirements of any other legal contract that is normally made in the field of commerce.

The written agreement is too important a legal document for you to attempt to draw it yourself. An attorney in your state who is involved in marital or family law, that is, who is either certified in family law (if your state certifies specialists in the law) or a member of the American Academy of Matrimonial Lawyers (a national organization of attorneys devoted to the practice of family law), should be sought out for guidance and the drafting of the formal agreement. Appendices B and C contain formal agreements that may be helpful in discerning the points to be covered and the structure to be followed. The agreement should contain an express disclaimer of future support or property division, if that is one's goal, or the exact sums to be paid or property divided when such obligations are accepted. In addition, to avoid the danger of being subject to the legal obligations that are imparted to married persons by virtue of contracting a common-law marriage, you should avoid living in the states of Alabama, Colorado, Georgia, Idaho, Iowa, Kansas, Montana, Ohio, Oklahoma, Pennsylvania, Rhode Island, South Carolina, and Texas, and the District of Columbia. This danger may also occur if you and your partner travel to a common-law state and hold yourselves out as being married, since your home state must then recognize the common-law marriage; this is because the full faith and credit clause of the U.S. Constitution requires states to recognize the laws of its sister states. The written agreement may enable you to avoid this result if it clearly negates the intent of you and your partner from ever holding yourselves out as husband and wife. For example, if you and your partner reside in New York, a state that does not recognize common-law marriage, and travel to a common-law state such as Pennsylvania and during the visit present yourselves as husband and wife to the people you come in contact with, you may find that you are deemed married and that your home state is obliged to recognize the common-law marriage found in Pennsylvania. Once this occurs, you will be treated as a married person in New York for all intents and purposes, which includes the obligation to pay alimony, the right to receive such payment, and the right to share marital property acquired during your relationship following the Pennsylvania liaison. Common-law marriage will be discussed more fully in a later chapter; it is important here to understand that it is possible to anticipate in the written agreement the possibility of traveling to or through a common-law state and to provide language that at least aids the court in determining that either it was or was not your intention to hold yourself and mate out as husband and wife (such an intention is a necessary ingredient in ultimately determining that a common-law marriage was, in fact, consummated).

In order to avoid being considered partners in a common-law marriage, it is recommended that one or more of the following clauses be included in the written agreement:

1. The parties intend to reside together as single persons and not hold themselves out as husband and wife. They shall maintain their own independent identities, last names, and bank accounts.
2. The parties acknowledge that they may travel to a state that recognizes common-law marriage, but they have no intention of being considered as married persons and will do nothing that can be deemed consistent with the acts of a married couple.
3. It is the express desire of both parties that they waive the provisions of any state law that would accord marital status to either of them without their having entered into a

formal ceremonial marriage performed following the obtainment of a bona fide marriage license issued by a state
of competent jurisdiction.

4. If by the laws of any state the parties shall be declared to be
husband and wife, then the terms of this agreement shall
be deemed to be a prenuptial agreement, which shall
waive support against either party and shall waive any
division of property acquired during marriage by the laws
of either equitable distribution or community property.

5. No oral agreement between the parties shall be binding,
and any agreement to be enforceable must be in writing
and signed by both parties before a notary public.

These clauses will certainly go a long way in eliminating the
potential financial danger that may occur because of your live-in
relationship by operation of law or because of expressed oral
promises made between you and your partner. They will go a long
way toward preventing a common-law marriage from being imputed because of certain conduct exhibited in a common-law state
during the time the two of you lived together. They will go a long
way toward preventing unwanted liability for ongoing support
similar to alimony or property division, but such protection obviously cannot be obtained if one of you is unwilling to go along
with such a transient nonfinancial commitment (chapter 5 deals
with common-law marriage at length).

Getting It in Writing: Limiting Your Liability

At times it may be necessary to negotiate the terms of a living-
together agreement in which absolute waivers are neither acceptable nor intended. When this is the goal, the agreement can be of
great value since it will limit the obligations in a manner consistent
with the intentions of you and your partner. If it is your understanding that if and when you separate in the future you will
provide support in a fixed sum for a limited specified period, the

agreement can state this explicitly. Sometimes you might wish to limit the period during which support is paid to no longer than one-half of the period shared together, or some other time thought to provide sufficient expenses for a reasonable adjustment and relocation. The supported person might have left a job or career to remain at home and tend to your needs, the household, and perhaps children and may require a longer period of rehabilitation and training. There are no fixed rules to apply to these circumstances; rather, an agreement must be fashioned that will be fair to both, consistent with the financial ability of one former partner to provide assistance and the reasonable needs of the other to receive it. In most respects, the negotiation of such an agreement is akin to that of a prenuptial agreement; unless it is handled delicately and with great sensitivity, it may lead to the termination of the parties' relationship even before it has had the opportunity to blossom. The partners should each employ their own attorney. There should be full mutual financial disclosure since if there is a misrepresentation as to income or assets by either party that a court might in the future find to constitute a fraud, it could be the basis for setting aside an otherwise entirely binding contract.

Overview

Let us review what we have discussed throughout this chapter. Couples who decide to live together may unwittingly enter into a contractual relationship with one another that might result in an obligation to pay support or a right to claim support, which might also include a division of property acquired during the relationship. These legal rights and obligations may occur because of the conduct of the parties, what is often referred to as an implied contract (similar to the one existing between the bootblack and his customer, discussed earlier in this chapter). Or there may be an expressed contract, that is, an agreement made by offer and acceptance, either orally or in writing. The *oral* promise to support and take care of another person and to divide property acquired during a relationship, coupled with the setting up of a joint household and the sharing of life's pursuits, can very well constitute an enforceable contract. Such an express contract will be limited to the parties' own language and mutual intentions. To eliminate any question of what was said or agreed upon (an issue that will ultimately be decided by a judge or jury in the event that a lawsuit is brought to enforce the contract), parties who contemplate living together may wish to explore entering into an expressed written agreement that will articulate all the terms of their understanding, including, for example, the amount and duration of support and the division, if any, of property acquired during the relationship. Because these agreements must comply with the prescription of local law to be valid, an attorney familiar with the complexities of family law should be consulted.

Where no written agreement is utilized and it is not the intent to incur legal obligations, caution should be exercised to negate any inference that a promise of support has been made by an oral representation. Disclaimers in words should be frequently spoken throughout the relationship not only to one's partner but to third persons with whom the parties have contact.

When living together, care should also be taken to preserve your separate identities and not present yourselves as a married couple. This is especially important when visiting a state that recognizes common-law marriage because your home state must recognize the laws of its sister states (in accordance with the full faith and credit clause of the U.S. Constitution). If marriage obligations are to be studiously avoided, it would be a good idea to remain out of and not travel through a common-law state.

By contrast, there may be situations where one wishes to impose marital obligations upon the live-in companion. By encouraging words of commitment for financial security and support, by holding yourselves out as husband and wife, by vacationing or living in a common-law state, and by obtaining an express written agreement, the right to receive financial benefits may be achieved when a court is called upon to resolve the question of whether a contract exists or whether a common-law marriage is to be imputed to the living-together couple.

Is the cup half full or half empty? One's perspective may only be a point of view, but in the field of human relations it may have a lasting impact on the way people conduct their lives following an unintended or even, at times, an intentional parting of the ways.

Note

1. New York Domestic Relations Law §236B(3).

    3. Agreement of the parties. An agreement by the parties, made before or during the marriage, shall be valid and enforceable in a matrimonial action if such agreement is in writing, subscribed by the parties, and acknowledged or proven in the manner required to entitle a deed to be recorded. Such an agreement may include (1) a contract to make a testamentary provision of any kind, or a waiver of any right to elect against the provisions of a will; (2) provision for the ownership, division or distribution of separate and marital property; (3) provision for the amount and duration of maintenance or other terms and conditions of the marriage relationship, subject to the provisions of section 5–311 of the general obligations law, and provided that such terms were fair and reasonable at the time of the making of the agreement and are not unconscionable at the time of entry of final judgment; and (4) provision for the custody, care, education and maintenance of any child of the parties, subject to the provisions of section two hundred forty of this chapter. Nothing in this subdivision shall be deemed to affect the validity of any agreement made prior to the effective date of this subdivision.

Chapter 4

Legal Obligations to Children and Their Effect on Your Relationship

When a couple decide to live together, often one or the other has custody of a child or children from a former marriage or relationship whom he or she wishes to have live with the two of them. If your partner is a noncustodial parent, the child will not share your living quarters, but certainly concern must be given for visitation periods that he or she will exercise on weekends and holidays and, perhaps, for a prolonged period during the summer. If both of you have children, the problem of space, both mental and physical, for yourselves and for the children, becomes a most serious concern. How will our children get along with each other? How will they accept and get along with my companion? How will the children affect our own relationship? Is it right to live together with the children? Can I afford to support them? All are questions that will race through your mind as the resolution of whether to live together or not draws closer. Living together with children creates special problems for the children. They may be ostracized by their peers at school; they may become confused and experience emotional distress because of your relationship. Societal approval may not necessarily follow your living arrangements. These matters must be fully explored and the potential harm to the children weighed before reaching a final determination.

Once these concerns are addressed and resolved, and you accept the fact that the children will play an integral role in your relationship, you may then decide to begin your search for suitable quarters to accommodate all of you, or decide that the present residence of one of you would be sufficient.

Unless you are prepared to accept your cohabitant's children as your own, which will require the full demands of parenthood, and to apportion your time, as well as your financial support, between them and your own children, it may be wise not to consider such amalgamation because of its inherent difficulties and potential adverse effects, especially if it is ended after a brief start since this may likely cause more severe emotional distress to the children than to the two of you.

Before making a decision, it may be helpful and beneficial to consult with a child psychologist, a psychiatrist, or a psychiatric social worker in order to receive advice and identify the potential problem areas that may arise when two families live as one. Knowing that the male (or female) head of the household is not their father (or mother) can create identity problems for children. It would be unwise to permit your children to refer to your companion as their parent because it is destructive to a child's relationship with the biological parent and is especially confusing to younger children. In addition, it will create great hostility in the biological parent toward you if he or she is maintaining close contact with the child.

A competent health care professional with experience in dealing with these problems can suggest ways to minimize, if not eliminate, these potential hazards. Almost all will counsel you to have open and truthful communications with the children regarding your plans to share one household together. This should never be sprung upon children as an afterthought or without sufficient time to permit them to adjust their thoughts and express the fears that the information that they will live in another home is sure to trigger. Most adults resist and fear change. Children are even more sensitive to a change in the status quo. Moving from a neighborhood where they have established friends, are comfortable in a school setting, and have found comfort and security is indeed traumatic for them. Even changing neighborhoods within the security of a stable, traditional family is difficult for a child. The added burden of adjusting to a new authority figure and the confusion between that person's role and that of the child's own parent are indeed intimidating and frightening for the child. Sharing with the child all of the details of your proposed move in frequent and ongoing chats, while both respecting and addressing the concerns of the child, will go a long way toward alleviating any lasting mental distress. There must be a period set aside to permit a child to adjust to and accept such impending change. This period should include frequent contacts in an informal setting with your companion and his or her children so that they can get to know one another. Going together as a group to enjoy a recreational activity is a natural way to become acquainted and to have some fun.

It is important at these initial meetings that they be unstructured and without great demands. You should never say to the children, "You must behave yourselves" or "I don't want you to cause a ruckus" or any other such negative or restrictive pronouncement that can only serve to create tension, heighten apprehension, and make more difficult an already taxing confrontation. It would be far better to let children know that the meeting will be an opportunity to meet in a relaxed and fun-filled atmosphere. "It will be a pleasant time for all of us, and I can't wait for you to meet the other children" is a far better approach.

This transitional problem exists for recently remarried couples whose children must accept a stepparent, as well as stepbrothers and sisters, into their lives, but because society approves of marriage the potential problems that will beset these children will normally be less severe than those facing children in a living-together arrangement. A health care professional will be invaluable in dealing with these most serious concerns.

The legal obligations to the children who may be imputed to

you because of your new living arrangements should now be looked at with great care. In most instances a person cannot be compelled to support a child unless he or she is the natural or adoptive parent of the child, but living together in the same household with a child and his or her natural parent may, in and of itself, give rise to a corresponding legal obligation to support the child (see Appendix J). The misconception that only the child's parents can be compelled to furnish support has been dispelled by recent case law. When a child is born to a married couple, the presumption in the law is that the child is the offspring of both husband and wife. This presumption of legitimacy is said to be the strongest presumption known to the law. Although there are circumstances in which the presumption is overcome and paternity is denied by the husband, it is indeed a very rare circumstance when such a finding will be made by the court.

The Paternity Suit

When a child is born to a woman who lives with a man out of wedlock, there is no such similar presumption. If the man with whom a woman is living when a child is born seeks to deny paternity and his obligation to support the child, the woman must then bring on a proceeding in the courts to establish paternity and ensure that the child will be able to receive support from the father. Paternity proceedings are normally brought in family court, where an attorney for the local government will prosecute the case on behalf of the mother (the petitioner) who seeks to establish a named person (the respondent) as the natural father and obtain his contribution for support of the child. The medical and hospital expenses incurred during the pregnancy and at delivery are also recoverable in most states.

Both parties involved in a paternity proceeding, that is, even the mother, who will have the case urged by a county or city attorney, may employ their own attorneys. It is far more important for the respondent to be represented, however, since a finding of paternity will result in a legal obligation to support the child until the age of majority, normally 18 or 21, depending upon state law. It is interesting to note that in New York, for example, although the age of majority is 18, the obligation to support a child who is not emancipated (self-supporting or married) continues for three years longer, until the age of 21.

The petitioner's case is rather uncomplicated. She must simply prove that she engaged in sexual relations solely with the named respondent during the period of gestation. Normally, there will be required only the testimony of the mother to establish these facts, but some states may require expert medical testimony concerning the period of gestation. Today many states can require blood or genetic tests to be administered to either establish or exclude paternity. In some states blood grouping tests can only be used as exclusionary evidence, so it would be essential for a respondent to request that a blood sample of himself and the child be drawn and the test administered in order to take advantage of this procedure.

In the trial of a paternity case, the respondent's only way out is to attempt to establish before the court that he did not have access to the petitioner during the period of gestation, which may require proof of an alibi witness, or that the petitioner engaged in sexual intercourse with one or more other men during the critical time of conception. Even with such proof, there is no assurance that a judge will believe such testimony and exclude the respondent as the father of the child. The defense of a paternity suit is complex and may rest upon the testimony of an expert medical witness. If you are the respondent, only an attorney familiar and seasoned in family law matters should be considered to represent you. Unless finances do not permit the retention of such an attorney, it would be foolhardy to attempt to defend yourself.

There are two aspects to every paternity case. Once the court concludes that the named respondent is the father of the child, then the focus will be on the proper amount of support to be paid based on the financial needs of the child and the financial ability of the father to provide. The court will also consider visitation rights for the father, once paternity has been established. As long as the father obeys the court order to support the child, he will have the absolute right to continue visitation. If as the child grows older the parents cannot agree on expanded visitation, the father may apply to the court in an attempt to gain greater contact with the child. In this regard the application before the court is no different from one involving a visitation dispute between a divorced couple. There has been a tendency throughout the country in recent years to accord equal status to visiting rights to those of the custodial parent. When problems of relocation crop up, there is a growing tendency in the courts to place the burden on the custodial parent to prove that a prospective move is in the best interest of the child (not necessarily of the parent) or that exceptional circumstances exist that require the move. Recent developing case law has made it generally more difficult to change the residence of a child to a distant state, especially when the parent who has visitation rights has established a close and loving relationship through ongoing and frequent contact with the child for a prolonged period prior to the application before the court seeking to change the child's home. Even when the change is motivated by a better job opportunity for the custodial parent or is required because of remarriage, there is no guarantee that a court will approve the move. It is frequently said in these situations that the custodial parent is free to move, but if he or she chooses to do so there may be a change of custody to the visiting parent. This is true because the courts recognize that there can be great disruption in the life of a child who is removed from longtime friends, a comfortable school environment, and perhaps members of an extended family in order to accommodate the needs of the parent seeking to change a residence. Exceptional circumstances that may be sufficient to win court approval for a move to a distant state certainly would include concerns for the health of the child, lack of support or contact by the noncustodial parent, and better educational opportunities for the child. Each case will be decided upon its own peculiar facts and circumstances, and it is difficult to predict with any reasonable degree of certainty how the court will react to a given case. One common thread, however, appears to be present in most decisions: custody is determined based upon what is in the best interests of the child, as opposed to the best interests of the parents.

Once paternity has either been established or acknowledged, the search by the parties or the court to decide upon the proper amount for child support begins. This problem, of course, will also be faced by living-together couples who have adopted a child. It may be addressed in a living-together agreement, discussed in chapter 10, or by later agreement or by decision of the court. In fixing the proper amount of annual support, most states have approved a predetermined formula to tie into the parents' gross annual income. For one child, 17% to 20% is a common percentage to apply to the combined gross income of the parties. Usually, there is a fixed upper limit of perhaps $80,000 where mandatory sums must be awarded. So, for example, in a situation in which the mother is unemployed, the father earns $50,000 in gross income, and the state applies a 20% factor for a single child, the annual child support amount would be $10,000 (20% of $50,000). Once the fixed maximum is reached, the court then would have the discretion of awarding additional monies; this sum is determined either according to the formula or to the judgment by the court as to what is fair and reasonable considering the earnings of the parents and the needs of the child. Frequently, the court will consider the preseparation standard of living in deciding discretionary amounts of child support. For example, if a father earned $100,000 and the percentage to apply is 20%, the child support formula mandates payment of $16,000 (20% of the first $80,000); that sum could be increased by any amount the court believes is proper, taking into consideration the financial needs of the father to maintain himself at a reasonable standard of living.

In resolving the issue of child support payments, the courts increasingly recognize that there must be a balance between the needs of the child and the financial capabilities of the parent to meet those needs. The fixed percentage approach has been adopted by all states because of a federal mandate to create numeric guidelines and the need to provide for more uniform child support payments throughout the country. Previously, child support awards varied greatly from judge to judge and state to state. The imposition of fixed percentages of gross income was mandated to make such awards more uniform. The formula approach has been perceived to be fairer to both parent and child. The amounts that are awarded are generally more generous now than in the past, when it was not unusual for some judges to fix weekly support of a child between $25 and $50, regardless of the parent's income. Today, the weekly sum will approximate $50 per week only when a parent earns $15,000 a year. The percentage formula adopted by the state in which you reside should be consulted in order to compute a more precise amount and to understand how the formula is applied.

It is to be noted that most states permit parents to ignore or "opt out" of the terms of this new law if they both acknowledge that they are aware of its terms but agree to modify the amount of child support for certain reasons, including labeling a more generous sum of money as alimony (maintenance in some states) or providing a more liberal division of property. Of course, where only the issue of child support is to be decided, the parent who will be the recipient of the child support payment would have little reason or incentive to accept a smaller weekly sum than would be computed by the formula. The decision to opt out should be based on the reality of some other financial benefit, such as payment of a lump sum or the undertaking of some additional expense of the child such as private school or camp.

It should be carefully noted and remembered that the agreements of parents to fix child support obligations are always subject to review by the courts and that the courts can intervene to modify the amounts of support agreed to by the parents when it is determined that the amounts are inadequate to meet the minimum living requirements of the child, based on the standard of living he or she enjoyed before the parents' separation, or when circumstances change in the future because of increased financial needs as the child grows older. In this respect, child support agreements can never be presumed to be binding, that is, not modifiable by the courts. Often, the courts will intervene in an appropriate case to increase the award, but it is rare that a downward modification or lesser sum will be ordered, except under exceptional financial circumstances, which could include prolonged illness and unemployment. By contrast, agreements between spouses or even cohabitants for maintenance (alimony) are less likely to be disturbed in any respect by the courts, unless it can be shown that the party making the payments is in extreme adverse financial circumstances or that the party receiving the support is in danger of becoming a public charge (a welfare recipient) because the agreed-upon amount is woefully inadequate to meet minimum support requirements.

Support of Children Not Adopted by You

There may be a danger that if the person you are involved with brings a child into the relationship and you live together for a number of years, treating the child as your own throughout this period of time, a court may later determine that you will be responsible to pay child support throughout the balance of the child's minority, in most states until age 21 (see Appendix J). This result seems likely since there are several states that have already held that a stepparent (i.e., a person who was married to another who brought children into the marriage but who never formally adopted those children) must pay child support, despite the fact that the stepparent never adopted the child, when he or she apparently promised to do so during the time of the marriage.

Recently, the Wisconsin Court of Appeals reached this decision in a case where the child's mother had also obtained an order terminating the child's biological father's rights, which, of course, eliminated his obligation to pay child support. The court remarked in reaching its decision that the stepfather had clearly indicated an intent to adopt the boy and that the mother would never have given up her right to receive child support had she not relied upon the stepfather's promise. The stepfather sought to avoid liability for child support by arguing that since he was not the natural or adoptive parent of the boy, he could not be compelled to support him. Other factors that weighed heavily in the court's determination was the fact that the stepfather held out the child as his own throughout the marriage. The test to apply in these cases is whether a stepparent unequivocally represents an intent to support a child and the natural parent relies on such promise to his or her detriment. If so, the court will deny the stepparent the right to raise any defense to discontinue support on the basis of the doctrine of *equitable estoppel*. Equitable estoppel simply is a principle of law that is utilized to prevent a person from raising an otherwise valid defense because of his or her previous conduct.

This case, as so do many others in the field of family law, rested upon its own peculiar fact pattern. The stepfather had openly and publicly expressed his intent to support the child until he was 18 years of age. As observed earlier, the stepfather's defense was that a court could not order him to support a child of whom he was neither the natural nor the adoptive father.

By contrast, in another case that was decided in Wisconsin, the court did not compel a stepfather to support a child in similar circumstances, basing its decision on the fact that although the stepfather had promised to love the child, there was no affirmative promise to support the child. There are other states throughout the country that have compelled a stepparent to pay child support, including California, Florida, Michigan, New York, Pennsylvania, Virginia, West Virginia, Maryland, New Jersey, and Utah. Perhaps a California court's philosophy is illustrative of that of other states that adopt this principle:

> There is an innate immorality in the conduct of an adult who for over a decade accepts and proclaims a child as his own, but then, in order to be relieved of the child's support, announces, and relies upon his bastardy. This is a cruel weapon, which works a lasting injury to the child and can bring in its aftermath social harm. (Clevenger v. Clevenger, 11 Cal Rptr, p. 710)

California would compel child support by a stepparent if the person seeking support could establish that an express agreement was made for the child's support or, as discussed earlier, could find an act of estoppel. It should be readily observed from a consideration of the cases discussed that there can be grave financial repercussions, based upon your conduct or words, concerning the support of children who are not born of your relationship or adopted by you. The courts will seek ways to avoid financial hardship to a child; they can do so by adopting the law of contracts or other legal theories. If the stepfather in the case discussed earlier had never indicated an intention to support the child and had never made this fact known to others during the time that the child resided with him, there may likely have been a different result reached by the court.

A court cannot find an express agreement to support unless a promise was actually made to be responsible for present as well as future support of a child. Thus, if you are a person who does not wish to be legally responsible for a stepchild in the event that you, in fact, marry your cohabitant—or even if you remain unmarried—a living-together agreement might incorporate language to eliminate your intention to support the child and might expressly state that the natural parent be solely responsible for such support during the time that you and your partner reside together, or in the event that you separate sometime in the future.

This is certainly another area in the law where cohabitants can wake up one morning and find that they are saddled with a legal obligation they may never have intended to incur. Accordingly, you must be most guarded before uttering statements of providing support or continued support for either your cohabitant or your cohabitant's children.[1]

A law may ultimately evolve that will require a person to continue to support a child he or she already supported for a prolonged period of time, whether or not that person has adopted the child or has married the child's natural parent. Some legal scholars have already written on the subject of "constructive adoption," in which the law would infer adoption of a child for the purposes of support on the basis of the prior conduct of and previous support by the person living with the child. Whether or not this will occur remains to be seen, but being forewarned is to be forearmed.

Deciphering these principles can become quite difficult and often will require the assistance of an attorney to properly present your plea to a court of law. However, in most every jurisdiction, a family court instead of a general court will make it far easier to proceed without counsel (i.e., *pro se*, "on behalf of yourself"), but the decision to do so should only be reached after careful thought. Abraham Lincoln once remarked that a lawyer who represents himself has a fool for a client. Only when your own finances prohibit the services of a lawyer should you appear in court in your own behalf. There may be circumstances where neither you nor your ex-partner is able to retain an attorney because of financial reasons. When this happens, the family court judge will, in an attempt to be fair to both of you, permit you wide latitude in the presentation of your evidence.

Considerations of Adoption

The occasion may arise when you will consider adopting the child of your live-in companion. There are moral as well as legal questions that should be considered before doing so. Since adoption proceedings must be sanctioned by the court, which will examine the background of the proposed adopting parent and the present living conditions of the child and natural parent, there may be some instances where there will not be approval of an adoption between unmarried partners. Adoption proceedings that involve two adopting parents become more complex. Such adoptions can come about by application to an agency or through a private agreement to adopt a child from a young mother who wishes to place her child at birth. Whichever method is chosen or becomes available, the adoption proceeding is monitored by the court, and in most states the natural mother is permitted to change her mind before a final order of adoption is approved.

The court's desire is to see to it that the proposed adoptive parents are of sufficient mental and moral integrity to assure the child proper care and a good home. Each state varies with respect to the requirements of adopting parents; these range from financial and religious considerations to psychological ones. Whether your state will even consider adoption by a single parent or an unmarried couple must be your initial concern before much else is done to find a child to adopt. The local court in your community, usually the family or surrogate court, will be able to furnish you with information regarding adoption proceedings. Again, it would be wise to consult with a family lawyer familiar with such proceedings if it is determined that your application will receive consideration in the first instance.

Adoption by a single parent appears to have received greater acceptance than adoption by an unmarried couple, although both have been approved where the courts have reached the conclusion that such adoption would not necessarily be adverse to the interests of the child. Perhaps where there are difficult placements to be made, such as a disabled child, the court may be more liberal in approving the adoptive parents (see chapter 6 for a discussion of adoption by a homosexual father of a special needs child).

Once an order of adoption has been made, the adopted child will be treated by the law no differently than a natural child. The right of inheritance and the right to receive support from the adopting parent, the two most significant legal aspects of adoption, are absolute and apply exactly as if the child had been born to one or both of the adopting parents. Although children may be left out of wills (i.e., no provision is made for them by the terms of a parent's will), they are not disinherited when a parent dies *intestate* (without a will). Then the laws of intestacy, which vary from state to state, will apply. Normally, when children survive the death of a parent, they are entitled to share, together with a surviving spouse, a portion of the deceased parent's estate. In the circumstance in which couples live together and never marry, there is no surviving spouse and the surviving child may be entitled to receive the entire estate of the deceased parent, or share it equally with other surviving children. In this respect, there is no difference between natural and adopted children; in the eyes of the law, they are treated equally.

In estate distribution it can readily be seen that an adopted child is much preferred over a surviving cohabitant. There is absolutely no right of inheritance that accrues to a cohabitant when death occurs (this area of concern is discussed more fully in chapter 9).

Decision Making: The Child Factor

When you become aware of the legal and psychological consequences that may affect your lives when bringing children into your relationship, the initial decision of whether to do so becomes far more important. No one should treat the decision lightly. Only when concerned thought is exercised and legal (and perhaps psychological) advice obtained will the ultimate resolution of this major problem be possible. Your happiness, as well as the child's, hangs in the balance.

Children: No Small Affair

The living-together couple may become involved in parenting through one or more of several ways: children may be brought into the relationship by one or both of the cohabitants, a child may be born to the living-together couple during their relationship, the couple may adopt a child if state law permits such a proceeding, or a child may result from conception involving one of several fertilization methods. Regardless of the way in which children come into the relationship, there are multiple ways in which legal obligations may attach to the unwary, be included in an agreement between the couples, or be imposed by operation of law. These legal obligations include the obligation to support a dependent child and the child's right to inherit from the parent, regardless of the manner in which parenthood occurs. When one seeks to ignore these obligations, legal repercussions will certainly accrue.

Once a separation has occurred between cohabitants who have a child, whether born of the relationship or adopted by one or both partners, issues of custody and visitation become troublesome. In addressing such issues, the courts in most states throughout the country, as observed earlier, currently determine what is in the best interests of the child, rather than of the competing parents, in making an award of custody or determining visitation rights to one or the other parent. In determining what is in the best interests of a child, the court may consider one or more of the following:

1. The emotional ties existing between the parents and the child
2. The parental capacity to exhibit to the child love, affection, guidance, education, and religious training
3. The financial capacity of the parents to provide the child with the necessities of life
4. The length of time the child has lived in a stable environment and the desirability of maintaining custody with the parent who has provided such environment
5. The moral, mental, and physical fitness of the parents
6. The preference of the child, if of sufficient age and maturity
7. The willingness of the proposed custodial parent to foster a loving relationship between the child and the other parent
8. Any other factors in a particular case that may bear upon the child's best interests

When parents contest custody in the courts, most states provide that they must be examined by a psychiatrist or psychologist, a social worker, and other investigators, all of whom together constitute "a forensic team." When a forensic examination is

ordered, both parents are interviewed by a health care professional who seeks to determine whether they are free from mental
disorders or personality defects and whether the home environment that they propose for the child will be suitable. If one or the
other competing parent is involved in another relationship, that
person will also be subject to examination and scrutiny. The
court's search is to find the parent who will make the more suitable
custodian for the child.

It is no longer necessary to prove the unfitness of the other
parent in order for you to obtain custody, although a finding of
unfitness may indeed cause a court to grant you custody of the
child. Unfitness normally includes alcoholism, physical abuse,
drug addiction, mental disorder, or other condition that would
render a parent incapable of providing for the needs of the child or
of permitting the child to grow into a well-adjusted adult. Most
custody cases, however, in today's enlightened society normally
involve parents whose relative fitness, rather than unfitness, must
be determined. The "tender years presumption," which places a
child of early years with his or her mother, no longer finds
acceptance in the vast number of states throughout the country.
This previous bent to normally place custody of a child with the
mother has been replaced by the best interest standard, discussed
earlier.

As it becomes more and more common for both parents to
pursue employment opportunities and careers, and therefore for
the child to be relegated to the care of a housekeeper or child care
center, it is increasingly difficult for a court to prefer one parent
over the other simply because of gender. Custody litigation can
really be viewed as the court's search for positives, rather than
negatives, in today's concern for finding the better custodian.
Expressed another way, the search may be to determine which
parent has been the more nurturing parent.

In order to demonstrate the contacts you have had with the
child and the depth of your involvement, it will be necessary not
only for you to testify in the courtroom but to call witnesses in
your behalf. Such witnesses will normally include neighbors,

school teachers, physicians, and any other person who has been exposed to you and your child, your interaction with each other, and the effects such interaction has had upon the child. Whether you win or lose custody in a court of law will depend on the testimony of you and your witnesses but, above all, on the testimony of a psychiatrist or psychologist who is able to testify regarding your abilities as a parent and your abilities to cope with the duties of a parent and to convince the court that you are a better choice for custodial parent than the child's other parent.

Sometimes a decision has to be made in a custody litigation whether or not the children themselves should be called as witnesses. Although a court will consider the wishes of a child of mature years, rarely will it consider those of a child who is less than eight or nine years old; and when it does so, the wishes of a child of younger years will not be controlling. However, courts give great weight to the wishes of a teenager, especially one who is approaching the age of majority (in most states, the age of 18). Some judges will urge the lawyers to permit them to examine children in their chambers rather than call them as a witness. Certainly, a very young child would not be a candidate for the witness chair, but, actually, if a child is of sufficient maturity to know right from wrong and the meaning of his or her oath, there would be no legal reason to forbid his or her appearance in the courtroom. However, the psychological damage that might result to a child from appearing in the courtroom to give testimony in a custody dispute must be given careful consideration by the parent. If you consider allowing your child to testify, it is necessary to discuss your plans with a psychiatrist or other health care professional to assess the psychological impact such testimony might have on the child. Only when you are convinced that calling the child will not seriously affect him or her psychologically should this choice be utilized. In the final analysis, it may well be better to go along with the court's wishes to conduct an interview in the judge's chambers rather than to subject the child to the rigors of the courtroom.

The goal you seek in a contested trial is to portray yourself as a caring, concerned, involved parent who has, among other things, taken the child to physicians when the occasion arose, attended all parent–teacher meetings, and actively supported the child's extracurricular activities, such as Little League, dance, art lessons, and so forth; above all, it is necessary to show that the focus in your life is your child and not your job or career. Moreover, it will be important to convince the judge that your priorities are such that you are willing to make adjustments in your own job or career in order to make sufficient time to be with your child at critical times, such as getting him or her off to school and perhaps returning after classes have ended to attend to the child's needs. If it is necessary to adjust your hours, then by all means let the court know in clear and certain terms that you intend to do so.

In establishing your claim as a nurturing parent, third party witnesses can prove invaluable. It is one thing for you to testify to all the school activities attended, doctors visited, sporting events shared but quite another matter to have an independent witness corroborate or bolster such assertions. This is true because most courts recognize that parents engaged in custody battles really have their own axes to grind and may, in certain instances, exaggerate claims of their own parenting. An array of witnesses called in your behalf, which may include the child's pediatrician, teacher, coach of Little League, and a priest or rabbi if the child has been in religious activities, as well as any other person who has witnessed your involvement with the child, may mean the difference between success and failure.

You must be prepared to sacrifice for your child if you wish to be considered as his or her custodial parent, and this willingness to sacrifice must be made known to the court. In this era of sexual equality, it is not unusual for both parents to have full-time jobs or careers. For example, if you are an advertising executive and your former spouse is a physician and you are both vying for custody of a young child, the court will be extremely interested to learn which one of you will be willing to modify office hours so as to be available to the child. When all other qualities of the parents appear to be equal, the availability of a parent to the child may be the single most important factor on which the court will base its decision. In this example, it would be wise for you if you work a ten-hour day, say from 9:00 A.M. to 7:00 P.M. or even later, to advise the court that you have received permission from your company to adjust your hours and to be away from the office on any occasion for which your child requires your attention. Certainly, you would like to highlight to the judge that you can continue to do this until the child is older and involved in school and extracurricular activities.

Custody litigation is an unwise choice, since it takes so much out of children emotionally when they become embroiled in such disputes with their parents. It is always far better to attempt to resolve a settlement between you and the child's other parent, which might include joint custody. Joint custody is being utilized more and more by couples seeking to avoid custody battles. If there is not a great amount of animosity between the parents, joint custody may be a very wise choice. It seems to work well when both parents reside within the same school district, especially if the parents live within the same neighborhood so that there is no detachment from friends or familiar surroundings when custody is exchanged between the parents. A joint custodial arrangement might include the child residing with one parent for one-half of a week and the other parent for the remainder of the week. Shared custody is sometimes on a monthly basis. Parents have even become involved in joint custodial arrangements that span a year or more before a shifting of residence takes place.

There are no fixed rules when you consider making a joint custodial arrangement, and whatever seems to work best for the child should be considered. Joint custodial agreements can be modified from time to time in order to adapt to the child's schedule and increasing activities as the child grows older. On the other hand, when parents do not reside in close proximity to one another, joint custody arrangements may prove troublesome, if not unworkable. Obviously, a child cannot attend two schools during a school semester, and shuttling back and forth on an annual basis between two different school systems certainly would not be in the child's best interest. It would appear that if you and your ex-partner desire to enter into a workable joint custodial arrangement, you should consider living at least in the same school district, if not the same community.

Joint custody can be an effective way to share children and their growth through adulthood. It can also be disastrous when parents continue to exhibit signs of hostility toward each other.

Note

1. Family Law Reporter, Bureau of National Affairs, June 18, 1991, Vol. 17, #32.

Chapter 5

Marriage by Common Law

The legal definition of a common-law marriage must be distinguished from the popular usage of this term since the former can in many states indicate a valid form of marriage. In casual conversation, the term may refer to an extralegal or meretricious relationship existing between two persons who do not intend to ever become married.

The legal definition of a common-law marriage, which is often accepted by judges throughout the country, is an agreement made between two persons who live together as husband and wife in a state of matrimony. It differs from a formal ceremonial marriage in that there is no requirement that the couple obtain a marriage license or that they exchange their vows before one or more witnesses. The essential ingredient of a common-law marriage that is recognized by the law is the present agreement of the parties to live together as husband and wife with the resulting obligations that may stem from such a relationship. At times the courts will interpret the words and actions of the parties in order to determine what their actual intent was during their relationship. It is important to note that an agreement to marry in the future is not sufficient, even if cohabitation takes place following such a promise. Whether or not a couple will be deemed to be legally married, whether by common-law statute or ceremonial marriage, is an important facet to determine eligibility for inheritance, death benefits, pensions, housing, and the right to share in property acquired during the couple's relationship.

Although many states throughout the country previously recognized common-law marriages, that is, a union of a man and woman sharing a common home who have not gone through a civil or religious ceremony and exchanged for.nal marital vows, today there are but 13 states remaining that do so: Alabama, Colorado, Georgia, Idaho, Iowa, Kansas, Montana, Ohio, Oklahoma, Pennsylvania, Rhode Island, South Carolina, and Texas, as well as the District of Columbia (see Appendix A). Common-law marriages come about or are imputed to cohabitants by virtue of their conduct. Common-law cohabitants have the identical rights and obligations that may be granted to or imposed upon husbands and wives by state law. These include division of marital property, alimony (or maintenance), and the right to inherit property of the deceased cohabitant or to elect against his or her will.

This *right of election* permits a surviving spouse to ignore the provisions of the will and choose to accept a certain specified sum or percentage from the estate that is fixed by state inheritance law. For example, a surviving spouse who has contracted a common-law marriage and who has been entirely eliminated as an heir by the express terms of the will may elect to receive the state percentage, normally a fixed dollar amount of $10,000 and one third of the gross estate. If the gross estate, that is, the value of all goods, monies, and properties owned by the deceased at the time of death, is valued at $100,000, the widow or widower who is not mentioned in this will could receive the first $10,000 and one third of the balance of the gross estate, or $30,000 ($100,000 less $10,000 = $90,000; one-third of $90,000 = $30,000). Each state's right of election may differ in amount of percentage. Most states provide that unless the will contains a direction that the surviving spouse receive the fixed statutory sum or percentage, the survivor may make such election. However, a provision of the will that requires the fixed percentage to be placed in trust, which would only permit the survivor to receive the income from the trust during his or her lifetime, would satisfy the legal requirement, even though the survivor would get a far smaller benefit than if the monies had been received outright. Some estate planners use this device to accomplish such a goal while at the same time complying with state law. This right of election applies only when a person dies testate, that is, with a valid will. The benefits resulting from the exercise of the right of a spouse to inherit when a person dies without a will (i.e., intestate) are far greater than those from the exercise of the right of election, since the percentage of the estate that will be inherited under the former circumstances will be received outright, not in trust or with other conditions.

The importance of being accorded marital status by virtue of a common-law marriage is readily apparent. Without such recognition, the rights of inheritance would be totally lost, as would the absolute right in the event of a termination of the parties' relationship to receive support or to receive property that is acquired during the relationship. Some persons are totally ignorant of these legal consequences and some are misinformed as to their rights.

Formation of a Common-Law Marriage

How can a common-law marriage come about? What conduct is necessary, in effect, to reach the conclusion that the unsuspecting couple are now subject to all the rights and obligations accorded a couple who exchanged formal marriage vows and have otherwise complied with their state's requirements for marriage, which includes the obtainment of a marriage license? To best comprehend how a common-law marriage can be formed, an exploration of the facts surrounding the high-profile case of actor William Hurt and his live-in companion, who bore him a child, will be helpful.

William Hurt and Sandra Jennings fell in love and began to live with one another. As the months passed, their ardor for one another increased. A baby was born and the couple continued to live together, but Hurt steadfastly disavowed that Sandra Jennings was his wife. Wherever the couple went and whomever they came in contact with, Hurt was careful to introduce Sandra Jennings as his live-in companion, his cohabitant, his lover, and the mother of his baby but never as his wife. At least this is the testimony Hurt gave to Justice Jacqueline Silberman in the New York County Supreme Court at a hearing to determine the claim by Sandra Jennings, a former dancer for the New York City Ballet, that she and Hurt had contracted a common-law marriage in the state of South Carolina during the ten-week filming of *The Big Chill*. Since New York had to recognize a common-law marriage if it was validly made by the laws of South Carolina, Sandra Jennings, if she had succeeded, would have been William Hurt's wife for all legal purposes in New York. New York was bound to give the laws of South Carolina full faith and credit as mandated by the United States Constitution. In this lawsuit, Sandra Jennings sought child support, ongoing alimony (termed "maintenance" in New York), and a division of all money and property acquired by the couple during the time they lived together following the common-law marriage. Interestingly, there was no claim by Sandra Jennings that there was an expressed promise by Hurt to support and divide their property following their "marriage" in South Carolina. An attempt to establish that she and Hurt were indeed married fell far short of the mark imposed by Jacqueline Silberman, who held that to prove a common-law marriage took place in South Carolina a "present intention" to be married had to be shown by "strong and competent evidence," especially since William Hurt was married in 1981 when the couple first began their relationship and did not become divorced until some time thereafter. Because of this fact, the court ruled, in order to be successful, Jennings had to overcome the presumption that the "illicit character" of their relationship had been removed.

Conflict of Laws

In all of these lawsuits in which a cohabitant seeks to impute a common-law marriage by virtue of the couple's conduct, the first legal question to answer is whether the state where the court proceeding will take place should apply its own law or the law of the common-law state visited. This is known as a conflict of laws question and is always resolved by looking to the common-law state involved and applying its rules of law to determine whether a couple residing within its boundaries would be deemed husband and wife.

States that recognize common-law marriage have different degrees of proof and different standards to apply when determining whether a given relationship can be considered a common-law marriage. Some states may require minimum contact and conduct to reach this determination while others may demand far greater proof and a holding out of a marital relationship. It depends upon state law and the judges who interpret them.

South Carolina is conservative in determining whether a couple's behavior qualifies for marital status. William Hurt became a beneficiary of such conservatism and Sandra Jennings an unfortunate victim of its provisions. When the trial began, Jennings seemed to have a lot in her favor. She had been living with Hurt for several years (between 1981 and 1984), had given up her career to be his constant companion, had borne him a son, and was no less a wife to him than any woman who has gone through a ceremonial marriage. Jennings thought that the law should help her receive her rightful share of the couple's property and that Hurt should be compelled to support her and the child, at least until she raised the baby and could return to work. As it turned out, she seriously miscalculated what the law would do for her and ultimately lost her lawsuit. The court decided that the proof she had introduced at the trial in an attempt to establish that she and Hurt were indeed married was insufficient. Jennings testified that during the filming of *The Big Chill*, she and Hurt lived together for ten weeks as husband and wife and that during that period Hurt told her, "We are married in the eyes of God" and "We're more married than married persons." The judge apparently did not believe her testimony.

Common-Law Marriage: Insurmountable Burden?

Can one conclude from the decision in the Jennings–Hurt case that it is far too difficult to meet the burden of proof that would cause a court to conclude that a common-law marriage had been consummated? Certainly not. To do so would be a most dangerous miscalculation; although the law was followed in the Hurt case, the facts presented to the judge were insufficient for her to conclude that the basic requirements necessary to establish a common-law marriage in the state of South Carolina had been met. Jennings lost because the court did not entirely believe her and the witnesses she called in her behalf. As with so many of these cases, the credibility of the party bringing the lawsuit (i.e., that person's ability to convince a judge or jury—the trier of the facts—that his or her testimony is to be believed and accepted as true) takes on major proportions because there are no eyewitnesses to the intimate contacts and conversations between cohabitants. Most cases are decided by the trier of the facts on the basis of a determination of which party is telling the truth.

To understand how the law may be applied to reach the conclusion that a common-law marriage was formed, consider the words of a judge in another case in South Carolina in interpreting that state's law in regard to the requirement of an intent to contract a common-law marriage:[1] "It is of the essence of every contract that the parties shall have a present contracting intention, at the time of perfecting their contract; otherwise no contract is made. However, I do not say that they must have a full understanding of the legal consequences of the contract they are forming." It is clear from this language that even if a person is not aware that a marriage can result from his or her conduct, a court can still determine that a common-law marriage exists if it can conclude that the parties have a "present intent" to be married. William Hurt was already married at the time he met Sandra Jennings, so there was an impediment to his remarrying until his divorce became effective. Much of the testimony that Jennings gave concerned Hurt's intention to be married at a time when he was not legally capable of entering into the state of matrimony, whether ceremonial or common-law. The lesson to be learned from the Hurt case is that there must be a clear and unequivocal intention made by words or acts that the parties regard each other as husband and wife. The law can certainly impute such intention from the parties' acts: registering in a hotel as husband and wife and introducing one's cohabitant as one's spouse may be all that is necessary to establish a common-law marriage in any of the 13 states that recognize such marriages (see Appendix A).

When his case was decided, William Hurt was already contributing over $60,000 a year to his son's support, and that certainly might have been a fact that the court considered in its overall decision (in a courtroom there is always the possibility that a case may turn upon a twist or nuance). Nonetheless, knowing that the law in a common-law state may impose a legal obligation based upon your words and deeds should make you especially guarded. With such knowledge you can protect yourself against unwanted legal obligations.

Persons living in states that recognize common-law marriage can be accorded the same rights as couples who have gone through a ceremonial marriage. To date, there has not been any move by those states' legislatures to repeal the common-law marriage statutes; since cohabitation is becoming even more acceptable in today's society, there appears to be little chance that repeal will come in the immediate future. At least in these common-law states cohabitants are being legally treated similarly to their formally married counterparts. Perhaps it is the feeling in these states that to deny relief to a woman who has played the traditional roles of mother, homemaker, confidant, and lover, and who may also have given up career as well as educational opportunities, would be extremely unjust (especially if the monied cohabitant can simply walk out of the relationship without any legal or financial responsibility whatsoever) and might also result in the state welfare department supporting such a woman. Each common-law state has its own standards that must be established before such equal status will be offered to the living-together couple. It is certainly within the realm of possibility that as more such couples proliferate and receive the increasing attention of the public, the courts in such states may become far more liberal in interpreting the laws, thus making it far easier to succeed in an attempt to be deemed a common-law spouse. And it is possible that other states may consider introducing legislation that, if not reviving common-law marriages, will afford some legal status to long-term cohabitants.

As with all litigation, the moment of truth occurs at the time of trial, and it is the preparation by the attorney, which includes his research of the law, that will win the day. It is necessary for the attorney to obtain the definition of common-law marriage in the state where the lawsuit is being tried and to break this into its common elements. The testimony and evidence that will be introduced must be of such character as to convince the court that the living-together couple have satisfied all of the state's requirements for recognition of the common-law relationship. In an Oklahoma case a reasonable definition was expressed as follows:[2]

> To constitute a valid common-law marriage, there must be an actual and mutual agreement to enter into the matrimonial relation, permanent and exclusive of all others, between parties capable of making such a contract, consummated by their cohabitation as man and wife, or their mutual assumption openly of marital duties.

Once an acceptable definition is obtained, it is important to prepare a listing of the elements of proof necessary to establish the existence of such a relationship, which can include the following: (1) a conversation between the parties that they were going to enter into a permanent marital relationship; (2) evidence that they always introduced themselves as husband and wife to relatives, friends, and neighbors; (3) evidence that they have lived together in a common household and cohabited during such period of time; (4) bank accounts held in their joint names as husband and wife; and (5) joint tax returns, deeds to property, credit card bills, driver's license, or social security cards indicating a common name.

A Case Illustration

A case in New York[3] is illustrative of many that have been decided throughout the country regarding the issue of common-law marriage and may be more instructive regarding the state of the law than the Hurt case. The facts are most interesting: Susan and Leonard McCullon began living together in a rented apartment in Buffalo, New York, in 1948. After six years they purchased a home in an adjoining suburb of Buffalo and continued to live there together for a period of 28 years. Susan and Leonard never entered into a ceremonial marriage. However, since Susan began living with Leonard, she used the surname *McCullon*, which was done with Leonard's full knowledge and apparent approval, and she was introduced to their friends and relatives as Leonard's wife. During their relationship they opened a joint savings account in the name of Susan and Leonard McCullon, and they filed federal and state income tax returns on which Susan was listed as Leonard's wife. During the time they lived together, Susan always wore a wedding ring on her left hand.

Before the couple began their living-together relationship, Susan worked as a nurse's aide, but for the 28 years they lived together she did not seek outside employment. At the trial Susan testified that she was a housewife and that her responsibilities consisted of preparing meals, doing the laundry, and caring for the defendant and their three children, who were born during the time they lived together. In return, Leonard supported Susan and their children and paid all of their necessary bills including food, clothing, entertainment, and the like. Susan also testified that when they began to live together, Leonard told her, "We should stick together and work at it and make a home for us and our children." For the first five years that they lived together, Susan was married to another person and did not become divorced until she and Leonard purchased their home in Blasdale, New York. Leonard was aware of Susan's marital status and knew that she had obtained a divorce in 1953. Throughout the period that they lived together before their separation, from 1948 to 1977, Susan and Leonard visited Leonard's parents in Pennsylvania between two and four weeks at a time. Susan was introduced to Leonard's relatives and friends as his wife. Throughout their relationship the couple slept together in one bedroom. Susan called as a witness in her behalf her daughter Laura, who testified that she always believed that her parents were married and that neither advised her to the contrary.

Based upon this set of facts, the New York court held that the couple were legally married by common-law under the laws of the state of Pennsylvania. The McCullon court cited another case in New York[4] that also involved a claim that a common-law marriage was established in the state of Pennsylvania; in that case the parties spent only three weeks in Pennsylvania. Since Leonard and Susan had held themselves out as husband and wife in both New York and Pennsylvania, the New York court held the marriage to be valid.

The court further held that the mere promise by Leonard that he would "always take care of" Susan, together with the fact that the couple had lived together for 28 years and that three children were born of their union, was a sufficient basis to constitute an implied promise for Susan to forbear employment and provide household services for Leonard. The court concluded that both on the grounds of common-law marriage in Pennsylvania and an implied contract in New York State, alimony was warranted (although the court indicated that it was not prepared to place its stamp of approval on every nonmarital relationship).

Changing Values, Changing Standards?

It is interesting to note that the McCullon decision was written in 1978 and referred to a *Time* magazine article indicating that 1.5 million Americans have taken to living together without benefit of marriage, a figure representing a 100% increase since 1970. Although no present statistics are available, it is probably true that there are at least 25 million Americans living together today without benefit of marriage.

The McCullon court also referred to a recent survey on changing social mores. One of the questions was, Is it morally wrong for a couple who are not married to live together? A negative answer was given by 52% of the respondents. The New York court reasoned that "these changing social mores in our society have given rise to inequities and hardships which arise with the dissolution of non-marital relationships." The court, quoting from a *Law Review* article, asserted, "As a result, the law can no longer plausibly ignore these relationships and the harm they may cause to one partner. Rather, sound policy requires that these family forums be acknowledged to the extent necessary to prevent hardship and injustice." The McCullon court then suggested that the following relief be afforded to such cohabitants:

1. If an unmarried couple enters an express contract to share property or make payments in return for property or service contributions, the agreement should be enforced according to its term, regardless of their non-marital cohabitation.
2. If the unmarried couple agree that their relationship should entail no property or monetary consequences, again, the agreement should govern.
3. If it can be gathered from the facts and circumstances that the unmarried parties have engaged in an implied partnership or joint enterprise, or there is an implied in fact contract or trust, recovery should be allowed in accordance with their implied expectations.
4. When there is no agreement one way or the other, the law should relieve in equity and hardship to one of them and prevent unjust enrichment of the other.

It is remarkable that these thoughts would appear in a judicial decision in 1978. There is no question that there is a decided trend in the courts throughout this land to embrace these principles, but their full fruition is yet to be reached.

Legal scholar Steven Waterbury, in a *Law Review* article entitled "Property Rights upon Termination of Unmarried Cohabitation,"[5] suggested that unmarried couples who cohabit for a period of more than three years intend from their relationship that property consequences shall result from their unmarried cohabitation and further suggested that this presumption in the law could be overcome by a written agreement between the parties evidencing a contrary intention.

In the arguments of a creative attorney new theories may also arise that may provide legal remedies where none now exist. The courts always stand ready to do equity in a proper case. They will not permit one party to take advantage of another where to do so would shock the conscience of the court, nor will the courts permit law to be used as a sword rather than a shield. In the future some states may consider adopting laws to provide financial protection for living-together cohabitants or may adopt common-law marriage laws. It would be interesting to look ahead to the next decade to see the direction the law will take.

Conclusions

Finally, it is sufficient for the reader to understand that common-law marital status can potentially be accorded in any state to cohabitants who have visited one of the 13 common-law states or the District of Columbia and who meet the statutory standards such states have established for legal recognition of a state of matrimony. Unless you are aware of these legal principles, unwanted financial obligations may be imposed—or, if you are on the opposite side of this situation, wanted financial benefits may be denied. To protect against the uncertainty of such results, cohabitants should consider written agreements that can override state requirements and permit them to make any financial provisions for support or division of property acquired during their relationship that they deem to be fair and equitable. Chapter 10 explores the length and breadth of such agreements and contains suggestions for both the working and the nonworking cohabitant, and for cohabitants with money and property and those with none.

Some states have already begun to give legal recognition to cohabitants and have enacted legislation that would protect a cohabitant, especially in the event of death. (Interestingly, in Latin America there are countries that have established a policy that affords protection to stable nonmarital relationships.) New Hampshire will treat the surviving partner as a surviving spouse, provided cohabitation is established for a period of three years. Indiana, Kansas, and Oklahoma have formulated quasi-partnership theories to achieve equitable results for a good-faith party to an invalid marriage. Community property states such as Louisiana and Texas have permitted recovery based on implied contract where there is to be found an agreement to enter into a joint venture or a pooling of funds and where unjust enrichment would otherwise result. Michigan has permitted recovery in cases where there was an express agreement between nonmarital spouses.

Most recently, the highest appellate court in the state of Washington approved a holding of a trial court that extended the equitable distribution of married couples to unmarried cohabitants who had a "pseudo-marital" relationship that spanned ten years in duration.[6] In this case the couple had built a home together, having contributed physical labor to the project, had taken title in their joint names, had shared joint bank accounts, and had combined their earnings. The court further reflected that it was not necessary for a couple to represent themselves as husband and wife to establish a pseudo-marital relationship, although this couple had, in fact, represented themselves as husband and wife in some social activities. Finally, the court reasoned that the fact that there was continuous cohabitation for over ten years, during which the parties conducted themselves as a married couple and pooled their resources, was enough to establish that the couple had a long-term relationship, a condition necessary to warrant division of the property.

Whether other states will adopt this view or enact similar legislation remains to be seen. Nevertheless, there appears to be at least some trend that is emerging to grant to cohabitants some of the legal benefits of marriage, especially the right to property division when the relationship ends.

Notes

1. *Fryer v. Fryer*, S. C. eq. 85 (S.C. App.)
2. *Bann v. Bann*, 96 P.2 76 (Okla. 1939)
3. *McCullon v. McCullon*, 96 Misc.2d 962 (N.Y. 1978)
4. *Skinner v. Skinner*, 4 Misc.2d 1013; 150 N.Y.S. 739, (Sup. Ct, N.Y. Cty 1956)
5. *90 Harvard Law Review*, 1708 (June, 1977)
6. *Foster v. Thilges*, Wash CtApp, No. 25053–1-I, 7/15/91

Chapter 6

The Legal Rights of Gay Persons

Many couples currently living together are gay and cannot formally marry. Their legal rights are in a state of flux, but there appears to be a beginning recognition of the gay couple as a family unit. There are pockets of gay communities that exist in many of our cities, such as San Francisco and New York. Gay couples live together throughout this country and share many of the same concerns as heterosexual couples, including the fear of legal entanglements. Although it appears that society has in some respects accorded legal rights to heterosexual couples living together, the law has failed to accord legal status, in the areas of support, property division, and housing laws, to the homosexual or lesbian couple residing together in the same household.

Despite this failure of almost every state to accord legal status to gay couples, there have been certain laws passed concerning housing that have been interpreted to give protection to the gay couple. For example, in New York City a recent ordinance that gave preferred housing to a "family" was not interpreted to include recognition of a gay couple. The law was then attacked by the couple as being unconstitutional, with the court determining that the law had to be interpreted to include a gay couple in the definition of a family. This ruling, and some others that have occurred throughout the states, has not as yet been extended to marital laws, which permit support of a dependent spouse and the division of property acquired during the course of a marriage.

At this writing, no state recognizes marriage between gay couples. However, since state laws relating to marriage and the obtainment of a marriage license do not refer to a person's sexual orientation, it may well be that such laws cannot withstand the constitutional attack of a gay couple seeking to marry who argue that they have not been afforded equal protection of the law, as required by the Fourteenth Amendment of the Constitution. Most states have a similar constitutional provision regarding due process, and any constitutional attack that will be made in the future will probably include an argument based on both the U.S. Constitution and the state constitution. Whether such a constitutional attack will be accepted by a court remains to be seen, but certainly a favorable result cannot be expected until the mores of society become far more liberal and can accept a definition of marriage that includes the union of two persons of the same sex.

Some lawsuits throughout the country have mounted a constitutional attack against discriminatory laws affecting gay persons but not concerning their right to marry. In a Supreme Court decision—*Bowers v. Hardwick* (106 S.C. 2841 [1986])—the high court refused to apply the due process clause to the claimed right of homosexuals to engage in sexual acts with one another. In that case, a Georgia sodomy law criminalizing homosexual acts was determined to be constitutional. This ruling was made even though the Supreme Court had previously held that many aspects of consensual, adult, private sexual conduct are deemed fundamental liberties and are protected from federal or state regulation. Although this decision must be limited to its facts, it is still an expression of the narrow view of gay rights taken by the Supreme Court.

Despite these past decisions by the court, it is to be noted that judges attempt to reflect the pulse of society and are themselves a product of society. Although it may be some time before the law reflects a laissez-faire attitude concerning sexual orientation, there is some evidence that a change is under way.

Are Homosexuals Unfit for Parenthood?

In 1991 a blockbuster case was decided in the state of Florida involving adoption by a homosexual.[1] Several years ago the Florida legislature adopted a law that expressly excluded homosexuals from adopting a child. The statute created a presumption that homosexuals would be unfit parents. Since the passage of this law, some 14 years ago, no homosexual had seen fit to challenge its constitutionality until Edward Seebol, whose attempt to adopt a special-needs child was denied because his application revealed that he was a homosexual, brought this case in the state of Florida. In agreeing with the arguments made by Seebol, the court struck down the statute and found that the law violates the privacy rights of homosexuals as well as their right to equal protection and due process under the Constitution. The court, in reaching this decision, reflected that during the years since the statute was adopted there was a notable increase of tolerance for homosexuality and that several states (Washington, New York, Alaska, Ohio, and Massachusetts) had determined that the homosexuality of parents should not be a bar either to custody or visitation of infant children.

In explaining the reasons for its decision, the court went on to note that the right to privacy in Florida ensures that individuals are free from governmental interference because of their sexual orientation. Significant was the language contained in the decision to strike down the statute:

> The law disqualifies not only prospective parents who engage in private sexual conduct, but also those who express orientation toward homosexuality, even if unaccompanied by homosexual behavior. We believe that the inquiry into sexual orientation and consideration thereof, without regard for the child's best interest, violates Florida's right to privacy.

The court then went on to determine whether the state had the right to even inquire into sexual orientation and remarked that even if the government had the right to do so, the best interests of the children to be adopted should be the paramount concern of the court and that that ultimate goal would be totally frustrated by excluding on the basis of their sexual orientation an entire class of potential parents.

The court then concluded that sexual orientation can only be a determining factor if it can be shown to directly and adversely affect the child. Noting that since the law being attacked conferred the right to apply for adoption to both married and unmarried adults, the exclusion of homosexuals deprived such persons of due process of law. In approving Seebol's application, the court concluded as follows:

> A special needs child requires great care and may be unsuitable for adoption by most families. It is in the best interest of such a child to be adopted by a caring homosexual parent rather than to languish alone and unwanted in a state institution. Thus, the government function involved completely fails to achieve its legislative intent of providing a permanent family life to all children who can benefit by it. The law deprives homosexuals of procedural due process.

This decision is especially remarkable in that Florida had an express law, rather than case determinations, forbidding adoption by a homosexual person. If this ruling is approved by the Florida appellate courts, it may well be the precursor for other lawsuits throughout the country attacking the constitutionality of any law that would prohibit homosexuals from marriage, adoption, entering into contracts for support or division of property—in fact, of any state law that would discriminate against a person because of his or her sexual orientation.

Gay Couples Living Together

Inasmuch as the Supreme Court has seen fit in the past to end sexual discrimination between heterosexuals when it disapproved of an Alabama law that would not permit the award of alimony to a male litigant,[2] such decision being responsible for today's gender-neutral approach to family law litigation throughout the country, there may well be a later decision from the country's highest court that will end discrimination based on sexual orientation. Of course, whether or not this will occur will depend on society's increasing tolerance for one's right to maintain one's private life as one sees fit and the disappearance of prejudice against a gay lifestyle.

These varying attitudes of the court pose several dilemmas to a gay couple who wish to reside with each other. Are there any jurisdictions that will accord such couples the same legal protection as married couples?

Although no state within the United States will permit two persons of the same sex to enter into a marriage contract, New York, California, and Florida have made some liberal determinations to accord equal status to all persons living together, regardless of sexual orientation. Once a state of residence has been chosen, the next question that will normally be considered is whether the laws of such a state will permit recognition of either an oral or written agreement between a gay couple concerning division of property acquired during the time that their relationship existed or concerning support of one by the other for a fixed or indefinite period following termination of the relationship. Some states have been called upon to determine whether a contract between gay couples will be enforced.[3] Still other states have refused to accord recognition to such agreements, usually deciding that the contract was based on sexual considerations and, as such, could not be enforced. Such cases are not different from those discussed in the earlier chapter in this book concerning contracts between unmarried heterosexual cohabitants. On the other hand, this consideration may be an excuse that the court is embracing in reaching its determination because of an inherent prejudice against such an unconventional living arrangement.[4]

It is extremely difficult to predict in any given situation whether a court in the state in which you reside will accord any rights to a gay couple who cohabit with each other—even if there has been an earlier precedent within your state that accords such legal rights to an unmarried heterosexual couple. Thus, a written agreement cannot *guarantee* that your wishes will be followed if there is a dispute at the time you separate. Nonetheless, it is better to have one in order to attempt to ensure a fair distribution of property and monies accumulated during the course of living together, as well as to provide for the support of one cohabitant by the other who may be financially capable of doing so.

Whatever the circumstances may be, the important question to resolve is what financial provisions should be made for each of you at the termination of the relationship. Making provisions in the event of death is a relatively simple matter; there are no legal impediments to doing so, unless you or your partner were formerly married and have not procured a divorce. If that is the case, in the event that you die first, you will leave a surviving spouse who will have full legal rights to inherit your property (in most states one-third or one-half of your estate, depending on the number of children surviving); if you leave a will that makes no provisions for your spouse, then he or she will be permitted to elect against your will, that is, to obtain money or property equal to the percentage permitted by state law (again, usually one-third to one-half of your estate, depending on the number of children who may survive you). If neither of you has been previously married or if you have obtained a divorce following a marriage, you can freely provide for the transfer of any property upon your death to your cohabitant, being bound only by prudence and what you perceive to be the needs of other members of your family, children, or friends whom you wish to remember.

Gay couples negotiating a written agreement that will make provisions for support and a division of property in the event of death or separation face the same problems and must consider the same issues as a heterosexual couple planning to live together without marriage (or the heterosexual couple who plan to be married at some point in the future). Whether to provide for a lump sum payment of money in lieu of periodic payments, whether to utilize life insurance proceeds for such planning, whether to base the amount and duration of such support on the length of the period in which you lived together preceding your death—all are common questions shared by all cohabitants, regardless of sexual orientation. These problems are discussed at length in chapter 9, which should be referred to for suggestions on negotiating such issues and reaching a meeting of the minds that will be incorporated by your attorneys into a formal contract.

Fashioning an agreement to make financial provisions in the event of your voluntary or involuntary separation is a much more difficult matter from a legal standpoint. As noted earlier, there are still some courts that may not recognize agreements between homosexual cohabitants, holding that such agreements are based on sexual considerations. It is extremely difficult to predict how such courts will react in the event that a challenge is made to the agreement following your separation. It is absolutely essential that you consult with a knowledgeable matrimonial or family lawyer who will be able to review the decisional law in your state and attempt to predict what result will be reached by the court if the agreement is later challenged. Even expressing such expert opinion, no lawyer will be able to guarantee a result that a court may make in the future. Nonetheless, consulting with a professional will enable you to weigh the risks of entering into such agreement and the odds of the agreement itself being enforced or set aside.

Problems concerning a gay couple's right to enter into financial agreements would only come into play in the event that one of you contests the agreement following your separation from each other. When no such legal attack of the agreement is made, then, of course, the agreement would be honored by both of you and your financial obligations to one another would be discharged as you had previously agreed to and set forth in your written agreement. There is an increasingly liberal view by the medical community that homosexuality is not a form of mental disease.[5] It appears that the American Psychiatric Association currently believes that the only relationship between mental illness and homosexuality is the anxiety that occurs as a result of a homosexual person's inability to recognize his or her sexual orientation, together with society's failure to accept that orientation.[6] Moreover, because of society's increased awareness of the gay community's existence and the fact that more and more gay persons are acknowledging their sexual orientation and entering into living-together relationships, even the most conservative state legislatures and courts may accord legal recognition to the contracts made between gay persons, either those made explicit by writing or the oral promises and representations made during the time that the couple reside together. When this change will occur is difficult to predict.

With these warnings in mind, the gay couple can then get down to the job of negotiating a living-together agreement with the give-and-take and myriad other problems experienced by all persons considering a living-together relationship or a subsequent marriage. Again, the reader is referred to chapter 10, which deals with these problems and discusses the needs of both the working and nonworking partner and the ways in which these needs can be addressed, offering suggestions for the division of monies and property acquired during the course of the relationship.

In the Best Interests of the Child

Children may enter the life of a gay person or gay couple in a number of ways. There are instances where a gay person (formerly heterosexual) was previously married and had a child born out of that relationship. Following the divorce, there may have been agreement between the former spouses that the gay person, despite the change in sexual orientation, should have custody of the child; or perhaps a custody battle ensued, following which the gay person received custody of the child from the courts. At the time of the court battle, the gay person may already have acknowledged his or her homosexuality, or he or she may have decided to adopt such a sexual lifestyle following the proceeding. The person may then have begun to live with another person of the same sex or may perhaps have proceeded to live alone as a single parent.

There may be other circumstances in which children are brought into the lives of gay couples. A child may be adopted through an agency or privately from a birth mother who may consent to placing her child with a single parent or a gay couple. Unorthodox adoption is possible through artificial insemination or embryo transplantation. Any gay person who has attempted to obtain custody of a child, adopt a child, or produce a child by artificial means has learned that society will not normally approve of such attempts; for a gay person to successfully obtain a child is indeed a most difficult task.

Regardless of the way in which children become involved in their lives, homosexual parents often find that overt prejudice spills over to their children, that the children may become objects of ridicule, and that their attempt to enlist the aid of the court to obtain custody of their children is frequently denied.

Should a person's sexual orientation be considered by a court in determining whether or not he or she can be a fit parent? This question has been addressed by many courts throughout this land, with decidedly mixed results. Today, it appears that the enlightened view is that children raised by homosexual parents are no more likely to adopt a homosexual than a heterosexual orientation. There seems to be little psychological support for the view that a child's sexual development is in any way directly related to his or her parents' sexual orientation. Although statistics indicate that most homosexual parents raise heterosexual children, suggesting that sexual orientation is not learned from parents, there is still a certain segment of society—and, indeed, some courts—that regards homosexuals and their ability and fitness to act as custodial parents with great suspicion.[7]

When custody is at issue, it is important for the gay person to determine the predilections of the court in the state in which he or she resides concerning the rights of gay parents. There are some jurisdictions, including Virginia and North Carolina, that harbor an actual presumption of unfitness with regard to a homosexual parent. There are other states that take a more liberal view and hold that it is not the mere fact of homosexuality that renders a person an unfit parent but, rather, the presence of a homosexual partner in the home or other evidence of active sexual activity. There are still other jurisdictions that treat a homosexual parent on a parity with a heterosexual one and simply determine the question of fitness on the basis of factors other than sexual orientation. So, for example, in New York there have been many instances of a court awarding sole custody to a gay mother or father.[8] In states that adopt the most liberal view, the one concern of the court is not whether the gay parent resides in the same home with a gay or straight lover but whether or not the child is being exposed to the sexual activity of the parent and his or her partner. In all custody disputes, the "best interests of the child" are the paramount concern of the court. If a gay parent resides in a jurisdiction that takes this liberal approach, he or she faces the same considerations as a heterosexual parent. These include the emotional ties existing between parent and child; the parent's capacity to exhibit to the child love, affection, guidance, education, and religious training; the length of time the child has lived in a stable environment with the parent; and the moral, mental, and physical fitness of the parent. These are but a few of the issues that will be decided by the court in arriving at its determination to award custody to one or the other parent.

The preference of a child, if the child is of sufficient age and maturity, will also be taken into consideration by the courts but will by no means be a controlling factor. Custody disputes can, of course, be resolved by agreement of the parents. It is only when agreement cannot be reached that the courts will become involved in such determinations. Of course, an agreement between parents concerning children is not binding upon the courts, and the court is free to make a contrary determination when it believes that doing so would be in the best interests of the child.

For a gay person to adopt a child from an individual or agency or apply to the courts to create a child by artificial methods is indeed a most serious move. Although you may feel that your sexual orientation should not be considered, societal nonacceptance of your chosen lifestyle can nevertheless have great impact upon a child who may become part of your household. Although you may be strong enough to resist the ostracism or overt hostility of your neighbors in the community in which you reside, a child may not be able to deal with the abuse perpetrated against him or her by peers. The extent to which the child will experience psychological damage may vary according to the nature of the child and the makeup of the persons living in your neighborhood. Of course, it undoubtedly will be far easier for the child if you live in a gay community with other couples who have children residing in their household. With the knowledge that there will be a difficult adjustment period and that the child may indeed be subject to psychological abuse, it is incumbent upon you to thoroughly investigate the risks involved with a health care professional before deciding to raise a child in your home.

Custody Disputes

If a custody dispute develops between you and your ex-spouse, or between you and your lover in the instance where you have a living-together arrangement, it will undoubtedly be the most gut-wrenching experience of your life. Not only will you be subject in most states to a searching forensic examination, conducted by a battery of psychiatrists, psychologists, and social workers who will look into every aspect of your life, your living quarters, and your ability to be a custodial parent, but the child will also be subject to such scrutiny, all in an effort to determine which of the two warring parents would make a more fit custodian to raise a child into adulthood. Although you would like to think that your homosexuality should not play a part in the court's determination of custody, in actual practice you will have to accept the fact that your sexual preference will cause a red flag to be waved, especially by a heterosexual parent, and that you will be called upon to defend your sexual preference against a charge that will, among other personal charges, undoubtedly be made concerning your fitness to serve as a custodial parent. It will be your job to enlist the aid of a highly competent psychiatrist who will be able to give expert testimony to the court indicating that children raised by homosexual parents are no more likely to become homosexuals than those raised by heterosexual parents.

To walk into a courtroom without recognizing that a prejudice exists against you is to fail to accept the realities of life. If you do not reside in a liberal jurisdiction, obtaining custody of a child in a contested case may prove to be extremely difficult, if not impossible. You must remember that until recently it was rare for a heterosexual father to obtain custody of a child of tender years, since there was a natural tendency in the courts to award custody in such cases to the child's mother. This was uniformly done—despite the fact that the father may have been possessed of equal parenting qualities and, indeed, may have been the child's nurturing parent—since during this era the mother–child relationship was considered inviolable. Family lawyers practicing in the sixties and seventies had to caution a male client that his chances of obtaining custody of a child between infancy and perhaps seven or eight years of age was extremely difficult, if not impossible. It was only in those cases where the child was of more advanced years and could express a preference to live with him that custody could be obtained by a father. This phenomenon was known in the legal profession as the *tender years presumption*. It took many decades before the courts rejected this as the basis for an award of custody and instead substituted the best interests of the child.

Whether the natural prejudice that exists against homosexual parents will be eliminated in future years remains to be seen. When you consider that today there are judges who will find that your sexual preference alone renders you unfit to be a custodial parent, it seems likely that it will be many years before sexual orientation ceases to be a factor in the custody courts and decisions will be based solely on qualities that bear upon the ability of a person to acquire parenting skills.

Some ten years ago the Supreme Court decided a landmark

case[9] which required that all statutes and laws pertaining to husbands and wives had to be gender-neutral. Put another way, the Supreme Court now required that spouses be treated equally in all respects, regardless of their sex. This case enabled men, for the first time, to seek alimony payments from their wives. Will the Supreme Court reach this determination concerning sexual orientation in the near future? That appears most unlikely, especially in light of the case of *Bowers v. Hardwick*, discussed earlier in this chapter.

There have been some notable decisions, both in Alaska and in New York, with regard to custody awards to gay parents. For example, a New York court awarded custody of a child to a gay mother, affirming the decision of a lower court that there was no finding that the mother's sexual orientation prevented her from fulfilling her parenting responsibilities. The lower court also took pains to point out that the sexual activity of this mother, like that of other parents, did not take place in the child's presence and should not be considered in reaching the determination of which parent to place the child with.[10]

There have been later cases decided in New York that have adopted a similar view, but by no means have the decisions been uniform. This lack of uniformity appears to take place in almost every jurisdiction, even in those states that have adopted a liberal view. One must understand that any custody dispute tried before a given judge will reflect that jurist's background, predilections, prejudices, and life experience. When a judge holds deep-rooted prejudices against homosexuality, there is little likelihood, even in a liberal environment, that such a judge will find in favor of a gay parent in a contested custody dispute.

In another liberal jurisdiction, Alaska, a lower court's determination to award custody to a heterosexual rather than a gay parent was disapproved and the lower court chastised because its decision was "tainted by . . . reliance upon the fact that the mother is a lesbian."[11] The decision by the appellate court in Alaska was even more remarkable when you consider that the mother was, at the time, maintaining an ongoing sexual relationship with her lover in the home where the child resided and previous cases in the past in the field of child custody seemed to disapprove of such living arrangements. The Alaska court carved out a rule that will permit awarding custody of a child to a gay parent, despite such living arrangements, as long as it can be shown that placing the child with the gay parent is the better choice in the contested custody dispute.

Because of the difficulty in predicting the outcome of litigation at trial as well as at the appellate level, custody litigation should not be treated lightly by the litigants. A tremendous expense may be incurred in seeking custody before the courts (it is not unusual for legal fees—as well as the fees of experts, such as psychiatrists, who must necessarily be called in such cases—to range in cost from $10,000 or $15,000 to $30,000 or $50,000. (This is because an experienced attorney who specializes or is certified in your state as a matrimonial expert may charge hourly rates between $200 and $400, especially in large cities like New York, Chicago, Los Angeles, San Francisco, and Miami, and the trial of a contested custody matter may involve perhaps 25 hours of preparation and 40 to 80 hours of trial time.) In addition, there will be untold emotional anguish to you and your child, which may result in scars that may take many years to heal. Keep in mind also that going through a contested trial and being awarded custody of your child by the courts does not mean that this decision cannot later be reversed by an appellate court or that when the child is older another challenge to custody cannot be made based on changed circumstances.

There will be additional attendant expense associated with an appeal. If you seek to overturn the decision of a lower court, you must arrange to prepare the record, which includes the testimony during the trial and all exhibits that may have been used; bear the expense of printing such records, as well as the legal briefs that will be prepared by your attorneys; and, of course, pay the fees of your attorney for his or her work in the appellate process. Most states provide for further appellate review under varying circumstances, so that even if you are the one who takes an appeal to an intermediate appellate court and are successful, you must nevertheless sustain this result in the state's highest appellate court, causing you further anguish and expense. Thus, you must clearly consider all of the potential problems and costs that you will encounter before you decide to seek the aid of the court to obtain custody of your child. In almost every instance it would be far better to attempt a negotiated settlement whereby the most liberal visitation rights are negotiated if you cannot obtain custody. Only after all such avenues have been exhausted, should the legal option be employed.

Notes

1. See Section 63.042(3), Fla. Stat. (1977), which provides that "no person eligible to adopt under this statute may adopt if that person is a homosexual."
2. *Orr v. Orr*, 99 S.Ct. 1102, 59 L.Ed.2d 306, 440 U.S. 268 (1979).
3. See, for example, Arkansas, *Bramlett v. Selman*, 597 S.W. 2d 80 (Ark. 1980); Oregon, *Ireland v. Flannagan*, 51 Or. App. 837 (1981); and Texas, *Small v. Harper*, 638 S.W. 2d 24 (Tex. Civ. App. 1982).
4. See *Jones v. Daly*, 122 Cal. App. 3d 500 (1981), where the court denied legal recognition.
5. The American Psychiatric Association no longer classifies homosexuality as a form of mental disease and has not done so since 1973.
6. See American Psychiatric Association, *Diagnostic and Statistical Manual of Mental Disorders*, 3rd ed. (Washington, DC: American Psychiatric Association, 1980), 281–282, 380.
7. Sexual identity of 37 children raised by homosexual parents, *American Journal of Psychiatry, 135* (1978), p. 692; and the avowed lesbian mother and her right to child custody, 12 San Diego L.Rev. 799 (1975).
8. See *Guinan v. Guinan*, 102 A.D.2d 963 (1984).
9. *Orr v. Orr*, 99 S.Ct. 1102, 59 L.Ed.2d 306, 440 U.S. 268 (1979).
10. See *Guinan v. Guinan*, 102 A.D.2d 963 (1984).
11. *S. N. E. v. R. L. V.*, 699 P.2d 875 (Alaska, 1985).

Chapter 7

AIDS and the Law

There is no doubt that acquired immune deficiency syndrome (AIDS) will have a greater impact on the law than any other topic in the twentieth century. While our scientists work feverishly toward a cure or treatment of this insidious disease that is inevitably fatal to its victims, our courts are only just beginning to grapple with the legal entanglement that will be caused by the transmittal of AIDS, or the human immunodeficiency virus (HIV), from one person to another, spouse to spouse, domestic partner to domestic partner. AIDS is no longer a disease confined to the gay community. It is a disease that knows no sexual boundaries today, nor those of race, nationality, or religion. A person who is a carrier of this virus may not even be aware of it, since the symptoms of this disease may not appear for many years following initial infection.

Because of this long incubation period, there undoubtedly are countless numbers of persons living together today who are infected with the disease and do not know it. Children born of infected couples will in many instances suffer from the disease. The number of persons who will die from AIDS in this country in the next several years is estimated to be in the hundreds of thousands.

It appeared that many persons throughout this country chose to ignore the magnitude of the AIDS epidemic, feeling secure in the false belief that AIDS was limited to homosexual practices or the use of infected drug needles by addicts. These myths were dramatically dispelled when one of this nation's most beloved athletes, Magic Johnson, went public with the fact that he, a married heterosexual, had contracted the HIV virus. Today, from every corner of the country, groups have sprung up to advance medical research to find the cause and perfect a cure or treatment for the victims of AIDS, as well as to promote "safe sex," a phrase that has recently entered our lexicon.

The sexual revolution that gave new freedom to consenting adults to freely enter into sexual liaisons has now given way to a fear of sexual contact and to increased use of condoms as a preferred means of disease prevention. Despite the fear of contracting AIDS or the HIV virus, sexual contacts proliferate among married as well as unmarried couples; it is more important to educate people about safe sexual practices than to advocate abstinence, which for many cannot be considered a viable alternative. In recent months courts throughout the country have been asked to determine whether contracting AIDS by a spouse constitutes grounds for a divorce, whether a person's request that a spouse submit to AIDS testing be granted, whether to deny visitation rights to a parent who has tested HIV positive, and whether AIDS itself is grounds for divorce[1] in those states that still require fault. One of the most important concerns to an unmarried person is to determine whether the partner has the disease or is a carrier of the HIV virus before entering into a living-together relationship. It is essential for any persons who now are in such a relationship or who anticipate entering one, as well as persons who plan to marry, to undergo an AIDS blood test. If this is not done and it is later determined that one person is infected with the virus, there will be significant medical, legal, emotional, and financial impact upon the partners and any children that may be born from the relationship.

While AIDS primarily is transmitted through sexual contact, there are indeed instances of persons contracting the disease from other, seemingly innocent, sources, including dental treatment and intravenous blood transfusion. These persons must be regarded as being unknowing victims of the disease, as distinguished from those who engage in unsafe sexual practices or drug use without regard to their potential consequences. Since AIDS can be contracted in innocent circumstances, it would be wise for all living-together (or domestic) partners, as well as married couples, to periodically undergo an AIDS blood test, especially if they are considering having a child. Although AIDS can be transmitted through sexual contact, blood transfusions, and shared needles, and from pregnant women to their fetuses, it does not appear from current scientific thinking that AIDS can be transmitted through casual contact, such as being in the presence of a person who is sneezing or coughing, or eating or drinking from common glasses, dishes, or utensils. Recently, federal public health officials predicted that at least 450,000 persons in this country will be diagnosed with AIDS by the end of 1993 and that as many as 100,000 new cases will be reported in that year alone. One need only to read the obituary columns to be found in urban newspapers to understand the magnitude of this problem. For the most part, people who die of illness in their twenties or thirties today are typically victims of the AIDS virus.

Although scientists are searching for a treatment, to date only a single drug, AZT, has been licensed by the Food and Drug Administration to treat the infection caused by the HIV virus. Approximately 60% of those persons who have been diagnosed with the disease for at least one year have already died. Statistics reveal further that the death rate increases to 70% some two years after diagnosis, although some persons have beaten the odds and are still alive seven years after diagnosis.

The Economic Implications of AIDS to Domestic Partners

As discussed in chapter 10 of this book, many domestic partners may be beset with a claim for a division of property that has been acquired during the relationship, as well as with a request for support that may be based upon an implied contract. Many times the courts will look to the adjustment of marital partners' rights when considering what to do with the claims of unmarried couples for these financial benefits. As observed earlier, the division of property acquired during marriage is uniformly recognized throughout the United States when the courts divide marital assets. Normally, the courts do not consider fault. However, in some states, such as New York, the doctrine of *egregious fault*, which has been defined as conduct that may shock the conscience of the court, has been recognized; its effect is to adjust the respective percentages that the parties may receive when marital property is divided. That is, if there has been a long history of profound spousal abuse and the court determines that such conduct is egregious, it can increase the amount of property that may be received by the innocent spouse by taking into account such wrongful conduct. For example, if under ordinary circumstances the court would divide marital property equally, it might decide, if egregious conduct exists, to punish the offending spouse by making a 40%:60% or perhaps even a 30%:70% division.

While few cases involving AIDS have yet to reach the appellate courts in New York or elsewhere, it appears likely that when AIDS is contracted through innocent conduct of the spouse, it will not affect the property distribution or be considered egregious. However, if a spouse has engaged in extramarital affairs or drug use and through such contacts contracts the AIDS virus, it would appear that this would constitute egregious conduct and would enable the court to make an unequal distribution of marital property. When one considers that transmitting AIDS is almost akin to issuing a death warrant, the court might well be so outraged by this conduct as to deprive the offending spouse of any benefits of the marital property and to award whatever financial benefits of the marriage exist entirely to the innocent spouse.

Domestic partners will undoubtedly be treated similarly when claims to division of property are made between them.

When AIDS has been contracted through innocent circumstances, it may well have no impact upon the property division. However, if the disease was contracted through unsafe sexual practices with another person or through IV drug use, most courts would adjust the division between the domestic partners unequally, favoring the party who becomes infected from sexual contacts with his or her live-in partner. However, it might be difficult for the courts to do so since, as has been indicated previously, the basis for a division of property between unmarried partners must rest in contract law until such time as the legislatures of the states pass laws that will actually treat living-together partners as marital partners. The courts might be much more liberal in making an award of support in claims founded in contract law between living-together partners since a promise to support a domestic partner without specifying the exact amount will permit the court to fix a weekly sum. When egregious fault is present, the court will obviously fashion the award and specify a weekly sum of money that is greater than it would normally be in order to punish the offending partner.

Money Damages for AIDS

In discussing AIDS, it should not be overlooked that a person who becomes infected from a marital or domestic partner, like an accident case victim, may have the ability to bring a lawsuit seeking extremely substantial money damages. Where it can be shown that a partner transmitted the disease with the knowledge that he or she had engaged in unsafe sexual practices with another person or where the partner had been an IV drug user and failed to disclose such information, that partner would undoubtedly be compelled to respond in a court of law for substantial money damages. The issue of whether the conduct of the partner transmitting the disease was intentional or negligent does not determine the innocent partner's right to recover: both negligent and intentional conduct are recognized by the law. The amount of damages a jury will award will normally be less for negligently transmitting a disease than intentionally doing so. Sometimes, *punitive damages* may be awarded in addition to regular compensatory damages. Punitive damages, sometimes referred to as "smart money," are an extra and significant amount of money awarded in order to "smarten up" other would-be offenders, that is, to serve as a lesson to others to refrain from similar conduct.

The pain and suffering experienced by a person learning that he or she has contracted AIDS is incalculable. It would appear that juries called upon to resolve the question of a reasonable sum of money to compensate a victim for such pain and suffering and eventual death may well return enormous money awards against the offending defendants. Those who believe that they have been infected by intention or negligence by another person should consult a personal injury lawyer who has had substantial experience in prosecuting AIDS-related cases. Of course, an award of a jury is only as good as the ability to recover such monies from the offending party. A million-dollar verdict rendered against a person whose assets are limited will be of no real value. Additionally, one should consider that a jury award obtained against an individual can be discharged in bankruptcy, provided the action of the party causing the transmittal of AIDS is negligent and not intentional; an intentional act, on the other hand, is not dischargeable in bankruptcy. Moreover, when it can be shown that the transmission of the disease was so reckless that it must be considered intentional, the courts may instruct the jury that it is free to award punitive damages in addition to compensatory damages for pain and suffering. Obviously, these lawsuits are most complex and require the aid of experienced personal injury lawyers. Local bar associations are able to refer attorneys particularly skilled in such matters.

Note that, generally, these lawsuits are handled on a *contingency basis* so that it is not necessary for a plaintiff to pay anything to the lawyer to accept the case. Contingency fees run anywhere from 25% to 33⅓% of the amount recovered in these matters. So it is important for a person who is contemplating bringing legal action to attempt to retain an attorney with the greatest experience and success rate with personal injury cases.

AIDS and Its Impact on Children

When disputes concerning matters of custody and visitation of children arise between domestic partners who have had children born of their relationship, the courts must consider whether one or the other parent has the HIV virus or AIDS itself. Since the courts must determine what is in the best interests of the child in deciding custody and visitation issues, a healthy ex-partner will be sure to raise the issue of AIDS in an attempt to prevent visitation or custody. Whether a person who has contracted AIDS can be considered an unfit parent remains for the courts to determine. Some may argue that there is no danger of HIV infection to the child since a child cannot contract the disease simply by residing with an infected parent; others may urge that the proper punishment for the transmission of the disease would be the denial to the infecting parent of both custody and visitation. However, since there appears to be no present scientific evidence that AIDS has ever been transmitted in the absence of high-risk behavior, such punitive arguments may fall on deaf ears. Because AIDS is a progressively debilitating illness it may certainly be argued that the resulting physical handicaps will prevent the discharge of a person's parental duties and, therefore, negatively impact upon the child; such handicaps would also affect the ability of the infected parent to exercise visitation rights. Certainly, the stronger argument would be that the parent suffering from this disease would not be as fit as the uninfected parent to have primary custody of the child; moreover, living with a terminally ill parent would subject the child to great emotional trauma and compel him or her to observe the progressive deterioration and eventual death of that parent.

There exists in this country, despite enlightenment in recent years, a social stigma to AIDS. Being placed in the custody of a parent with the disease may cause the child untold emotional trauma from his peers; the child may be the object of ridicule and contempt, not to mention fear, in the school environment. It may very well be necessary for children of infected parents to be seen by a psychiatrist or a psychologist to help them cope with the emotional and social repercussions of a parent's terminal illness— and the social stigma it may impart. When the courts are called upon to decide custody and visitation disputes involving AIDS-infected parents, they must also consider the potential psychological damage of their decision to a child who is aware that his or her parent will become disabled and die.

On the other hand, there are circumstances in which AIDS, whether contracted by innocent or willful conduct, should not prevent a parent from contacts with the child, although it may well be that custody might be better placed with the uninfected parent. Visitation should be encouraged. Children are not deprived of parents during serious illnesses such as cancer. It would seem unwise, then, to refuse out of vindictiveness to allow a child to visit an AIDS-infected parent. Children must be given the opportunity to come to terms with a parent's death.

The needs of the individual child must always prevail, and both parents must be sensitive to the psychological needs of their child. Only when this is done, can custody and visitation matters be resolved without the aid of the court. All parties—parents and children—are best served by avoiding the trauma and cost of becoming embroiled in a long court battle. Parents beset with these difficulties are urged to seek counseling from health care professionals and attorneys so as to deal with these problems and prevent them from escalating into a courtroom drama.

Note

1. *Doe v. Roe*, 526 N.Y.S.2d 718 (1988).

Chapter 8

Support and Property Division Laws

The concept of "palimony," although fanciful, has not been approved by any state, including California, where the word was first coined and urged as a remedy before a court of law. Alimony is a creature of statute, which simply means that unless state law makes an express provision for it, alimony simply is not available as a legal remedy. Alimony has been approved only for a legally married spouse who otherwise cannot be self-supporting. No state has extended its support laws (which grant alimony or, in some states, "maintenance") to include unmarried persons living together. So the term *palimony* is a misnomer; the attempt to include nonmarried live-in companions as eligible persons to receive support has failed. The reason for this result appears to be that most courts wish to send a message to cohabitants that their relationship will not be given the approval afforded to married persons, perhaps because marriage is regarded by many as the strength of the American fabric.

Disapproving of palimony is surely a way to sharpen the distinction between cohabitants and married persons. However, it should be noted that although the live-in companion, Michele Triola, in the widely publicized Lee Marvin case[1] failed to obtain palimony, the California court actually ruled that cohabitants could enter into express contracts concerning financial matters following separation or that contracts might be inferred to exist because of the relationship. Although no such contract was found to exist between Marvin and Triola, the lower court awarded Triola $104,000 for rehabilitation; this award was later dismissed. The case made an impact throughout the country since it was one of the first to acknowledge that cohabitants might, under certain circumstances, obtain financial or property rights and enforce such obligations by virtue of their relationship.

This chapter focuses on the size of a property division or alimony award that can be made by the courts to a married person and explores community property and equitable distribution laws, which permit in every state the distribution of property acquired during marriage regardless of *title*, the legal word used for ownership. An understanding of these principles and of the size and scope of the award that may be made by a court is essential knowledge when considering what terms should be included in a prenuptial or cohabitation agreement.

Alimony

Alimony is defined in many dated dictionaries[2] as "(1) an allowance paid to a woman by her husband or former husband, granted by a court upon a legal separation or a divorce, or while an action is pending, or (2) supply of the means of living, maintenance." Since the decision of the Supreme Court in *Orr v. Orr*, all alimony laws throughout the land have been constitutionally sanitized and rendered gender-neutral; that is to say, today either spouse, husband or wife, is eligible to receive, or can be compelled to pay, support on the basis of their respective financial circumstances.

In determining the proper amount to be awarded as alimony in a given case, the courts must balance the respective needs and abilities of the parties. The court does not seek to prefer one spouse at the expense of the other; rather, it seeks to accommodate both parties' needs in arriving at a sum it deems fair after considering a number of factors. The following factors are taken into account by a majority of the courts throughout the country:

1. Current respective income and future earning capacity
2. Duration of marriage
3. Respective physical and mental conditions, including need for special medical care
4. Need to remain in the marital home, especially where young children are living in the household
5. Length of time required to acquire new skills or renew old ones in an effort to become self-supporting
6. Reduction or loss of earnings or earning capacity because partner may have foregone or delayed education, training, employment, or career opportunities during marriage in order to act as the primary homemaker or parent
7. Need to support minor children and the amount of such support that is awarded by the court
8. Tax consequences, that is, the tax effect of paying alimony (deductible by the paying spouse) or receiving it (includable as income to the receiving spouse and, therefore, reduced by taxes by about 28%–33%, depending on the tax bracket)
9. A party's contribution to the marriage, as a wage earner or homemaker, or to the career of the supporting spouse
10. Waste of any marital asset (for any of a myriad of reasons, including greed, gambling, and drug addiction)
11. Transfer of a marital asset without a genuine reason for the express purpose of placing it out of the reach of the court and without receiving the fair market value for such transferred asset
12. Preseparation standard of living, an assessment of which would include the home lived in, vacations taken, clubs and theaters attended, restaurants enjoyed, and, gener-

ally, any other factors that would reflect the quality of life enjoyed during the happier years of the marriage

These are but some of the factors most courts will consider when attempting to balance the financial circumstances of the parties when awarding support to a needy spouse. They are by no means intended to exclude other considerations that may be pertinent to this search for fairness. Many states permit the court wide latitude in reaching a final award and permit the consideration of any other relevant factors that a court might find to have some economic bearing on the final sum of money considered proper. Can anyone predict with exactness the size of the award to be made? No, not unless that person is clairvoyant, since there are so many variables that enter into consideration; it is a mistake to rely on a history of past awards. It would be extremely dangerous for someone considering divorce to anticipate the same amount of alimony awarded to a friend or relative who has gone through a divorce proceeding, because even if the financial factors are almost identical in the two cases, the philosophy and background of the judges making the awards may be more responsible for the result than the income of the parties. That is to say, there are some judges who are much more liberal than others in making alimony awards. Since one cannot select the judge who will hear the case (oftimes selection is made by computer, a rotation list, or luck of the draw), the ability to predict the amount of support to be awarded is much akin to predicting the numbers of a winning lottery ticket.

Is there a rule of thumb that is used by the matrimonial or family courts to arrive at a reasonable amount of support? If you would ask any judge who decides such matters, the odds are he or she would deny such a rule exists. Nonetheless, experience dictates that certain parameters are utilized, especially in cases involving working or middle-class families. In the final analysis, common sense will prevail over legal theories. For example, if you are earning $300 a week, and your take-home pay is but $225, there is little chance that a court could award more than $75 weekly as alimony, since you would have remaining but $150 weekly for all of your own living expenses. The court would also have to consider that your spouse should be able to earn $75 weekly, even if employed part-time or at home, assuming, of course, that no physical disabilities exist and that there are no small children involved. The court must give great weight to the working spouse's needs for the necessities of life before even thinking of the standard of living of the parties: no court would award a sum for support that would have the effect of rendering the working spouse unable to pay for his or her own rent, food, and clothing. Thus, when limited incomes are involved, it is rare to see more than 25% to 33⅓% of the wage earner's net income, or 50% of gross income, awarded as alimony.

When larger incomes are involved, the courts can then consider the couple's preseparation standard of living and the lifestyle they enjoyed. When the needs of the spouse who does not work or earns less require about $350 a week, the amount of that spouse's income, say $125 weekly, must be deducted from such an amount to establish a deficiency of $225 weekly. This is the starting point. If the major breadwinner's gross income is $750 weekly, there is a good likelihood that the shortfall of $225 will be awarded in alimony, since there would remain $525 for the supporting spouse to apply to his or her own living expenses. In this example, a 30% award of *gross* income enables a nice balancing of the needs of both parties and includes a consideration of the preseparation standard of living.

If you are wealthy, your exposure to liability for larger sums becomes greater. If you enjoy gross income of $250,000 or more and your spouse can prove that in order for him or her to maintain the preseparation standard of living $75,000 annually (approximately $1,440 a week) is required, the court might very well award the entire sum requested, since you would retain $175,000 for your own purposes. In this example, again, the percentage of gross income awarded is about one-third. The larger your income, the greater the likelihood that the court, upon an application for alimony, will award the amount requested. If awarding an amount sufficient to maintain the supported spouse's status quo will not impose an undue financial burden upon the supporting spouse, the court will normally grant the amount requested.

Perhaps the most difficult dilemma for a court is to decide support applications where incomes between $25,000 and $75,000 are involved, because it becomes very difficult to balance the needs of the spouse who requires support against those of the spouse who will be paying such support. The court, in attempting to avoid preference of one party over the other, must do a nice balancing act to arrive at a fair decision. In these cases, the preseparation standard of living becomes a less important consideration. There would be no point in the court's creating a crushing financial burden for a working spouse; doing so would only encourage flight to another state or remove the incentive to be gainfully employed. Of course, an oppressive award to either party will normally result in an appeal to a higher court to adjust any apparent inequities. Most appellate courts are receptive to appeals of lower court orders that fail to consider carefully the needs of each litigant. Put another way, a one-sided award (perhaps $125 weekly from gross weekly income of $200) is destined to be set aside or materially reduced by an appeals court.

As you have probably observed, it is far easier to predict a court result when dealing with either very small or very large incomes. The harder job is to predict, with a reasonable degree of accuracy, a court's determination for a middle-income couple. This is perhaps the single most compelling reason to enter into a written agreement that will make certain what the future rights and obligations will be for both you and your partner and will enable you both to avoid the trauma and unnecessary expense that a court proceeding will generate. Agreements between parties are always encouraged by the courts, and they afford you the finality that is necessary to move on with your lives in the event that the two of you separate at some time in the future. Lawyers frequently remark that even a questionable settlement is better than a long and bitter lawsuit where nerves are frazzled and emotional scars are inflicted.

Despite these difficulties, in order to successfully negotiate a prenuptial or cohabitation agreement, you must nevertheless weigh your exposure to receive or pay alimony and obtain a feeling for the amounts that may be granted. Of course, a reluctance by one partner to do so can result in aborting the plan to live together or marry; the consideration of these subjects is a very delicate matter indeed (see chapter 10). Having a good idea of what may lie ahead in the courtroom will make you a better, more informed client and better able to communicate with your chosen attorney on these matters.

Before moving on to discuss how different courts treat the division of property acquired during marriage or other relationships, it is interesting to observe that not every state permits an award of alimony or maintenance. For example, Texas prohibits such spousal support and, instead, looks to the parties' properties and, to some degree, child support in order to fashion a financial package for separating or divorcing persons.

A "Taxing" Thought

Before leaving the subject of alimony, consideration must be given to the income tax implications of the payment or receipt of alimony. Alimony or maintenance payments (which must be conditional upon the death, but not the remarriage of the recipient in order that it be tax deductible) made according to an agreement or court order are deductible by the paying spouse and includable as income to the spouse receiving such payments. However, the tax law only recognizes married persons in granting such treatment concerning support payments. Accordingly, if partners do not marry following the signing of their agreement, no tax implications would be imposed on the agreement of support; that is, the support payments would not be deductible from the supporting partner's gross income when filing the annual tax return, and the supported partner would not be required to include receipt of such payments as income. The application of these rules can have a marked arithmetic impact. For example, if we assume that you are married and in the 30% combined tax bracket for both federal and state income taxes (assuming further you reside in a state that imposes a personal income tax) and you are the person who agrees to pay $100 weekly in alimony or maintenance, the cost to you after taxes would be but $70 weekly, since the effect of the tax deduction would trim $30 off each week's payment. In this sense, the federal and state governments would share in your obligation to make support payments to the extent of $30 weekly. On the other hand, if you are the now-divorced recipient of such payments, you would have a corresponding loss of $30, assuming you did not have other income tax deductions that could wipe out the payment; as such, the net monies you would have available for use, after the payment of state and federal income taxes, would be but $70 weekly. The numbers may change, but the formula remains the same. No one should agree on a support arrangement without carefully considering the tax consequences that will flow from such payments. It would be most wise to consult with an attorney or certified public accountant who is highly skilled in tax matters affecting divorcing couples to obtain specific advice on these complex tax matters.

The never-married couple, as noted earlier, will not be concerned with these arithmetic changes based on the tax laws. No benefit or loss will be occasioned by either party. Although there is a trend today to accord some benefits to gay persons who reside together (see chapter 6), such as considering them a family unit under some local building codes, such a trend in no way means that favorable income tax treatment will be accorded to such persons. Because the gay communities have become more vocal and aggressive in seeking legislative change throughout the country, their needs are now being seriously addressed. There is no similar lobby for the needs of heterosexual cohabitants, but as more persons adopt this lifestyle as an alternative to marriage, their needs may be similarly addressed. Many of the court decisions today that seek to provide financial relief, apart from an award of alimony or a division of property pursuant to community property or equitable distribution, do so under the guise of contract enforcement and other creative legal theories. Some laws already exist that give equal rights to cohabitants in acquiring or retaining housing; whether such legal approval will spill over to other areas remains to be seen.

Property Divisions

Almost every state in the union during the past 15 years has enacted laws that provide for the distribution at the time of divorce of any property acquired during marriage, regardless of whose name the title is held in. For example, a piece of real estate acquired in your sole name or held jointly with your spouse or a bank account or shares of stock held in your spouse's sole name at the time of divorce are all treated as marital property, and the courts may compel you or your spouse to share the assets equally or equitably, depending upon what your state laws direct. Title in the name of only one spouse no longer prevents the court from making a division of the asset in some fashion. New York, for example, is an equitable distribution state, California a community property state. Presently, there are 37 states that have adopted equitable distribution laws and only 11 that have approved of community property. This is probably true because equitable distribution allows the court to take into account the myriad financial circumstances of the parties involved whereas the concept of community property compels an equal arithmetic distribution. However, there are many community property states[3] that now permit the courts to consider other than arithmetic factors in dividing the marital estate.

Today, most states permit and encourage prenuptial agreements that include provisions for support and division of assets. Some states permit agreements to be made during marriage that will address the same issues. The considerations reviewed in the following pages will enhance your ability to arrive at fair provisions that will be acceptable to you and your fiancé, spouse, or cohabitant.

The primary concern of most people when they contemplate these agreements and their impending relationship is to protect an asset that may have been in the family for many years or property or a business interest that might be purchased or received as a gift from a family member. To begin with, you must know the difference between marital and separate property. In most states *marital property* is defined as property obtained during marriage, except by gift or inheritance; in some states this also includes monies received during marriage as an award from a personal injuries lawsuit. *Separate property* is defined as all other property owned prior to marriage or acquired by gift, inheritance, or the result of a personal injuries claim. In some states the definition of marital property includes the increase in value, sometimes referred to as the appreciated value, of separate property. This can come about if you own a business prior to marriage that, let's say, is worth $50,000 and increases in value at the time of divorce to $100,000; the increased (or appreciated) value of $50,000 ($100,000 less $50,000) would be considered marital property and therefore subject to distribution upon divorce.

A similar result obtains when a share of stock, real estate, or bank account increases in value, although some courts first determine whether the increase was brought about by the active, rather than the passive, participation of the person owning such separate property. When the increase is due to market conditions alone, it is said to be caused by passive forces and is therefore not included in the marital estate. Expressed another way, increases that occur in the value of an asset by no active participation by the spouse who has ownership of such asset will not qualify as a marital asset. Only when some affirmative act of the partner (e.g., managing a business, stock portfolio, or investment real estate) is responsible for the enhanced value will the courts determine such increase to be a marital asset. These distinctions can be very difficult to make, and the advice and counsel of an experienced matrimonial lawyer is essential in these matters.

The desire to protect family assets, or to protect accumulated assets, for the benefit of your children if you have been previously divorced is an understandable motive. In order to protect these assets, you must be aware of how courts will first define, and then divide, marital property. Most people grasp the concept that property owned before marriage is separate property and that property acquired during marriage by inheritance or a gift from other than one's spouse is also defined and treated as separate property. As explained before, in many states throughout the country the increased, or appreciated, value of such separate assets, if the increase was brought about by some active participation (e.g., working to make a business grow, trading securities to enhance the value of the portfolio, or some other such hands-on control of a separate asset), will convert the increased value of the separate asset into a marital asset. Once this is accomplished, the added value then drops into the marital pot and the court is free to lower its ladle into the stew and portion out as much as it deems fair onto each partner's plate. Deciding whether a given asset is marital or separate property has produced fierce battles in the courts and has been the subject of much litigation. You and your partner can, of course, resolve such questions in the negotiation stages of your premarital agreement, which is one of the most important reasons to have one.

Having discussed the nature of such property and identified what property will eventually be placed into the marital stew, thought must now be directed to the division of such assets, which depends on whether you reside in a community property or equitable distribution state.

Today there are 11 community property states: Arizona, California, Idaho, Louisiana, Nevada, New Mexico, North Carolina, Oregon, Washington, West Virginia, and Wisconsin. All others have adopted equitable distribution laws, with the exception of Mississippi, which alone stands as a title state. The law favoring equitable distribution evolved so that courts can consider other than arithmetic factors when they divide marital property. It is to be noted, however, that even of the community property states, only ten require that the court must consider that the law creates a *presumption* of equality, which means that the judge must start with the concept that the property can be equally divided and only alter such division if he or she finds compelling other circumstances, such as advanced age or physical or mental disability. Presumptions in the law make it much more difficult for a court to disapprove making an equal division because the burden is on the party seeking to overcome the presumption to offer acceptable proof to the court to disregard it. This rule does give the court some flexibility to make an other-than-equal distribution but not nearly as much as the community property states of Nevada and Arizona, which permit equitable considerations to vary the arithmetic division.

The trend in the law in both equitable distribution and community property states is to attempt to treat equally spouses who have been involved in long-term relationships. A long-term marriage is not normally defined by state law, but court decisions have helped shape such a definition. Any marriage that has spanned 20 or more years seems to be accorded "long-duration" treatment. Some marriages in which there are several children seem also to receive this preferred status. It is rare to find a court refer to a marriage of less than ten years as a marriage of long duration. Once a court reaches the conclusion that spouses have been involved in a long-term relationship, there is a natural tendency by most courts to try to equally divide whatever marital assets have been accumulated.

Experience has dictated that if assets are not divided equally in marriages of long duration, the working spouse who runs a business or has been responsible for creating the assets will be preferred over the spouse who has assumed a more traditional role and has remained at home to bring up the children and run the household. The degree of such preference is meaningful, but not severe, in larger marital estates. It appears that in the majority of court decisions that discuss these aspects, divisions of 60%:40% to 66$\frac{2}{3}$%:33$\frac{1}{3}$% are not uncommon. Divisions of 75%:25% or larger are becoming more rare. In all states where the division of marital property made by the lower courts greatly varies from the aforementioned divisions an appellate court will seek to right any wrong that has befallen the aggrieved parties. This is the check and balance system, which has evolved in American jurisprudence to protect a litigant from a judgment that is against the weight of the facts or the law or the body of the case decisions that have been made in the given state balancing the financial interests of married couples who apply to the courts for a divorce.

One other aspect of dividing marital property is of extreme importance: valuation. How much is your husband's dry cleaning store worth? What about your wife's law degree? How much is a medical or other professional license worth? Does an advanced degree earned by your spouse during the course of your marriage that enables him or her to enjoy enhanced earnings also have value? At what date should marital assets be valued? Should they be valued at the time the action for divorce is commenced or when the case is reached for trial?

These and other questions concerning the valuation of marital assets must be considered and answered because they are so important to the bottom line in divorce cases, that is, the final dollar amount that can be reasonably anticipated after all the dust settles.

The spouse who owns and operates a business obviously wishes to have the court set a figure on such assets that is low or as low as possible, especially since in almost every case a court will not divide the asset and make a warring spouse a partner in the business. Rather, the court will fix a value on the business and award to the other spouse a sum of money equal to a percentage of the fixed value. This is known as a *distributive award* in most equitable distribution and community property states. How this is accomplished can be best understood through a concrete example.

Case Illustration

The parties have been married for 25 years, have three children, and reside in an equitable distribution state. The husband is in the retail auto business, the wife a homemaker. Both adult sons work in the business and plan to remain there as their life's work. The husband argues to the court that the value of his business is its net worth, that is, its net assets less its liabilities. In computing such a value he argues that the real estate he owns, which is carried on his books at the price he paid for it when it was first acquired, less depreciation, is the value the court should consider. He urges the court to further reduce these values because his sales are down, the automobile business generally is in a recession, and he fears that he will do even worse in the years ahead. Because of these uncertainties and declining sales, he requests that the court divide the assets 75% to himself and 25% to his wife. He also points out to the court that it should consider the tax impact on him when a division of marital assets is made, observing that although there is no tax consequence to him or his wife when he makes payment to his wife of the sum fixed by the court, he will have to pay a capital gains tax, which the wife will not share, when he sells the business in the future. The 75%:25% division would thus take into consideration these concerns and be fair to him.

The wife, by contrast, urges that she has given up her own career pursuits and ability to obtain an advanced education because her husband wanted her to remain at home and raise a family. She argues that in addition to raising the couple's three children single-handedly, she entertained her husband's business clients extensively in their home, was responsible for suggesting certain marketing techniques that enabled the husband to become engaged in an international leasing operation, and, after the children began school, started to work with her husband in his executive offices and helped make many important business decisions.

Faced with this state of facts, a court would then try to sift through the various pros and cons, the pluses and minuses, and attempt to fashion an award that would not provide a financial windfall to one spouse at the expense of the other.

It appears clear that because the wife was solely responsible for the rearing of the couple's three children and contributed to the husband's business pursuits by entertaining business guests and later participating in business decisions, and because the marriage spanned 25 years in duration, the wife's share, whether this case is determined in an equitable distribution or a community property state, should be a full 50%. More troublesome to the court would be the husband's argument that his business had substantially declined and that his future prospects were grim and that whatever value is fixed must take into account a potential capital gains tax that will have to be paid when the business is sold.

At first blush, it appears that the husband has made some very compelling arguments. However, it must be noted that most courts do not take into consideration future prospects because it is felt that to do so would be highly speculative. The automobile business, being cyclical in nature, has historically experienced the hills and valleys of economic rise and fall. A court could then logically conclude that if the husband were to continue the operation of the business, he might recoup any potential immediate decline by an economic turnaround in the future. Thus, it would not be unusual for a court to totally discount the husband's plea.

The argument for tax relief is frequently made in divorce cases and must be given consideration in this illustration. Here, however, the business has been family-run for some time and the couple's sons planned to remain in the business indefinitely; the husband, when he retires, will most likely pass the baton to his two sons. To accept the husband's tax argument that the value placed on the business should be reduced by the amount of capital gains taxes that will be imposed upon the sale ignores the fact that the business may never be sold by the husband to a third party and that the likelihood is great that the sons will continue to operate the business. Resolving the tax relief argument requires additional speculation as to acts that may occur in the future. Although there may be some courts that are willing to speculate and that would adjust the percentage to be paid to the wife by the amount of a capital gains tax that may ultimately be assessed, many courts, given the set of facts in this illustration, would argue that since there is no sale that is presently or in the immediate future contemplated, the computation of such tax is too speculative to consider when valuing the husband's business (though such a court might well consider the husband's claim that he should be given some consideration for the declining sales brought about by economic forces).

Having resolved the tax issue, there is left for discussion the valuation of the husband's business for purposes of division upon divorce. A business is generally valued in divorce cases by attempting to determine its fair market value. Fair market value is commonly defined as what a buyer is willing to pay to a seller in an arm's length transaction (i.e., where there is no compulsion to buy or sell by either buyer or seller for anything more or less than what the current market demands). What is the fair market value of a given business? The answer may be subject to differing opinions and customs of the industry and always requires expert testimony of business brokers, forensic accountants, or other owners of similar businesses who are familiar with current market conditions. For example, a retail automobile business is frequently sold on a "multiple of earnings" approach. If the dealership earned $500,000 and the industry multiple is three, the value of the business would then be $1,500,000 (3 × $500,000). The fixation of the property multiple at 2, 3, or 4 can vary the dollar value tremendously. The correct multiple is often subject to differing opinions, so the court must carefully consider the credibility of the expert who appears and testifies before it. When the experts' opinions are very close to each other, it is not unusual for the court to split the difference (e.g., if the multiple urged by the husband is 1 and the wife urges 2, the court might choose a multiple of 1.5 to adjust the variance). However, when the multiples recommended are widely different (say, a multiple of 1 against a multiple of 10), it is far more likely for the court to adopt the testimony of whichever witness the judge decides deserves to be accorded the greatest credibility and has the best credentials.

Any plea by the husband in our illustration that the court should only consider the net asset value (which gives no consideration for "good will," which is included in the multiple approach) will fall on deaf ears. In the real world auto dealerships are sold on multiple values of income, which include good will.

Real estate values, carried on the business's books at cost of acquisition less accumulated depreciation, simply do not reflect fair market values. Nor does simply considering the book assets less the book liabilities enable one to arrive at a fair market value.

Although it contains some difficult legal concepts, this discussion is necessary to obtain a feel for the evaluation process and how it may be applied by a court. This knowledge will also enable you to discuss these problems far more intelligently with an attorney and assess any offers of settlement or proposed terms of an agreement.

Today, the bulk of marital litigation focuses on the worth of property, rather than on fault. If you have drawn the conclusion that there is wide latitude and discretion exercised by the court in arriving at its ultimate valuation of property, you are entirely correct. Valuation is an art form, not a science. There are no tables to consult to fix the value of a going business. There can be wide variances, depending upon the jurisdiction in which you reside and the judge before whom you may go, in resolving this issue. Again, the inability to accurately predict the precise value and the ultimate division by the court is the strongest argument for attempting to reach a negotiated written agreement with your partner in order to remove the uncertainty of outcome and the added expense of years of litigation that a lawsuit can engender.

These issues that must be dealt with as a prelude to a prenuptial agreement, which eliminates them from being considered upon divorce, are the very same ones that a divorcing couple without a prior agreement must resolve. When litigants to divorce enter a written agreement, the agreement will be termed either a *stipulation of settlement* or a *separation agreement*. Regardless of which name is applied, this agreement falls into the same category and is subject to the same laws and pitfalls as a prenuptial, marital, or cohabitants' agreement. The goal of all must be to reach a fair settlement that cannot be subject to later attack because of a claim of fraud, of overreaching by either party, or other irregularities.

Notes

1. *Marvin v. Marvin*, 18 Cal.3d 665, 557 P.2d 106 (1976), thereafter remanded for a consideration as to whether a contract was made and then reversed a money award as improper, 122 Cal. App. 3d 8717, 176 Cal. Reptr. 555 (1981).
2. See, for example, *The Random House College Dictionary* (1973). Based on *The Random House Dictionary of the English Language—The Unabridged Edition*, Copyright 1973, 1971, 1970, 1969, 1967, 1966 by Random House, Inc.
3. Community property states include Arizona, California, Idaho, Louisiana, Nevada, New Mexico, Texas, Washington, and Wisconsin.

Chapter 9

Estate and Inheritance Laws

What your partner may ask you to give up in the event of his or her death or what you may ask your partner to give up if you predecease him or her must be known by both of you in order to intelligently negotiate a prenuptial, marital, or cohabitants' agreement. A common-law marriage can be recognized in seven common-law states, and even if you do not reside in such a state but travel and have some substantial contacts there and later return to your home state, you may have to deal with the laws of inheritance in the same way as ceremonial married persons or persons contemplating a ceremonial marriage.

What will be your principal concerns in the event of death? Persons considering a second marriage will most certainly be primarily concerned with preserving for the benefit of their children, parents, or other members of their family assets they accumulated prior to the contemplated marriage. Without an agreement, a surviving spouse (but not a cohabitant) is entitled in almost every state to do the following:

1. Elect against (choose) the terms of your will to obtain a percentage of assets left in your estate, despite the lack of any provision in the will and despite any terms of the will that may provide for less than a fixed sum as provided by law.

2. Act as the administrator of your estate if you die without having left a will (which may entitle him or her to earn a commission).

3. Share in your estate, if you fail to leave a will, to the extent provided by the laws of your state (usually the entire estate if no children or parents are surviving, or one-third to one-half with such survivors).

The *right of election*, as the first choice listed is referred to in legal jargon, will permit your surviving spouse, in most states, to receive a specified percentage (usually one-third) and sometimes other benefits, such as homestead, from your estate despite the provisions of the will itself that either omit your spouse entirely or provide less than the statutory percentage that prevails in your state.

Illustration: You prepare a will that leaves $5,000 to your spouse. There are no children involved. Your estate consists of money and property worth $100,000. The state where you live provides that a spouse must be left at least one-third of the value of the gross assets of the estate. Since the requirement would be to provide $33,300, either directly or in trust for the benefit of your spouse, and you provided only $5,000 by the terms of your will, your spouse would elect to "take" against your estate the additional sum of $28,300 ($28,300 + 5,000 = $33,300).

Illustration: You die without a will and leave two surviving children. No prenuptial agreement exists. Your estate consists of money and property worth $500,000. Your surviving spouse would be entitled to be appointed as the administrator of your estate (a spouse is normally accorded a higher priority than a surviving child), which carries with it great control over the monies and properties left by you and also the right to receive fees from the estate, which may be as much as 5% of the gross estate. In addition, since there are two children surviving, your spouse would be entitled to receive one-third of your estate (or one-half if there is only one child) in most states.

A person can disinherit a child by drawing a will and making no provision for the child but cannot disinherit a spouse because of the right of election and the laws of intestacy that prevail in each state. There is no similar right of election for a child in most jurisdictions.

Since it is possible to enter into a prenuptial agreement that can override these estate laws, it is absolutely essential to have one if you wish to preserve assets for the benefit of children or other family members. Again, it is important to remind the reader at the risk of repetition that the rights discussed in this chapter are only accorded to a spouse (whether by common law or ceremonial marriage) and do not apply to living-together partners. Unless it can be established that a marriage took place, there are absolutely no estate rights *presently* recognized in the law that would offer any financial protection to a surviving live-in companion, although the law may rapidly change. With a prenuptial agreement, it is possible to vary these estate laws and make provisions that you and your partner believe to be fair and desirable. In order to protect yourself if your state begins to accord such estate rights or if you unwittingly enter a common law marriage, you should always consider discussing such estate matters. Moreover, if you live together and later become married, these agreements can protect against unwanted results.

Contents of the Agreement

Turning now to the various provisions that can be made upon death in a prenuptial agreement, you should consider the following possibilities:

1. The amount of support to provide, if any, and over what period of time
2. The amount of any lump-sum payment
3. Gifts of any specific properties, whether real estate, stocks and bonds, jewelry, or items that may have sentimental value

4. Whether life insurance should be used in order to fund these specific provisions
5. What provision should be made to permit your husband or wife to remain in the marital residence, giving consideration to whether any school-age children are involved and their need to remain in the same school district, and whether the residence ought to be left to your survivor

There are some concerns about the prenuptial agreement that are common to couples contemplating a first marriage and those anticipating a second or later marriage, but there are also some very different considerations, which are discussed in the following paragraphs.

When considering the terms of a prenuptial agreement when you are contemplating a first marriage, there may be property that you own that has been in your family for some time that you may wish to protect in the event of your death. For example, if you own an interest in a family business or enter the marriage with large sums of money or property that has been inherited from a parent, grandparent, or other family member, or received as a gift, you may wish to exclude your spouse-to-be from receiving such interest or property, especially if you have an untimely death. Your thinking may change after you have been married for ten or more years. On the other hand, you may not wish to alter your spouse's estate rights at all, confining the prenuptial agreement to support and property division in the event of divorce. However, only after you become aware of what your state's inheritance laws provide can you make an intelligent decision in this area.

Conditional Provisions Based on Time

Many persons accommodate their concerns by making conditional provisions in the prenuptial agreement that are based on the number of years married at the time of death. A schedule can be incorporated into an agreement that will provide for increased sums in five- or ten-year segments, or any other period of time that you feel will be fair and appropriate. These provisions, conditioned upon the length of marriage, can apply to lump sum payments, moneys to be paid in equal weekly installments, or the right to receive property. For example, if you wish to leave to your spouse a valuable painting, you may wish to condition the gift upon your marriage spanning at least five years in duration. If you should die before this period of time has elapsed, the painting would not pass to your spouse but, rather, to someone else as designated by the terms of your will.

Most persons would probably choose to be more generous, providing for a larger lump sum or a greater amount of weekly support, as the marriage matures and as children are born. Schedules contained within a prenuptial agreement can accommodate such concerns. A complete prenuptial agreement is contained in Appendix D and comprehensively illustrates how these conditional provisions can be best utilized. The concerns of a person entering a first marriage without children are far different from those of a person who contemplates a second or later marriage and who may have one or more children born of an earlier marriage. The latter's desire to provide for the financial security of a child may temper the desire to be more liberal to the second spouse. When such concerns are present, there are many options available, depending upon the size of the estate or the nature of the property that you own. The suggestions made in this chapter can also be utilized to reflect the needs of former family members.

The law permits a person to waive the rights afforded by a state's inheritance law when entering into a prenuptial agreement. Both the right of election and the right to share in the estate of a deceased spouse who has left no will (i.e., who has died *intestate*) can be eliminated. However, when this is done, couples then attempt to provide alternative provisions in their prenuptial agreement that both will find satisfactory after considering their respective needs and obligations. The use of life insurance, which is discussed more fully later in this chapter, may be an excellent device for providing financial protection at a limited cost, without disturbing or diverting other assets for this purpose. Life insurance can be used solely for this purpose or to augment other monies.

Lump Sum versus Periodic Payment

Whether to make provision for a lump sum or for a periodic installment depends upon your appraisal of your prospective spouse's ability to manage money. Certainly, to receive a lump sum payment affords the recipient greater flexibility. Sometimes, following the trauma of the loss of a loved one, there may be a psychological need to remove oneself from past familiar surroundings because remaining in the same household may bring on, or cause to linger, difficult or painful memories. One's mate is gone and there is a painful silence within the home brought about by the loss. Although not all persons suffer such psychological consequences, those who do will require new living quarters and will incur the immediate expense of moving and relocation. Furnishings do not always fit into a new apartment or home, and public transportation may no longer be available; the expenditure of a large sum of money may be required for new furniture or an automobile. Providing a lump sum bequest will enable the survivor to meet these immediate expenses and invest the balance of the gift into a certificate of deposit, treasury note, or other income-producing asset. If the need arises for further funds, the asset invested can always be drawn upon and the remaining income used periodically. However, if you are fearful that your intended spouse will have difficulty managing or investing a lump sum payment, you may choose to ignore such an option and, instead, provide that a fixed weekly or monthly sum of money, based upon your lifestyle and anticipated standard of living, be paid from your estate. If you choose to elect to make provision for a periodic sum, then it will be required that you establish a trust fund.

Trusts

Trusts that are established by a last will and testament are known as *testamentary trusts*; those established during your lifetime are referred to as *inter vivos trusts* (living trusts). Depending upon the nature of your assets and your financial condition, either may be selected for your use. For example, if you have an income-producing asset, such as a common stock that yields $10,000 a year, you might wish to consider placing the security into a trust that would pay a fixed weekly sum of $192.30 ($10,000 divided by 52 = $192.30) during the lifetime of your spouse or until he or she remarries, or until some other specified event. Thereafter, the shares themselves can be gifted to another person whom you may designate. If, however, your assets are limited, and the bulk of your estate will be provided by life insurance, or you cannot give up the use of income producing assets, a testamentary trust would be a better choice.

The trust may be either a living trust or a testamentary trust, which will only come into being upon your death. It is necessary that you name a person or institution, (e.g., a friend, relative, or bank) to act as trustee to administer the trust according to your wishes. It is also possible to leave instructions that your trustee can use his or her discretion to use a portion of the securities (i.e., sell off a part to raise monies), if the need arises, to cover an expenditure that will make your spouse's life less financially difficult. When an asset is sold in this fashion, it is said that the trustee has been given the power to invade the principle of the trust. Some persons give their trustee the ability to invade their trust in order to make payments for the general benefit of their spouse in matters pertaining to health, education, or general welfare. These trusts can eliminate the choice of making a lump sum versus a periodic distribution, since you can instruct your trustee to do both as the need or the occasion arises. In the previous example, a sum of money could have been given to the spouse for moving expenses and to purchase an automobile while retaining the balance of the trust fund to provide income that would be paid weekly.

There are costs and fees associated with setting up and administering trust funds, but they are generally fixed by state law and are not terribly costly. Most commercial banks maintain trust and estate departments, and a visit to your local bank's trust office will provide invaluable information concerning the use and costs of lifetime or testamentary trusts. Of course, an attorney or accountant may also provide a source of information and should be consulted when you are ready to work out the terms of a prenuptial agreement. There may be some tax consequences associated with the use of trusts, and they should be explored before you reach a final decision.

Nonprobate versus Estate Assets

In a first marriage, couples sometimes decide to exclude from the possibility of distribution certain previously owned assets and, for the most part, are content to share other properties acquired during marriage. It is quite common for such couples to purchase a home, condominium, or cooperative apartment in their joint names. The legal effect of doing so is that the survivor will own the residence upon death of the spouse without the need to take any further steps to accomplish legal ownership. The obtainment of title upon death by the survivor when parties own real property jointly (joint tenants have rights of survivorship) is said to be "by operation of law"; there is no need in such circumstances to apply to the surrogate, probate or estate courts to transfer or approve or participate in the transfer of title from joint to individual ownership. A property that passes by operation of law is also referred to in legal jargon as being a *nonprobate asset* (i.e., an asset whose ownership legally passes upon death without the need to apply to the probate court). Examples of nonprobate assets include joint bank accounts, bank accounts held in trust for a named person, real property held jointly with another, and proceeds of a life insurance policy that are paid to a named beneficiary. Life insurance policies are really contracts. The life insurance company is bound to pay the face amount of the policy to the person you name as beneficiary in the event of your death. Unless you make an irrevocable designation of a beneficiary, you are free to change the person named from time to time, according to your own wishes. (Naming a person as irrevocable beneficiary is not a good idea, since it will not be possible to make a change in the future, no matter what the reason.)

All properties held in a person's *sole* name at death, whether real estate, bank accounts, stocks or bonds, certificates of deposit, or assets held in some other form, are deemed *estate assets*, that is, assets that must be dealt with by the terms of the person's will or, in the absence of a will, that will pass to heirs according to the laws of intestacy in the state where the deceased resided. All such assets require the estate to be administered in the probate or surrogate's court. If a person dies with a will, the will must be offered for probate and its proper execution proved by the methods fixed by statute (law) in your state. Generally, all persons named in the will and all heirs must be notified. The witnesses to the will must be produced and the other formalities required by local law met in order to "admit the will for probate." When these legal requirements have been fulfilled, the court will issue *letters testamentary* to the person you named as executor and that person will be able to take charge and distribute your assets. Once this is done, your wishes, as expressed in the will, can be complied with and monies and properties given to the persons you selected.

Dying without a Will

Where no will is left, the proceedings become somewhat more complicated. A surviving relative, either a spouse, child, or parent, would normally seek to obtain *letters of administration* to become the legal representative of the deceased's estate. The person selected by the court will be known as the *administrator* of the estate (as opposed to an *executor* if you die with a will). The deceased's property will then be searched for and identified, and later distributed to heirs according to the laws of intestacy in the state. A surviving spouse, when there are no children, will inherit the entire estate. Where a spouse and children survive, the estate will generally be divided one-third to the surviving spouse, and two-thirds to the surviving children. Once it is determined who will act as administrator and the persons who will share in the distribution of the estate are identified, the assets left in the deceased's name will be reduced to cash or distributed in kind to the persons entitled by law to receive them.

Failing to make a will is not recommended and is not, by any stretch of the imagination, an intelligent choice. It is strongly urged that all persons make a legal will to prevent assets from being distributed in a haphazard way. A will enables all of your money and property to pass to the persons *you* desire and not those determined by the state in which you live. It is far better to have control over the distribution of your worldly possessions, which a will can provide, than to leave such important matters to chance. Not only will you have a sense of security and certainty concerning your wishes to provide for those who survive you, but the persons you wish to protect will be better off for your having the foresight to plan for an event in life that cannot be avoided.

Homeowners Contemplating Marriage

Having this knowledge of the world of wills and estates will enable you to make provisions in your prenuptial agreement in the event of death of you or your partner and to give special consideration to the home you may purchase, which will probably be the largest asset you will acquire during your marriage. If you already own a home, you may wish, whether you are contemplating a first or subsequent marriage, to make special provisions for your spouse regarding the use of the residence without actually transferring ownership in the home. You must understand that under such circumstances you cannot place ownership to your home in your joint names (*joint tenancy* or *tenancy by the entirety*), since doing so, as we observed earlier, will create a nonprobate asset and cause a transfer of sole ownership to the named joint tenant—despite contrary provisions in a prenuptial agreement or will. Once title of a home is placed in your joint names, it can never be changed, except by mutual consent, and you effectively lose control to make a later provision for the use and enjoyment of the home.

Provided title remains in your sole name, the prenuptial agreement can make whatever you desire become a reality. So, for example, if you own a residence that has been in your family for many generations and has a substantial value, you might choose, if your death occurs in the earlier years of your marriage, to provide your spouse with a lump sum of money, have your estate purchase another residence for your spouse's use, or pay for a rental for a fixed period of time instead of allowing your spouse to remain in the residence or receive any ownership in the property. As an alternative, you might also wish to consider permitting your spouse to remain in your residence for a fixed period of time, which could be as little as a few years or as much as his or her lifetime. A *life estate*, as the right to remain in the real property for as long as a person lives is referred to in the law, can be used to retain ownership of the marital residence within the family while at the same time permitting your spouse the use and enjoyment of it. Upon the death of your spouse, title and possession could then be given to a child or other family member. In this way, you can accomplish the dual ends of permitting your spouse to be secure during his or her lifetime in the home you shared together while at the same time preserving the ownership of the home for another family member.

Whether you wish to use this technique depends upon many nonlegal considerations. If this is a first marriage you are contemplating, there may be no thought of preserving ownership of a residence acquired during marriage for another family member. However, if this is a subsequent marriage, you may desire to retain a home that has been owned by you or your family for several generations, an end that can be accomplished through the life estate device. Then, too, your wish to protect a child may also have to be considered. In negotiating a satisfactory agreement with your spouse-to-be, the life estate provision may be the sole way to ensure that you will reach agreement and exchange marital vows.

There is a certain give-and-take in all negotiations. Those involving marital partners or single persons living together or contemplating marriage are always more delicate and may require even more elasticity concerning your respective positions.

Reaching Agreement

As you can see, there are no fixed rules that will apply to every case. Rather, there must be a nice balancing between the needs of both parties before a meeting of the minds can be reached and a satisfactory agreement drawn. The provisions that may be contained in your prenuptial agreement relating to death will obviously become more liberal with the passage of time; that is to say, the longer the marriage, the more generous the provision for a surviving spouse should be. If death occurs after 20 years of marriage, it would seem that there would be no cogent reason to withhold or limit support that would be necessary in order to maintain the preseparation standard of living or to make other restrictive provisions that would make difficult the continuance of the lifestyles enjoyed by the two of you during the marriage.

The major difficulties that will be encountered in attempting to provide liberal terms in the event of a marriage of long duration most frequently are experienced by couples who are about to embark upon a second or subsequent marriage and who simply cannot part with a family residence. For them, the desire to make provisions for the financial security of a child, or perhaps even a parent or other relative, may take on a major priority.

If a second or subsequent marriage occurs later in life, there are, in discussing the terms of a prenuptial agreement, even greater concerns to protect against a marriage of short duration, especially among people of advanced years. The motive is really quite easy to understand. Persons who have worked hard throughout their lifetime and struggled to accumulate some assets for their family and old age may not be willing to risk entering into a marriage that may soon end because of their premature or sudden death and having their heirs lose their inheritance. This is especially true if the parties contemplating a second marriage have had the prior unpleasant experience of a divorce proceeding. In fact, for persons to enter into a second marriage without the security of a prenuptial agreement would indeed be foolhardy, whether the previous marriage was severed by divorce or death.

The Use of Life Insurance

If you view marriage as a full partnership that includes the financial aspects of the relationship, then it may not be difficult to reach the conclusion that only assets acquired during the course of the marriage should be included in your estate planning for economic security in the event that your relationship is curtailed by death. If this is the case, it appears that the use of life insurance proceeds is a most reasonable way to fund the needs of your partner in the event of your death. If, however, the present health and/or age of you or your prospective spouse or live-in companion is such that it would make life insurance either unavailable or prohibitive in cost, then an alternative method must be utilized.

Even with persons who are experiencing some form of health problem or are of advanced age at the time the prenuptial or living-together agreement is about to be entered, there may be preexisting policies that would not be affected by such factors and that could be utilized to fund the support provisions, specified in the agreement, that would be payable upon your death. For example, if there is a provision contained in your agreement that would prohibit your spouse or live-in companion from continuing to occupy the marital residence, the proceeds from a life insurance policy could possibly be placed in trust for the benefit of your spouse, with a direction to the trustee that all or a portion of the funds be used to purchase or lease a new residence. As was discussed earlier in this chapter, these trust provisions can offer great flexibility in providing for the needs of your surviving spouse or companion while, at the same time, keeping control over the monies so that if there is a fund remaining at the time of your companion or spouse's remarriage or death, the remaining portion of the trust fund can be paid out to persons designated by you, which may include your children or other family members. The proceeds of an insurance policy need not be payable to a named beneficiary and are often made payable to a person's estate. The trustee who will be appointed by your will, or designated in your prenuptial agreement, will then be able to administer the trust as you have indicated. It matters not whether the trust is funded through monies that are in existence at the time of your death or through monies that will be paid to the trust from the proceeds of your life insurance policy.

In the final analysis, before you can attempt to sit down and discuss provisions in your prenuptial agreement that will apply in the event of your untimely passing, you must have full knowledge of the laws of intestacy that are provided in your state, as well as the extent of the right of election you may choose to select in the event that a will is left by your spouse that makes insufficient or no provision for you. There is no substitute for consulting a competent attorney conversant with these estate matters, particularly with prenuptial agreements. Whatever special needs you may bring to the negotiating table can be addressed with the attorney at an initial meeting. Once you are able to consider what the law may provide without any intervention by you through the use of a prenuptial agreement, you will then be in a position to have a meeting with your intended spouse to discuss some of the concerns you may have, such as those regarding the retention of certain properties for the support of children of a prior marriage or, perhaps, aged parents.

After these concerns have been exchanged and addressed by the two of you, it will then be possible to begin, without undue hardship to either of you, the give-and-take that naturally will take place concerning the particular needs of each of you and your mutual goal to satisfy them. Chapter 10 explores in detail these negotiating techniques.

Chapter 10

Drafting Prenuptial and Other Written Agreements between Cohabitants

In order to make certain that the oral promises exchanged between you and the person with whom you desire to live will be held to be legally binding by the courts and not misconstrued, it is wise to consider adopting a written agreement that will comply with your state's requirements to be considered a binding contract. As noted earlier, many states will recognize express oral promises made by the living-together couple, while still others will infer promises to exist because of the conduct of the parties. However, two states, Minnesota and Texas, will accord no legal status to the oral promises of such persons and require that there be a written agreement before the courts can grant relief.

What financial concerns should be considered and covered in these written agreements? Essentially, what will happen when your relationship terminates by either death or separation. The focus of your concern should be (1) the division of any moneys or other property, and (2) support for yourself and any children born during your relationship.

Before discussing the various financial arrangements that may be made, a threshold question must first be posed and answered: Do you wish to incur any financial rights or obligations during the time you live together; if not, is there a way to avoid doing so? If the first part of the question is answered in the negative, then a written agreement may be the best way to achieve such a goal, rather than play Russian roulette with the laws of 50 states and some of our territories. Just one of these 50 or more chambers may be loaded and may inflict a mortal wound.

Playing Russian Roulette with an Unloaded Gun

To prevent a court from later ordering you to divide your property, pay support to your former live-in companion, or pay for the support of children, a written agreement attesting to the fact that neither cohabitant will have the obligation to support the other or to divide money or property upon separation will be almost universally recognized. Of course, the courts are never bound by the agreements of parents when the best interest of a child is not served. Nevertheless, where an agreement as to child support is fair and reasonable and provides the child with the necessities of life as enjoyed before separation occurred, such an agreement will be accorded validity by the courts.

If your goal is to escape all financial obligations when separation or death occurs, then the written agreement must so provide. It would be wise to set forth that the legal rights and obligations of both parties have been explored and explained, that the parties have each had their own attorneys advise them concerning such issues, that there has been full financial disclosure between the couple before the agreement was reached, and that the parties evidenced their consent to such terms when they finally placed their signatures on the formal document. See Appendixes B and C for cohabitants' agreements disclaiming all liability.

Why should such formality be followed? Why is it necessary to exchange financial information if your ultimate goal is to have no financial entanglements? The questions are easy to answer. It is necessary in order to avoid a later challenge that the written agreement was induced by fraud, overreaching, misunderstanding, or lack of fairness. Some states, such as New York, require that a written agreement between marital partners must be "fair" when made and not "unconscionable" at the time when their separation or divorce becomes a judgment of the court. Most states permit any contract to be set aside because of fraud, duress, overreaching, or mutual mistake of the parties as to the terms of the writing. The basic right of any party to set aside a written contract on these grounds makes clear the need for cohabitants to avoid these pitfalls and to ensure that their written contract will not be later voided by the courts on any of these grounds. A more complete discussion of the application of such rules to cohabitants' contracts and how they may be used to avoid legal obligations is to be found in chapter 3 of this book. This chapter examines the various clauses that can be used and the negotiating techniques that may be employed in order to arrive at an agreement that will withstand a later attack by either party and will contain fair and appropriate terms to abide by in the event of death or separation.

Are Prenuptial Agreements for Everybody?

It seems everyone is doing it, from Donald Trump to Donald Jones. People contemplating marriage, whether for a first or subsequent time, are entering into prenuptial agreements with increasing regularity. In fact, the June 10, 1991, edition of *Forbes* magazine, which depicted on its cover a cigar-smoking cherub with attaché case in one hand that was pierced by arrows, and a bow in the other, sported the following headline: "Ah, June, feeling romantic? Better consult your lawyer." According to an article entitled "Share and Share Unalike" in that magazine: "No matter how romantic a newly married couple may feel, they can't ignore the statistics: 50–50 they'll end up divorced. A prenuptial agreement can avoid great future pain at the cost of a little present unpleasantness." It should also be added that the cost of obtaining a prenuptial agreement pales in comparison to the amounts that can be preserved to the signatories in the event of divorce or separation.

The laws of different states can yield bizarre results. Some states, the most notable being New York, regard professional licenses and advanced academic degrees as marital assets subject to valuation and distribution upon divorce. Although such states are in the distinct minority, you must be in a position to understand the law of your state concerning the acquisition of assets during the time of marriage in order to successfully negotiate and plan a prenuptial agreement. Each state can take a different view. For example, inherited property in the state of New York is considered separate property and cannot be considered by the courts in distributing marital assets whereas, by contrast, the state of Connecticut deems inherited property as marital property (so that if you receive an inheritance during marriage and later become separated or divorced, your former spouse can walk off with as much as one-half of the monies that you inherited from your relative).

As will be observed later, it is also important to know whether you reside in a community property state or an equitable distribution state. (Community property states include California, Arkansas, Idaho, Louisiana, Nevada, New Mexico, North Carolina, and Texas; the others are equitable distribution states). If you are going to consider negotiating a prenuptial agreement, you must understand that there is no guarantee that the agreement will stand up to the scrutiny of the court if it is later challenged. There have been cases in which courts have struck down prenuptial agreements that were unfair or unconscionable by their terms, that failed to make full financial disclosure as to income and assets of one party or were otherwise induced by fraud or coercion, or that were signed by a party who was not represented by an attorney and did not understand the legal implications of the agreement. All of these problems are discussed at length in this chapter.

Considerations for Cohabitants

Cohabitants' agreements are quite similar to prenuptial agreements by couples who will later marry. The concerns surely parallel one another. Financial provisions in the event of death will be far easier to agree upon than those that will take effect only upon separation or divorce. Death creates an unwanted and, for most, an unanticipated circumstance. Many cohabitants may wish to provide financial security for the other in the event of their untimely death, although there may be greater reluctance to do so in the event of a separation. A separation is much akin to a divorce and evokes many of the same emotional reactions to one's partner during the uncoupling period. Nonetheless, the security of fixing one's obligations and rights when such an event may occur is the strongest argument to include such provisions in a living-together agreement.

What are the different ways in which you may provide for your live-in companion in the event of death? Initially, thought should be given to providing an ongoing income to replace the monies you normally contribute for food, shelter, clothing, entertainment, and the like. The sum provided should attempt to approximate the standard of living that was enjoyed by the two of you, if your personal finances will permit such generosity. This can be accomplished in a variety of ways. One that is financially painless is to create a trust whereby income generated from the principal of the trust can be utilized for support of your cohabitant but whose assets can later be diverted to another person of your choosing. For example, if you have stocks, bonds, a certificate of deposit, or other income-producing property that will yield a sum of money deemed adequate for the weekly needs of your companion, such an asset may be placed in trust, with a direction to a person that you name as trustee to pay such income during either a specified period or the lifetime of your companion. But upon the death of the latter, the asset itself can be transferred to another person you designate—a relative, child, or any unrelated person of your own choosing. In this way, you can preserve the asset for the benefit of another person of your choosing while, for a limited period, providing support for your cohabitant.

The Use of Life Insurance

Another way to accomplish the same result, without making an outright gift of the asset itself, is to provide that the proceeds of a life insurance policy be placed in trust for the benefit of your companion during his or her lifetime. This insurance trust device is quite similar to a *testamentary trust* (a trust that is created by the terms of your will and is only implemented upon your death), but it is far simpler to administer and potentially far less costly. Any independent insurance broker who is a Charter Life Underwriter (referred to as a CLU) will be competent to advise you on how this insurance trust can be set up and utilized. The use of an insurance trust to provide financial protection to your cohabitant is perhaps the most economical way to arrange for such protection, and it will preserve your other assets from being even partially used for this purpose. Term insurance (i.e., insurance that contains no cash surrender value) is by far the cheapest type of life insurance that can be bought. For example, a man aged 55 may purchase $500,000 of term insurance for an annual premium of approximately $1,160 (see Appendix E). While it is true that the life insurance premium will increase with increasing age, such increase is not significant until advanced years are reached. In any event, one can always elect to terminate the coverage if the premium appears to be too costly. The substitution of another asset can accomplish the desired result. Another benefit of the use of an insurance trust is that the insurance company itself can be named as trustee, thereby eliminating the designation of an independent trustee who may charge greater fees to administer the trust. And, of course, a trust created by a will requires a probate proceeding in a surrogate or estate court, with its attendant costs. If no other assets are owned that require a will to be drawn in order to transfer ownership of property to a named person, then both the making of a will and the need to go through the courts to complete such transfers are eliminated. This may occur when money or property is held jointly with another named individual, such as in a joint bank account, stocks held in joint names, or a bank account in your name that you hold in trust for another individual. Collectively, assets so maintained are referred to as *nonprobate assets* (i.e., it is unnecessary to apply to an estate court to probate or process a will in order to distribute such assets). Nonprobate assets are transferred "by operation of law"; that is to say, when death occurs, the survivor is deemed by law to solely own the asset. All one need do in such circumstances is obtain a death certificate, apply for estate tax waivers, where necessary, and present these documents to the bank where the account is maintained, or to the brokerage house or wherever else the property is located. When these documents are delivered, you will be able to obtain sole title to the account, and a passbook or the shares of stock will then be reissued in your own name. This example illustrates the ease with which nonprobate assets can be transferred. It is no wonder that various types of joint ownership are so popular with married couples, cohabitants, and others who wish to have rights of survivorship to a joint asset without the expense and inconvenience of processing this transfer through estate courts.

When considering joint ownership of real estate, an attorney should be consulted in order to make certain that the result you wish to achieve will be possible in the state in which you reside. Real estate transactions are far more complex than the transfer of monies and other personal property. Most states accord some greater rights to married couples in this regard. So, for example, in states that recognize a *tenancy by the entirety* (a term used to denote ownership of property by a husband and wife) that can only be created by persons who have been validly married (including a valid common-law marriage), the survivor will receive sole title to the real estate upon death of the co-owner. *Joint tenancies* are similar but not identical to tenancies by the entirety; they also allow for the survivor to take all but do not give the identical protection from attacks by creditors. The important fact to remember is that tenancies by the entirety and joint tenancies both permit the survivor to take all and become the sole owner of the property.

A *tenancy in common* is another popular form of real estate ownership but does not include rights of survivorship. Each tenant in common owns a one-half interest in the property. Upon his or her death, such one-half interest will not pass to the surviving tenant in common but will be given to a designated individual either by the terms of a will or, if no will exists, by your state's laws of descent and distribution.

To review, if a house is purchased by you and your cohabitant and title is placed in both of your names as *joint tenants*, you would become the sole owner of the entire property if your cohabitant dies. By contrast, if title was taken by the two of you as *tenants in common* (which does not accord survivor's rights) and your cohabitant dies, you would not receive any greater interest in the property; your cohabitant's half interest would be given to a person named in your cohabitant's will or, if no will was made, then to your cohabitant's heir (such as a child or parent), according to the estate law specified in the state where death occurred. These additional forms of ownership can be used effectively in estate and separation planning by married as well as unmarried couples.

These observations with respect to the various forms of ownership of real property and other personal assets may make it easier for you to understand how you can transfer assets, apart from a written agreement or will provisions, in order to provide financial security for a cohabitant. However, placing ownership of an asset in joint names should never be used when your sole objective is to provide your cohabitant with income derived from the asset but to preserve the asset itself for transfer to another person whom you wish to ultimately have its use and enjoyment.

How Much Is Enough?

Following our discussion concerning the methods by which monies can be made available to your cohabitant following your death, the next question should be, What is the proper amount of such support? It is necessary to consider two important factors in order to answer this question: (1) the length of time that your relationship may span prior to your death and (2) the standard of living you may have established during the time you and your partner lived together. You, of course, must balance your desire to provide sufficient money to reflect such factors with the ability of your estate to meet such obligations. Provided that upon your death there will be enough monies available to do what your feelings and conscience dictate, one way to accomplish this end is to make a provision in your living-together agreement that will reflect adequately upon the length of your involvement with one another and the lifestyle you have enjoyed. A graduated formula approach would be a perfect way to accomplish this end.

The following example will best illustrate the utilization of a graduated formula provision. Say that at the time of your death you and your partner had lived together for one to five years, without any children born of the relationship, and that reasonable living requirements were $10,000 annually. This sum could be paid to your cohabitant upon your death in equal weekly or monthly installments, either (1) during your cohabitant's lifetime or such lesser fixed period that you may designate; (2) until his or her remarriage; or (3) until he or she resumes cohabitation with another person.

Payments would cease upon the earliest occurrence of any of these three events.

It is also possible to limit the support to a fixed period of time by designating an outside date, such as five years following your death. The length of time support should be paid, as well as all other details regarding your financial involvements, will be decided by the two of you over the negotiation table. By and large, the longer the span of years preceding death, the larger the amount and the longer the duration of support you should consider. The following is a sample schedule that incorporates this notion of graduated increases:

Length of time preceding death	Duration of support	Amount of support
6–10 years	5 years	$15,000 per year
11–15 years	7 years	20,000 per year
16–20 years	10 years	25,000 per year

There is no magic in arriving at this schedule formula. Whatever appears fair to both parties and reflects your pre-death standard of living and your ability to provide should be the proper guideline to follow to arrive at the details to include in your own schedule. Greater flexibility is afforded the parties in their financial planning by utilizing a schedule rather than a fixed approach. You and your partner can then fashion an agreement that will reflect your wishes as well as take into consideration the period of time your relationship lasts.

Increasing the amount of support as the period preceding death grows longer is sound planning and is often utilized in estate planning as well as in prenuptial agreements. Planning financial aid for a cohabitant is hardly different. The graduated formula approach is by no means the only way to recognize a matured and seasoned personal relationship. The only real parameters for this most important aspect of support planning should be the bounds of the imagination and creativity necessary to enable you to reach a "meeting of the minds," an expression the law frequently uses in discussing contract issues. Obviously, if you enter into the negotiation process with the goal of overreaching or attempting to obtain your partner's consent through coercion or fraud (e.g., a false and knowing misstatement of your finances) or if you deny your partner legal representation or suggest that he or she waive the right to use an attorney in the preparation of the written agreement, with the goal of extracting your partner's consent to obviously unfair or unconscionable terms, you may find that the courts might determine that the agreement must be set aside because of one or more of these irregularities if the agreement is later attacked following your separation or your death. A further discussion of the ways in which a separation, prenuptial, or cohabitants' agreement can be set aside for legal irregularities is contained in chapter 12.

Lump Sum

Instead of making a periodic support provision, either directly from your estate or through the various forms of trusts explained earlier, you might wish instead to provide for a lump sum payment. This would depend upon your assessment of your companion's ability to manage and/or invest monies. Leaving a sum of money outright, with no conditions attached, which are often found in trust arrangements, certainly will provide greater flexibility for the recipient. It will enable your survivor to use the money for whatever he or she may find to be the most necessary purpose. Moving or educational expenses, as well as other economic rehabilitative measures, can be paid for as the need arises. In many instances, the survivor may face greater financial needs and challenges immediately following the death of a loved one than at a later time. This is especially true when you consider the resultant depression and immediate inability to face new financial demands that follow an emotional trauma. There must be a sufficient time for grieving and adjustment. Many persons find themselves in an emotional straightjacket, unable to cope with life's basic demands. This period is perhaps the time of greatest need for financial support, and a lump sum payment might well be the most welcomed form of aid.

Selecting the proper lump sum of money to provide for a loved one gives rise to certain difficulties but is similar to the dilemma facing you when you attempt to arrive at a proper periodic weekly amount, as discussed earlier in this chapter. Your holdings and assets, as well as other persons you may wish to make provisions for, including children from a prior marriage or elderly and infirm parents, will certainly enter your judgment. Providing a sum of money commensurate with the length of your relationship with your partner is again a much-used device in financial estate planning. For example, the following table could be utilized for this purpose (but is by no means offered as a definitive schedule):

Length of time between signing of agreement and death	Lump sum amount
1–5 years	$ 5,000
6–10 years	10,000
11–15 years	20,000
16–20 years	35,000
21–25 years	45,000
More than 25 years	100,000

These payments to your surviving companion can be achieved by making a provision in your will to pay such sum outright from your remaining assets, by establishing a joint bank or stock account that will pass to your companion at the time of your death by "operation of law" (discussed earlier), or by naming your cohabitant as beneficiary of a life insurance policy.

If life insurance is the vehicle you select to make payment of the lump sum amount, conditions can be incorporated into the life insurance policy itself that will ensure that the sum payable reflects the length of your relationship with your partner preceding your death. If a life insurance policy of $100,000 is maintained and the sum required to be paid according to your agreement is $50,000, the balance should be directed to be paid to another person or to your estate. This device is known as the appointment of a *contingent beneficiary*. Most life insurance companies and independent life insurance agents will be able to assist you or your attorney in tailoring the terms of your life insurance policy to the exact provisions of your agreement with your cohabitant.

Provisions in the Event of Separation Occurring Other Than by Death

What we have already learned concerning financial provisions in the event of death may not necessarily apply to the negotiations and preparation of the agreement with regard to termination of the relationship through a separation. If you and your companion mutually decide that your relationship should end, that continuing to live together is not in either party's best interest, the separation may be less painful than when the breach occurs because of the decision of but one of you. However, the necessity of providing or receiving support under the latter circumstance is a most difficult topic for the two of you to discuss at the negotiation table when you attempt to reach a living-together agreement prior to actually sharing the same residence. These dissimilar interests may result in one or both of you deciding that you cannot share your lives together, causing you and your companion to separate even before your living-together relationship has begun. This delicate issue is one that is also addressed by persons who plan to marry, and more than one wedding has been canceled because of an inability to reach financial terms before wedding bells chime.

Nonetheless, even though it is extremely difficult to reach agreement on the topic of financial obligation in the event the relationship terminates by mutual or unilateral separation, if your companion insists that the ongoing relationship be contingent upon an agreement being made, it is wise to adjust your thinking and be prepared to offer or request a fair proposal, namely, one that will meet the reasonable needs of the person needing support while giving consideration to the financial ability of the other to provide such support.

When married couples divorce and attempt to make a separation agreement, when cohabitants separate, and when single people negotiate a prenuptial agreement, their concerns are entirely similar. There must always be a delicate balance between the needs of each party. The need for periodic support caused by a breach of your relationship should be considered together with the length of time the relationship endured before the breach. Just as concern for the span of years involved is factored into estate planning, so too should it be a basis for a formula approach for the determination of weekly or other periodic support payments if separation occurs for reasons other than death. The following table illustrates one such plan:

Length of time between signing of agreement and separation	Weekly amount
1–5 years	$100
6–10 years	200
11–15 years	300
16–20 years	400
More than 25 years	500

Again, the division of the relationship's length into intervals that correspond to increases in the amount of support, as well as the amounts themselves, will depend upon your respective financial circumstances and the lifestyle and standard of living that is anticipated by the two of you. It can, of course, be stipulated that these periodic payments end at your death, when marriage of the supported person occurs, or when he or she resumes cohabitation with someone else. This provision is most important to ensure that support will end after the need for it no longer exists. It would be grossly unfair to request or to agree to provide otherwise. Support should not be thought of as a punishment of the supporting partner by the recipient.

It may be that when separation occurs because of discord, both of you can agree on a lump sum payment instead of ongoing periodic payments. A lump sum, as was observed earlier, can fix with certainty the total amount of support that will be paid and will not be conditional (except, of course, to the extent that the amount to be paid will correspond to the duration of the relationship preceding separation). The table included in the estate planning section should be referred to and considered when a lump sum payment is to be used.

The portion of this chapter pertaining to prenuptial agreements should also be considered and read by cohabitants who have no intention of marrying, since the financial concerns of persons in both situations may be similar. Reaching an agreement that will be acceptable to you and your partner, that will be fair to you both, and that accommodates your respective needs is your primary goal. A lawyer skilled in these matters should always be consulted. A member of the American Academy of Matrimonial Lawyers, a national organization with chapters in most populous states, will be highly trained in family and cohabitants' rights and will be able to advise and represent you. If your state certifies legal specialists, an attorney who is certified in domestic relations matters will also have the knowledge and experience in this area of the law. Knowing some of the ways in which agreements can be structured will enable you to work more effectively with an attorney and to explore areas of concern. Although under some state laws it would be possible for an attorney to devise a cohabitants' agreement and represent both parties, it would be wise for each to obtain independent counsel. It has frequently been observed that one servant cannot effectively serve two masters. This is especially true in the negotiations of cohabitant or prenuptial agreements since the needs of the parties are quite different and require special attention.

Prenuptial Agreements

Written agreements between cohabitants can take several forms. A prenuptial agreement is no more or less than an agreement between two persons who may or may not already cohabit and who plan to later marry. A prenuptial agreement is distinguished from a cohabitants' agreement by the condition that it will only become valid when the parties enter into a ceremonial marriage; all prenuptial agreements contain this condition. Prenuptial agreements are made between persons who have not been previously married or, more commonly, between those who are about to enter into a second or later marriage. Today, couples who wish to enter into prenuptial agreements can normally address almost every legal aspect of the termination of the marital relationship, including support, division of marital property, custody and support of children, and, theoretically, other terms and conditions of the marriage relationship. Prenuptial agreements can also include provisions for support and a division of property in the event of death and can vary the estate and inheritance laws that exist in your home state (see chapter 9 for an extensive discussion of state inheritance laws).

The negotiation of a prenuptial agreement is indeed a delicate affair. If you seek to get the last drop of juice out of the orange, you may be doing a great disservice to yourself, since such attempts may lead to the abandonment of your wedding plans. The conflict becomes readily apparent: do you continue to press for all points that are in your best interest or do you relax your vigor for the very sake of the impending marriage? It should be uppermost in your mind that greed can never be countenanced and that it would be improper to attempt to obtain an unfair advantage in these dealings. When considering these matters, Henry Fielding, in his novel *Tom Jones*, observed: "If this be the motive which prompted the desire to fashion an ante-nuptial agreement, not only the agreement, but the marriage itself, is doomed to failure." Once you have realized this potential problem, earnest negotiations that seek a fair and equitable agreement can be begun.

Whether you are the prospective spouse with assets and income will make a considerable difference in the approach you take to the negotiations. For example, the question of whether previously owned property should be entirely excluded from the definition of marital assets must be addressed at an early stage. If such property is to be entirely excluded, the next question to consider is whether its appreciation during marriage should be included in the definition and therefore subject to division in the event that you later divorce. These determinations are important since almost every state has adopted either equitable distribution or community property laws, which permit distribution of marital property (i.e., any property acquired during the marriage, regardless of ownership) to be made upon divorce.

Prenuptial agreements are important because they can remove the guesswork and anxiety of attempting to look into a crystal ball to determine what a court would do in a divorce proceeding. Rather than have the court fix their obligations and rights concerning property and support, many couples now opt to enter into written agreements that remove such uncertainties. A prenuptial agreement will also ensure that there will not be a drawn-out legal battle in the courts over these property and support issues, including appeals from lower court determinations, which can be extremely costly and may drag on for months and, possibly, years.

There is always the danger that a prenuptial agreement can later be attacked by one of the parties. In order to avoid having a court set aside a prenuptial agreement because of some irregularity, it is best to take the following precautions: have separate attorneys represent you and your prospective spouse, and make certain that there is a complete exchange of financial information. In this way, neither of you can claim that the agreement was unfair when made, that you did not have proper independent representation, or that you were defrauded because of your lack of information regarding the income enjoyed and the assets owned by the other party. If you have taken the effort and incurred the expense to formalize your agreement concerning your financial rights and obligations, you should do everything in your power to ensure that the agreement will be sustained by the courts in the event that it is later attacked by a disgruntled spouse. Some attorneys have suggested that the signing and final negotiations should be placed on video tape.

What we have considered should alert you to the extreme delicacy that must be employed when you are beginning to negotiate the terms of a prenuptial agreement. To win a battle at the negotiating table and lose your prospective spouse would certainly not be in your best interest. But if you and your future spouse decide to have a prenuptial agreement, you should attempt to remove any ambiguities or questionable conduct during the negotiation process in order to avoid a later legal attack upon that agreement.

Prenuptial agreements come about more frequently with second or later marriages than with initial unions. Most subsequent marriages occur in mid-life; normally, the people involved have children and have acquired some money and property during the prior marriage. Having previously made a mistake in a choice of a mate, which ended in a divorce, a person entering a subsequent marriage may be somewhat more guarded than someone who has yet to be married. Certainly, it would not be unreasonable for you to wish, in the event of a divorce, to preserve for your own benefit or for the benefit of your children assets that you bring into the marriage. This would also be true if a first marriage ended because of the death of your spouse. The problem really becomes how to balance the goal of preservation of money and property against the desire to treat your spouse-to-be fairly. Some persons seem to resolve this dilemma by making a compromise that excludes the money or property brought into the marriage but not the appreciation in value of such money or property. For example, if you come into a second marriage with a bank account and equity (the market value less the amount of an existing mortgage) in real estate, you might consider making a provision in a prenuptial agreement that would exclude the present value of the bank account and real estate but would permit any increment in value that occurs during the marriage to be deemed marital property, or subject to the laws of inheritance. Put another way, any increase in value of the real estate or the bank account would be able to be divided by the courts in the event of a divorce, and such increased value would form part of your estate in the event of death.

Perhaps an arithmetic explanation would be helpful at this juncture to understand how this prenuptial agreement provision would be implemented in the event of death or divorce. Say that you have been married for a period of ten years when either death or divorce occurs, that the bank account that you brought into the marriage originally in the sum of $50,000 has increased to $70,000 simply by drawing interest over that ten-year period, and that the real estate that you owned with an original equity of $100,000 has increased in value to $170,000. There would be a total appreciation of money and property of $90,000, which sum of money would be considered a marital asset ($70,000 − $50,000 = $20,000 and $170,000 − $100,000 = $70,000; $20,000 + $70,000 = $90,000). The original bank account of $50,000 and the earlier value in the real estate of $100,000 would be excluded from consideration by the court. Only the increased or appreciated value of $90,000 would be treated as marital property. What you have accomplished by this device is to preserve for yourself, or your heirs, the moneys brought into the marriage while at the same time affording your spouse of ten years the ability to share at least a portion of the appreciated value of $90,000. This compromise provision is only a suggestion, something for you to consider when negotiating a prenuptial or cohabitants' agreement.

By contrast, there are many persons who feel that whatever assets they bring into the marriage should remain their separate property and should not be shared with their new spouse in any way. Persons who hold such feelings regard the increase in value of such assets to be a normal increment that should not form part of the couple's marital property. Those who share this view would not be willing to insert such a clause in a prenuptial agreement and would stipulate that only money or property acquired during the time the parties live together (but not the increments to previously owned property) preceding a death or divorce be considered as marital property, and thus subject to division. This view includes the belief that marriage is an economic partnership and that only the financial fruits acquired during the partnership should be subject to division upon death or divorce.

There may be many different ways to arrive at a prenuptial agreement that will be acceptable to both you and your prospective spouse. These may include the use of life insurance, trusts, annuities, or any other financial instrument that can provide the necessary moneys that will be used to satisfy any claim against property or for the support of a spouse or child. These methods can be explored at length with an attorney, accountant, or financial planner.

Chapter 8, "Support and Property Division Laws," should be reviewed in order to ascertain what amounts of maintenance and/ or child support might be reasonably anticipated to be made by the courts in the event of a divorce or separation, as well as what division of property will be made in either an equitable distribution or community property state. Once this knowledge is gained, it can form the basis for successfully negotiating the amount and duration of support and division of property within the prenuptial agreement. In those states, such as New York, that permit premarital agreements to be set aside if they are unfair when made or unconscionable at the time the parties come before the court, your goal is to agree on terms that will stand up to the scrutiny of the court in the event of an attack.

Certainly, it would be dangerous to negotiate a prenuptial agreement that would essentially give you everything and your intended spouse absolutely nothing in the event of a divorce or a separation. However, if there was complete financial disclosure, if independent attorneys represented both sides when the agreement was made, and if the agreement specifically sets forth that the party who is to receive no support or property in the event of a divorce or separation had his or her rights explained and that if no such agreement is signed he or she could apply to the court for support and a property division, there may be some possibility, where the finances are not drastically lopsided, that such an agreement could withstand attack. However, because the courts regard those who make prenuptial agreements as persons who have not yet entered into the confidential relationship of husband and wife, these waiver clauses may have a slightly better chance of being upheld than those that may appear in a separation agreement between a married couple, or an agreement between cohabitants whose relationship has spanned a number of years. Including a waiver clause is still a dangerous choice and one that might meet with the disapproval of the court. Certainly, in states that apply a fairness or unconscionable test to these agreements, the odds are greatly in favor of the agreement being set aside if it provides for a total waiver, especially in circumstances where one of the parties enjoys a large income and many assets while the other party has no income or assets whatsoever.

Whether a prenuptial agreement or simply an agreement between two cohabitants who never plan to marry is contemplated, the same techniques can be employed in order to accommodate both partners' interests. Remember that prenuptial agreements are conditioned upon marriage while cohabitants' agreements are not; however, the goals of the partners and the drafting techniques utilized can be quite similar.

Chapter 11

Senior Citizens

Living together may occur at many different times of life. Some persons begin living together as a prelude to a first marriage when they are in their late teens and early twenties, while others enter into such a relationship in mid-life. The decision of senior citizens to live together rather than marry may create some special problems that will not be faced by persons of younger years.

Separations that occur late in life are caused more frequently by death of the spouse than by divorce, and separating from a partner at age 60 or later can be one of life's most difficult events. Having experienced both the joys and the difficulties of a long marriage, including parenthood and the children's departure from home, the natural tendency, as one grows older, is to become more concerned with companionship and security. Even for couples whose relationship has been more stormy than serene, divorce, with the initial loneliness and the financial demands that must be faced alone, becomes less of an option. Some such persons may feel that under the circumstances it is far better to try to overlook the shortcomings of their spouse and spend the twilight years together, rather than alone. Nonetheless, there are others who do not regard the prospect of continuing a bad marriage until death do them part as a viable alternative, preferring to go it alone rather than continue in an unfulfilling relationship. Still others are left alone to face old age without a partner, perhaps after a long illness in which they tended to the physical, emotional, and financial needs of their spouse.

Whether such separation occurs because of an untimely death or because of divorce, senior citizens must make very important decisions concerning their future.

Senior citizens who decide to live together are also a subject addressed in this book. Whether to marry or not may depend upon what loss of social security benefits may occur if marital vows are taken. In addition, a senior citizen must be especially cautious entering into such a relationship because of the likelihood of illness accompanying advanced years. When illness strikes a senior citizen, his or her partner, whether married or not, may very well incur substantial financial obligations for medical treatment, hospitalization, nursing, and nursing-home expenses.

Dealing with a terminal illness presents other problems that are addressed in this work. In 1990 the United States Supreme Court recognized the growing desire of citizens to refuse medical treatment or to designate a person who could make medical decisions for them in the event of mental or physical incapacity. The *Cruzan* case established the right of every person to refuse medical treatment, whether conscious or comatose, as long as his or her wishes have been made known to a treating physician. *Cruzan* also recognized the right of a surrogate to act on behalf of a disabled person. The Supreme Court directed that the states set their own standards for "clear and convincing evidence" of a patient's wishes.

The enactment by Congress of the Patient Self-Determination Act of 1990 will go a long way in furthering treatment. While it appears to make sense to combine a living will and health care power of attorney into a single document, some state laws may forbid such practice, since the terms of living wills and health care proxies in such states may not be compatible. Because of these disparate statutes, it is most important for senior citizens to fully explore and understand the law of the state in which they live, especially if residence is maintained in more than one state. The chapter dealing with senior citizens explores these various options, and the appendices that follow the text include sample documents.

Adjustment Is Necessary at All Ages

The adjustments to separation may be harder for a person of advanced years, especially when the separation occurs because of death. Such a loss creates a major impact and, at times, a great crisis in one's life. The loss of a spouse is especially difficult when one has lived with that person for most of one's adult life, sharing the joys as well as the challenges that beset all couples, raising children and seeing them through the minor problems of childhood and the more difficult adolescent years until they themselves have left home and have taken their place in the adult world, marrying and bearing children. Many of the emotional problems that beset persons following separation are magnified in the minds of the elderly. These emotional problems need to be addressed as rapidly as possible in order for the senior citizen to return to the mainstream of life.

After the emotional problems have been resolved and after a reasonable period of mourning, the older person begins to again have social contacts. Neighbors, friends, and relatives furnish emotional support and attempt to introduce the newly single senior to persons of similar age in the social stream:

> "I have a person who just lost his wife that I want you to meet."
>
> "There is this wonderful lady that I recently met who lost her husband, and I'm sure you would enjoy her company; why don't you give her a call and tell her that I suggested that you meet?"
>
> "It's been over a year now since your husband [wife] passed away and I really think that you must consider getting back to enjoying life again. Why don't you come over to the house next week. I'm inviting a few people over, and I'm sure you will enjoy getting to know some of our friends."

All are suggestions made by persons in the senior's life who wish to see him or her regain the zest for living that was previously enjoyed.

When a first contact is made following these meaningful suggestions by friends, the senior citizen will undoubtedly feel most uncomfortable. Returning to the social mainstream and meeting new persons and learning to get along with them is not the easiest thing to do following a period of mourning. Most people by nature are shy and find it emotionally draining to meet persons for the first time, perhaps because of the fear that they will not be accepted or that they will not be thought of as attractive, both intellectually and physically. Advanced age is a tremendous obstacle on the road to social recovery. In this country, youth receives a premium while old age is frequently looked upon with disdain. One needs only to thumb through the ads of a newspaper or magazine or flick on the television set to know that youth is "in" and old age is "out."

Despite these apparent prejudices in favor of youth, there is a vast population in this country of persons 60 and over who have become single by virtue of death or divorce and who have made new meaningful lives for themselves. Their needs for social relationships are no different from those of the young or middle-aged person who may be looking to find a new mate following a first marriage. In a phrase, we are all very different but very much alike. The need for companionship, for love and affection, for sharing and caring, really knows no age limit. Mature adults, having experienced so much of life, may find it more difficult to adjust to change, but their desire to do so is no less strong than that of a much younger person.

What other things concern the mature adult and the senior citizen? The need for companionship must, of course, be the most compelling reason to seek out new relationships, followed closely by financial concerns. The following are thoughts that may rapidly pass through a senior's mind or, perhaps, dwell there for extended periods. They are real concerns, ones that must be carefully considered and addressed.

"Will I be able to make it on the monies I have left?"
"Can I continue to live in our home by myself?"
"Is there enough money to take care of me in the event that I suffer an illness?"
"Will the children think of me as a burden now that their father [mother] has passed away?"

Once serious thought is given to these issues, one must then consider if one's finances appear to be sufficient to go it alone or whether it will be necessary to turn to the children for financial help or, perhaps, whether one might choose to share expenses with another person. Should this other person be someone of the same sex, or should you look to share your life with a person of the opposite sex? If you consider seeking out a person of the opposite sex, the next issue to decide is whether a commitment for marriage should be considered or whether it would be better not to undertake the legal obligations that a marriage will necessarily incur but to simply live together in a common residence and share all expenses.

Whether to marry or instead live together must necessarily include an examination of the legal consequences that were discussed earlier in this book, as well as a consideration of the loss of certain benefits that may be provided by the terms of a will, a divorce settlement, a prenuptial agreement, or Social Security benefits. To marry or not; that is the question. The answer can have profound emotional as well as legal impact. It may be that you will never have to decide whether to live with or marry someone, because you have concluded that it would be too much of an emotional drain to enter into such a relationship and take the risk that your new partner may become seriously ill or that you may divorce, forcing you to go through another most trying emotional period. This fear of losing yet another partner may be all that is needed for you to reach the conclusion that it would be far better for you to remain alone and face the challenges of life by yourself. And those persons of advanced years who had a previous bad relationship or marriage may similarly opt to live alone. This choice spares one the necessity of having to make new social contacts, adapt one's lifestyle to that of another person, or risk becoming disappointed in another person or involved in a most unpleasant emotional conflict.

Nonetheless, there are still many persons who will risk suffering these myriad disappointments and emotional difficulties and decide that they would rather not live alone. Sometimes this choice includes joining another family member, often an adult child, in his or her residence. This choice can be a good one for both the senior citizen and the grown child if the living quarters are large enough to provide the senior with a comfortable separate bedroom and if both the child and his or her spouse, as well as any grandchildren that may reside in the home, enjoy a close and warm relationship with the elderly one. It may be to the mutual benefit of all parties concerned if you elect to move in to the home of your child and become a part of his or her family. The advantage of doing so for your child may be that he or she is able to return to the work force while you provide child care for your grand-children. Moreover, you will have the gratification of knowing that you are not only providing loving care for your grandchildren but are helping your child financially as well.

You must be convinced that your child has made the offer to you with the full consent and support of his or her spouse and that your acceptance of the offer will not in any way create a burden to the children or the grandchildren or interfere with their lifestyle. If you reach the conclusion that you will intrude upon their privacy or that you will not be accepted without reservation, then this option should be rejected by you. While there are many instances of parents who later in life become part of their children's household, not all these living arrangements are satisfactory. Some who accept that initial offer to share the residence of their children find, after a period of time, that living together is unworkable and causes resentment in the son- or daughter-in-law. Others find that they must give up the privacy they have enjoyed through most of their lives. Moreover, the demands of the grandchildren, especially in situations where a child returns to the work force, may, in reality, be too difficult for a senior to cope with. Having been independent for the many years that one has lived either alone or with a spouse makes it far more difficult to adjust to communal living.

Once the decision has been made to live by oneself (perhaps after a living arrangement with a child that proved unsatisfactory), the desire for companionship becomes most prevalent in one's mind. There are essentially no legal impediments to remaining single and not entering into a relationship with another person. It is only when, either by choice or by happenstance, you find yourself in a relationship where you are sharing the same living quarters, although not contemplating marriage, that legal issues arise. These are considered in the following pages and can be grouped into five categories: (1) loss of social security benefits, (2) loss of rights created by a will or trust, (3) loss of alimony or maintenance payments, (4) loss of health care insurance, and (5) compulsion to support a companion who has become disabled and/or institutionalized.

Loss of Social Security Benefits

Unless you have qualified on your own for full Social Security benefits, the major benefits that you will receive from Social Security are survivor benefits, the benefit afforded to a surviving spouse. These payments will be made pursuant to the Social Security Law until you die or remarry. Remarriage has not as yet been defined to include your living together in the same household with an unrelated male, so that there would be no loss of benefits if you decided to live with another person without formal marriage. However, marriage could cause the loss of Social Security benefits not only to you but to the person that you choose to marry. In many cases, the loss of these benefits could prevent the older couple from maintaining a reasonable standard of living, or even from obtaining the necessities of life.

It is for this reason alone that many senior couples choose to live together without the benefit of marriage. In recent years, the mores of our society actually accept such living-together relationships, even though it may be difficult for the participants themselves, who grew up in another era. Nonetheless, when faced with the dilemma of whether to live together or marry, financial considerations may well transcend any pangs of morality that the mature person may experience.

Social Security benefits for a surviving spouse that are based on the contribution of the deceased spouse can be modest or, at times, fairly substantial. Appendix F includes a schedule of Social Security benefits. Sometimes a survivor is not eligible to receive such benefits because of a lack of contribution to the Social Security fund by the deceased spouse. A retired couple contemplating marriage must be willing and able to give up the advantage of Social Security benefits, since marriage can eliminate a monthly check of $800 or more. By contrast, if they simply live together, there will be no such loss of payments. This financial loss may well be the deciding factor against entering into a marital relationship.

There are still other financial considerations that may lead senior citizens to decide not to marry, including the extraordinary expense of a mental or physical incapacity. What happens if they can no longer care for themselves? How will their financial decisions—such as paying bills, withdrawing money from the bank, and dealing with the local Social Security office regarding payments—be made? Also, there are many health care decisions that must be attended to, involving receiving or refusing medical treatment, entering a hospital, choosing a nursing home or other health care facility, and selecting a physician, psychiatrist, or other health care professional. Once a disability is upon you, it is often too late to make plans for your personal life and for the disposition of your finances. In the event that you become mentally incapacitated, there is great likelihood that your relatives will petition to have the court appoint a conservator, that is, one who will be responsible for making all of your personal and financial decisions, which, of course, may not be made in the direction you would have chosen.

Advance Planning

There are other personal decisions that should be given attention, including choosing a place to live and disposing of your money and property. While every individual has an absolute right to live with dignity and to make decisions concerning day-to-day living, these rights cannot be enjoyed unless one expresses in writing one's decisions about these personal, health care, and financial concerns. If you fail to draw up such a formal document, you may well lose control over these decisions in the event of your mental disability. Moreover, if you become physically disabled, although mentally alert, you may not be able to attend to the chores required to put your financial house in order. This is much akin to failing to leave a will and permitting your hard-earned money to be distributed according to local or state law and, perhaps, to persons other than those whom you would choose. It is a result that you should avoid at all costs.

Today, there are a variety of legal tools available in almost every state within this country to enable you to avoid these results. One of the most common devices being utilized today is a *durable power of attorney*, which retains its legal effect even in the event that you become physically or mentally disabled. A durable power of attorney is a legal document similar to an ordinary power of attorney that does not lose its legal effect in the event of your mental disability. It can provide for the orderly management of all of your financial matters, including the payment of current bills, the investment and reinvestment of your assets, and the application of your own funds for your day-to-day needs, or those of a loved one. A durable power of attorney can be limited to certain areas or, if you choose, unlimited in scope. Whether to draw a durable power of attorney that is limited or unlimited depends on your own desires and the nature and extent of your holdings. It is a personal decision that should only be made after consultation with an attorney, financial adviser, accountant, or other person you deem to be expert in the field of finances. If you have decided that a durable power of attorney is right for you, then your next consideration should be the selection of someone as your attorney-in-fact, that is, a person who will act in your behalf in all matters pertaining to your care and your finances, which will, of course, include matters regarding not only your own support but also that of your spouse, your live in companion, and other persons for whom you bear responsibility, such as an aged parent or a child.

It may also be possible to prepare a conditional durable power of attorney. In states that permit these powers, the device is known as a *springing power of attorney*, which will only become effective upon the occurrence of a specified event, such as a catastrophic illness. Because of the complexities of the different types of powers of attorney that can be utilized, it is recommended that you always employ an attorney who understands the needs of the elderly, as well as the legal devices available to them for protecting their assets and the financial security of their loved ones, in order to draw up a document that will be certain to accommodate your wishes.

Who should act as your attorney-in-fact? You should only choose a person you have complete trust in, one whose judgment you respect, one whom you can rely upon to make a proper decision that will accommodate your needs as well as the needs of your spouse, live-in companion, parent of advanced years, or child. You may decide to choose your spouse or live-in companion or some member of your family to act in this capacity if you determine that this person possesses the necessary skills to administer the financial aspects of your life.

Instead of employing a durable power of attorney, some persons choose to establish trusts, which will accomplish the same end. A trust that will come into being during your own lifetime is often referred to as a *living trust*. It can be funded immediately by placing one or more of your assets into the trust for a specific use, for example, to support yourself, your spouse, or other loved ones. If you choose, you can make a provision that the trust will only come into being upon the occurrence of a specified event, similar to the provision employed when drawing up a durable power of attorney. For example, a trust can be drawn up that will not spring into being unless you are declared mentally incompetent or so physically disabled that you cannot act in your own behalf. Either a trust instrument or the durable power of attorney will avoid having the court appoint a conservator when your capacity to manage your own personal affairs has become impaired because of illness, advanced age, or mental incapacity.

There is another advantage to a trust: to preserve assets from invasion by an institution in the event that you ever become a Medicare or Medicaid recipient. However, in order to accomplish this goal, you must, in effect, give up all control over the asset placed in trust. You should most certainly consult with an attorney or an accountant, and perhaps both, in planning such a trust.

Health Care Decision Making

As noted earlier, it is very important to provide for decision making in the event of an illness, especially since the illness itself may prevent you from making decisions. You must remember that unless you draw up a document known in most states as a *health care proxy*, decisions regarding the doctor you will see or the hospital you will enter will be made by the state (see Appendix H) in the event that you become stricken with a catastrophic illness or disability and lose your capacity to make these decisions on your own. If you have not made a health care proxy designating a member of your family or other person to act in your behalf, the court in your state will appoint a person known as a "committee" or "guardian" to make decisions in your behalf. Such a person will not be familiar with your own wishes and undoubtedly will not be as sensitive to your needs as a spouse, live-in companion, or other member of your family.

All persons have the fundamental right to make their own decisions regarding their medical destiny, decisions that cannot be vetoed by their spouse, their adult children, a friend, a physician, or any other person who seeks to intervene. By preparing a health care proxy, you will permit the person named in the document to act in your own behalf, free of interference from others. A health care proxy is similar but not identical to a living will (discussed in the next section), which is limited to life-prolonging procedures, but a health care proxy can include whatever directions you wish concerning your medical treatment. However, granting a proxy to a named individual will not permit that person to decide whether you are to receive nutrition and hydration while ill unless you yourself have clearly expressed your desires in a written document. Nonetheless, a person to whom you have given a health proxy will have access to all medical records that pertain to you and will be able to select a physician to treat you and the hospital where you will be admitted.

Living Will

A living will is a written document that will incorporate your health care declaration concerning the use of life-prolonging medical procedures if you become terminally ill or lack the capacity to make your own health care decisions because of mental incompetence. Recent court decisions throughout the country have made clear that a proper living will or health care proxy made by a patient prior to his or her illness will be followed if it is clear in its terms regarding the use of life-prolonging medical procedures, which can include resuscitation, blood transfusions, or other heroic methods. There are a number of organizations that have prepared living wills, which are available to and can be adopted by the general public, including The Right to Die, Concern for Dying, and the American Association of Retired Persons (AARP). Although these documents are freely available (and one is contained in Appendix I of this book), it is not recommended that they be used by you without consultation with a professional who deals with the problems of the elderly. If you clearly do not wish to have any extraordinary methods utilized to prolong your life in the event of a stroke or other catastrophic illness, such as cancer or heart disease, you must execute a living will. You must remember that if the issue is brought before the court, it undoubtedly will be resolved in favor of utilizing prolonged treatment.

Some states have enacted legislation to permit you, in the absence of a health care proxy or a living will, to declare that cardiopulmonary resuscitation that may be medically required or indicated in your case not be performed upon you (see Appendix G). A Do Not Resuscitate declaration can be made either in writing or orally if it is attested to by the number of witnesses required to give legal status to the declaration.

All persons of advanced years (and perhaps young people as well) should have the presence of mind not only to prepare a will that will protect their loved ones but also to adopt the various health care documents that may be necessary in order to plan for the future in the event of their physical or mental incapacity. These decisions should not be left to chance or to the whims of others. If you have not, in fact, made your wishes known concerning, for example, the prolongation of your life through a feeding tube or other artificial means if you are in a comatose or vegetative state, your relatives or loved ones will not be able to refuse such treatment in your behalf—even if that is your wish.

Medicare and Medicaid

How will you be able to deal with a catastrophic illness that will require extensive medical treatment and hospitalization for yourself or the person with whom you live? How will you be able to meet the needs of your spouse or live-in companion who may become ill, infirm, or mentally incompetent and require admission to a nursing home or other health care facility? Will your spouse or live-in companion be responsible for your care or treatment? Put another way, will the state be able to take away from such persons their own assets in order to support you in a facility? It is important to determine the resources you and your partner possess and whether advance planning can prevent the state from taking away from you any of the assets that you may own or have previously conveyed by gift to others. To answer these questions, state Medicaid laws, as well as Medicare eligibility (see Appendix L), must be examined carefully. Most states have provisions concerning the treatment of income and assets of spouses, not live-in companions. Whether the assets are owned or whether either party has made any transfers of assets preceding the time when Medicaid benefits are to be paid will determine whether these monies can be reached. Medicare is the federal act that provides basic health insurance benefits while Medicaid generally is supplemental assistance by a state to provide health care benefits over and above, or in absence of, Medicare payments.

All of the Medicare and Medicaid laws pertain to spouses and not live-in companions; this legal distinction may cause you to determine that it would be wise for you and your partner to live together rather than become formally married, since the assets and income of the nondisabled live-in companion cannot be considered in determining the eligibility of the disabled companion for Medicare or Medicaid benefits. The rules are indeed complex, and there are varying formulas of eligibility and ineligibility contained in each state's laws. Most states give a certain resource allowance to the nondisabled spouse, usually referred to as the "community spouse," which will permit him or her to retain a certain amount of assets as well as a fixed minimum monthly income, thus protecting these funds from contribution to the care of the institutionalized spouse.

There are also varying rules pertaining to the transfer of assets that can render a person ineligible for Medicaid: for example, if a transfer of assets has taken place, there must be a waiting period of 30 months following the transfer before one can become eligible for Medicaid assistance. There are certain exemptions of property, which normally includes a person's homestead. The law allows even the transfer of a homestead during this 30-month waiting period if the transfer is made to a spouse, child, or other family member. Such laws, which have been recently adopted in most states, stem from the Medicare Catastrophic Coverage Act of 1988, or MCCA. If assets were transferred 30 months or more before application was made for Medicaid benefits, then, of course, they would be secure from attack by the state.

If you are a senior citizen and must determine whether to live with another person with or without benefit of marriage, you must know the Medicaid laws that apply in your state, as well as what Social Security benefits may be lost if you decide to get married. Unless you have some extremely strong religious or moral reservation, marriage may not be the right financial choice for you. This, of course, is a personal decision and should only be made after careful consideration, but unless you are aware of the matters discussed within this chapter, it would be impossible for you to make an intelligent decision.

Overview

Married senior citizens should utilize the knowledge in this chapter to prepare a living will or a health care proxy to make certain that their wishes will be followed during a final illness. There are some remarkable circumstances that may even lead persons to obtain a divorce in order to preserve assets for the use of a nondisabled spouse. Of course, if you and a live-in companion have substantial assets of your own, choosing not to marry will not protect your own assets in the event that you become incapacitated. Although failing to marry (or divorcing) will insulate your own assets in the event that your partner is the one who becomes incapacitated, it cannot accomplish the same result for you, unless, of course, you make provision to gift your property to others at least 30 months prior to the time you may need to apply for Medicaid assistance.

There appears to be no prohibition against your making gifts to members of your family, such as your adult children, of whatever money or property you choose, provided it is accomplished 30 months prior to applying for Medicaid assistance. In turn, if your children desire, they can make periodic gifts to you in order to meet your living requirements. This may be the one device available to you enabling you to place your assets out of the reach of the state while, at the same time, preserving these assets for your children or other loved ones. Since the Medicaid laws will include not only your assets but, if you are married, your spouse's, a gift to a spouse could not accomplish this result. However, there are some state laws that look to the extended family, which can include children, when determining Medicaid eligibility. In such states, gifts to your family will not do the trick; in fact, Florida has passed just such a law, since there are so many senior citizens who reside there. Again, before any planning is considered or attempts are made to implement such plans, you should consult with a professional who will be able to advise you concerning the specific laws that exist in your home state.

The law is rapidly changing in the area of senior citizens' rights, and it is hoped that there will be major reforms that will enable such persons to complete their lives with dignity and financial security.

Chapter 12

Becoming Unwound:

Ways to Successfully Prosecute or Defend Lawsuits Stemming from Unwanted Separations

Having explored the various living-together arrangements that can be made, as well as the legal and psychological implications that flow from such arrangements, it is appropriate at this point in the book to examine the many ways people can become unwound from such situations and both the psychological and legal implications of doing so.

If your living-together relationship began without benefit of a written agreement, whether you live in a state that recognizes common-law marriages may be of great significance to you if you have now come to the realization that the person with whom you have been residing for a period of time is no longer someone you choose to remain living with. A break occurring by mutual consent is the least painful and will cause little psychological damage. There may be no hard feelings between the two of you, let alone a vindictive bent to "get even" and explore ways in which to reap some financial benefit or windfall; in fact, you may continue to have genuine affection for each other.

It is only when there is a unilateral desire to end the relationship that vindictive motives surface. Moreover, when only one party wishes to terminate the living-together relationship, the other party, who has no such similar desire and may even be shocked by this wish, may experience psychological trauma much akin to that suffered by a divorcing person. Reactions differ. A large percentage of cohabitants who are extremely hurt by the reality that they can no longer have the security of a stable home environment will, nevertheless, accept such news without choosing to take any legal action to obtain support or other financial betterment. Normally, these persons who do not seek to enforce a legal right that may exist have incomes of their own, are essentially self-supporting, and do not wish to embroil themselves in a drawn-out lawsuit that will undoubtedly cause extreme animosity and bitterness, as well as require a substantial investment in legal fees.

To those persons who recognize the pitfalls of pursuing a legal option, the choice of whether to do so or not may be less difficult. They may feel that dealing with the disappointment, frustration, and anxiety that may surface after the breakup may require all the strength they can muster and may not permit a consideration of legal remedies. Some persons may experience a deep depression that will require professional treatment by a health care professional. Others will be able to handle the trauma of separation by themselves or with the support of friends and family.

Lawsuits between Cohabitants: Some Considerations

Lawsuits between unmarried couples normally occur when one party cannot support himself or herself or does not have sufficient financial means to continue to maintain the preseparation standard of living that the couple established during the time that they lived together. This financial bind may occur for a variety of reasons, which can include the insistence of one party on being the sole wage earner while requiring that the other be freely available socially and emotionally, without obligation to a job or career. When such cohabitation has spanned a very long period of time, the financial impact on the dependent partner can be severe. The ability to obtain employment that will produce a meaningful income may be all but removed for the partner who remained out of the job market by curtailing a career or not pursuing advanced education. The pursuit of a legal option may be the only choice available to such an individual in an attempt to preserve some semblance of financial security following the breakup.

The best way to explore your legal rights and the ways they can be enforced is by retaining an attorney who is a certified family law practitioner, if your state has adopted certification of specialties by lawyers, or whose practice, if your state does not have such certification, is limited to family law matters. There are many ways to find such attorneys. Your local bar association will be more than willing to provide you with a list of certified attorneys in the field of matrimonial or family law. *Martindale-Hubbell*, which can be found in most law and public libraries, compiles a list of attorneys throughout the country and rates them by peer review. An AV-rated attorney is one who receives the highest recognition for competency and ethics. Almost every attorney in your state will be listed by name and geographical location, and biographical information regarding his or her experience, background, and training will be included. You should look for an attorney who specializes in domestic relations matters, has written in the field, and has been involved in specialty bar groups, such as the family or matrimonial sections of the county and state bar associations or of the American Bar Association, participating in their programs either as a lecturer or author.

In selecting such an attorney, you should also be aware of the American Academy of Matrimonial Lawyers, which is a national organization composed of local state chapters of matrimonial attorneys who have practiced for a period of at least ten years in the field of matrimonial and family law, have passed an oral or written examination given by the local chapter in your state, and have been recommended by at least two fellows of the Academy and one or more judges within your state. The American Academy of Matrimonial Lawyers was organized to preserve the best interests of the family and of society and to improve the practice, elevate the standards, and advance the cause of matrimonial law. Its members participate in continuing legal education programs on an annual basis and are generally the leading lawyers of the matrimonial community in each state. A local chapter will provide you with a list of the members or, in some instances, will recommend a fellow within the Academy who can best satisfy your particular needs.

There is no better way to select an attorney, after making an investigation into his or her background, than to receive a recommendation from a friend or relative who has been involved in a similar type of legal problem. Remember that today is the age of consumerism. The right of the consumer to obtain knowledge to make an intelligent decision applies to the service industry as well as the retail industry. You should interview several attorneys before you make a final selection. It is most essential that you feel comfortable with and can relate to the person you choose to represent you in this most difficult area of the law. The lawyer should be patient and willing to listen; he or she should be someone with whom you have a rapport and in whom you have confidence. You should not select as your attorney a person with whom you have difficulty communicating, no matter how highly recommended he or she is or how outstanding his or her credentials may be. Selecting a competent, experienced attorney, one you can work with, is the most important decision you will make. It should not be treated lightly or made without careful investigation and thought.

In making this selection, you should also look for an attorney who is creative, one who will be willing to take on a case that may have no precedent within your jurisdiction. Put another way, an attorney should be willing to attempt to break new ground, especially in the areas of human relations, where society is adopting a liberal attitude toward persons living together without benefit of marriage.

Once an attorney is selected, there must be full exploration of all possible claims, known in the legal jargon as *causes of action*, that may exist in order to provide you with proper representation in the courts of your state. The more knowledgeable you are concerning such possible rights, the better able you will be to understand the various options that may be presented to you by an attorney and to weigh the possibilities and ultimate opportunity for success. While you will make your decision on the basis of your attorney's professional advice, nonetheless, you will be responsible for ultimately making a determination of the way in which to proceed and for selecting the cause of action. (The selection of an attorney is more thoroughly examined in chapter 13.)

In drawing such ultimate conclusion, you must also consider the cost effectiveness of your legal representation. If an attorney indicates to you that a protracted litigation appears to be required, that legal fees could range in the area of $25,000 to $30,000, and that your hope of recovering property or receiving periodic support would not substantially exceed the cost of such fees, it would be foolhardy to pursue such a legal remedy. On the other hand, when your attorney believes, on the basis of the financial circumstances of your case, that the recovery can far exceed the legal expense and that a solid lawsuit will result in your favor, then it would appear to be far more cost effective to invest such monies and attempt to obtain what you feel you are rightly entitled to.

Before considering bringing on a lawsuit, you must be prepared to invest a substantial sum of money for legal fees and must understand that you may ultimately be unsuccessful and recover no monies. Bringing on a lawsuit that has no precedent in your state makes your decision even more difficult. You must be prepared to gamble; if your makeup is such that you are unable to assume risks, you should not consider entering the legal arena or investing any monies in such a lawsuit.

Sometimes it may be possible to serve a summons and complaint, which is a descriptive narrative of the facts that a person alleges will entitle him or her to relief from the courts, and shortly after serving such papers, which is the first step in instituting a lawsuit, wind up with a settlement. This frequently happens because an ex-partner may feel it better to compromise than to expend considerable legal fees, time, and energy in defending the lawsuit. The ex-partner may also feel that his or her defense will ultimately be unsuccessful and that a settlement will be effected that will reduce his or her monies. In addition, the finality of a settlement between litigants can be attractive to both parties.

Once a settlement is made that is a full resolution of all matters by the parties without court intervention it will eliminate the right of appeal. This alone can save additional legal expense, as well as the trauma of enduring months, or possibly years, of remaining in the court's appellate process. No such settlement can ever be achieved if the papers served are not well thought out and properly drafted or if they fail to comply with the law in your state. A meticulously drafted complaint that will be able to withstand an early motion to dismiss the lawsuit may, in fact, form the basis for beginning talks to attempt to settle the parties' respective claims. A settlement will avoid rolling the dice and obtaining an unpredictable legal result.

Starting a lawsuit by the service of a summons and complaint does not necessarily mean that the case will ever come to trial, since, historically, more lawsuits are settled than actually tried. Nonetheless, you must also understand that merely starting an action in your behalf will not necessarily result in a settlement, and unless the relief you seek can be substantiated in the courtroom by proper testimony and evidence, you should not consider bringing a lawsuit in the first place.

It should readily be seen from the foregoing discussion that the selection of a competent attorney, skilled in these matters, can make the difference between success and failure. Embarking on a course of legal combat is not for the thin-skinned or faint-hearted. You must have the emotional stability and stick-to-itiveness to last through a very long and difficult legal entanglement. If you are not prepared to accept such demands or the expense that will necessarily be involved, you should not consider the litigation option.

Attacking the Written Agreement

If you have the benefit of a written agreement between yourself and your partner, you may expect your quest to enforce your legal rights to be far easier than the attempt by those persons who lack such an agreement. However, the mere fact that an agreement was negotiated and signed by the two of you does not, of itself, guarantee that you will be able to derive the benefits provided under the terms of the agreement for a variety of reasons. Where there is great bitterness and hostility following a separation, the person who is obligated to make payments may attempt to resist doing so, even in the face of a written agreement, and may attempt to set the agreement aside on a legal basis. Traditional grounds to set aside an otherwise valid written agreement include fraud, duress, or a failure of consideration, all of which have been discussed in previous chapters of this book. It is rare to see a court setting aside a written agreement between cohabitants based upon allegations of fraud or duress, although where an actual fraud can be proven, the court would have to declare the agreement a nullity.

If the grounds for your attack are fraud, it will be necessary for you to prove that your partner made a false representation to you of some material fact that you relied upon to your detriment. For example, if at the time of negotiating your cohabitation agreement, your partner gave to you a false net worth statement that contained a misleading list of assets and liabilities and it turns out that there was a material misrepresentation, the agreement may be set aside. Not all misrepresentations are viewed as material. For example, if an asset was falsely stated to be worth $25,000 rather than $25,100, the misrepresentation would not be considered material. On the other hand, if the reported value was $25,000 and the real value was $50,000, the judge hearing the case could certainly conclude that this is a material misrepresentation. Judges will apply common sense and fairness to reach such conclusions. Assume in this example that there was a bank account listed as $50,000 that, in fact, had a value of $250,000, or a stock account listed as $10,000 that, in fact, had a value of $150,000, and that you, in signing the agreement, relied upon the truth of the value stated in the net worth statement; a court might well find that your consent was induced by the fraud of your partner and, accordingly, will strike down the agreement.

Whatever grounds are used to get out from under the strict letter of the cohabitants' agreement, you must understand that if you cannot prove an express promise of support or one to divide property acquired during your relationship, you may find that you have achieved but a Pyrrhic victory, since, as noted earlier, cohabitants do not enjoy the same legal rights as a married couple and cannot receive alimony or community property or equitable distribution. There is no basis for a court to award alimony or property to an unmarried cohabitant except under the theory of contract or where a common-law marriage can be established in a jurisdiction that still recognizes such unorthodox marital relationships, although it seems that a court that would reach a determination that fraud had been perpetrated upon one cohabitant might well reach for a way to find another legal basis to permit a more equitable award to be made. There is an old adage in the law that a wrongdoer cannot profit from his own wrongdoing. When a couple enters into a cohabitation agreement and later the agreement is set aside for fraud, the court might reasonably infer from the existence of such agreement a promise to equitably divide property or provide support and might then proceed to fix a sum of money for support or order a division of property that it deems fair and equitable under all of the circumstances. And if it is possible to prove that the cohabitants actually held themselves out as husband and wife in a common-law jurisdiction, thereby establishing a common-law marriage, the courts would then be free to treat the cohabitants as a married couple and grant a full measure of alimony and a division of property if it felt these measures were required under all of the facts of the case. No one can pull the wool over the eyes of the court, although many have tried to do so in the past. The court will not permit a wrong to go unpunished if it can find any legal basis whatsoever to restore a defrauded party to a position of equality with his or her contractual partner.

In observing some of the ways in which a party who is to receive benefits from a cohabitants' agreement seeks to obtain more property or support because of retrospective knowledge that the supporting partner misled him or her into believing that the supporting partner enjoyed less income or property, we did not take into consideration the ways in which a party who is required to make payments can also find a way in which to avoid his or her contractual obligation. In actual practice, the number of persons seeking to avoid their legal obligation to make payments far exceeds the number of those who seek to set aside agreements requiring payments to them in order to obtain a larger piece of the pie. This is especially true since the person who sets aside the agreement would have no other legal remedy if there cannot be shown to exist an implied contract of support or a division of property or a common-law marriage and could find himself or herself walking out of court without even the benefits of the original contract.[1]

What are the grounds available to avoid the obligations imposed by a cohabitants' agreement that was negotiated between you and your partner when each of you had the benefit of an independent attorney and the agreement was certified by a formal writing? There are several grounds that can be employed, including fraud and a lack of a legal consideration.

The person who is obliged to pay and seeks to set aside such agreement really has nothing to lose. His or her obligations to make payments of support or divide property are already set forth by the terms of the written agreement. Without bringing on a lawsuit to avoid such obligations, there would be no basis upon which to avoid liability. Although no one wishes to send good money after bad, the expenditure of legal fees in such a circumstance might after all be a good investment if, of course, your attorney advises you that within your state cohabitants' agreements have been held suspect and set aside because of a public policy to discourage other than marital relationships. Being successful in such a lawsuit is like hitting a home run with the bases loaded in the bottom of the ninth inning with the score 3 to 1 against you. Having a court set aside your agreement will eliminate all of your obligations, which may have included sharing property or supporting your partner following a separation.

Without the Benefit of an Agreement

Where no agreement exists between cohabitants and a separation occurs, the party seeking to obtain some financial benefit from years of living together must seek a remedy based upon express contract or determine whether a common-law marriage was contracted. Establishing an express contract depends upon your credibility as a witness in the courtroom and your ability to recall the promises made when your relationship first began. An express contract is limited by its terms. In order for your attempt to be successful, complete terms must have been expressed in the promise, since the court is unable to infer the agreement of the parties or to speculate upon what the parties themselves ought to include in their arrangement to live together. For example, it would be insufficient to simply allege that when you and your partner began to live together, he or she promised to "take care of things" without a specific promise that he or she would support you during and/or after the relationship ended. Moreover, it must also be shown that a specific promise was made that any property that was acquired during the time you lived together would be shared equally by you during the time of your cohabitation or in the event that you separated from one another at a later time. Expressed another way, it is extremely important to prove that all of the precise terms of your arrangement were agreed upon during the time preceding the actual beginning of your cohabitation or during the time that you, in fact, lived together. You must, of course, spend a considerable amount of time in preparing notes for your meeting with your attorney so that the exact words spoken and the dates and places that such conversations took place can be established. This will enable your attorney to frame a complaint that will be legally sufficient to support your claim. You cannot be successful by merely expressing generalities in a complaint; if you do so, it is more than likely that the court will dismiss your lawsuit because it has not "stated a legal cause of action."

When you are on the other side of this lawsuit and your cohabitant seeks to establish that an oral agreement was made but fails to set forth allegations with specificity, your attorney should seek to have the matter dismissed on the complaint alone without doing anything further to defend the lawsuit and await trial. This device is sometimes known as a *motion for summary judgment*, or *a motion to dismiss the complaint for failure to state a cause of action*. Your lawyer will be able to explain the technical difference to you in order to select the proper motion to best protect your interests. If your cohabitant can resist a motion to dismiss and continue with the lawsuit, your preparation for trial then becomes vital. If your lawyer does not suggest that you spend several hours together going over your testimony and participating in a mock cross-examination, you should insist that you do so. It is only through these mock trial sessions that you can understand the cross-examination process and prepare the testimony you will be called upon to give in the courtroom.

Trials are governed by rules similar to those in a sporting event. There are rules of evidence and rules of law and procedure that are employed in all trials. If you do not play within the rules, you will be severely penalized. For example, you cannot testify to your feelings and emotions, but you are permitted to testify to conversations that took place between you and your cohabitant. If during such conversations you expressed your feelings and emotions, the court would be bound to admit the conversation into evidence, although it could not otherwise allow you to testify as to how you feel. As long as you testify to the exact words uttered by each of you, whether or not there was any witness to the conversation, the court would permit the entire conversation to be admitted into evidence. In addition, the conversation can supply the express terms of your contract. For example, the following dialogue is illustrative of such devices:

QUESTION: Did you have a conversation with John prior to actually sharing the same residence with him?

ANSWER: Yes, I did.

QUESTION: When did that conversation take place?

ANSWER: Some time in February of 1990, approximately one week before we signed a lease on our apartment in Manhattan.

QUESTION: Who was present during the time that the conversation took place?

ANSWER: Just myself and John.

QUESTION: Where did the conversation take place?

ANSWER: At my home in Great Neck, New York.

QUESTION: Now will you tell the court what you said to him and what he said to you?

ANSWER: I said, "John, we have been seeing each other now for some time and you want me to give up my home, come to Manhattan, and take an apartment in the city together. I'm frightened and apprehensive. I can't do that unless I know that you will provide for me while we live together and, in the event that we find that it is a mistake for us to live together, that you will support me for at least two years so I can get back on my feet and earn sufficient monies to take care of myself." John then said, "Mary, I love you. I want you to be with me, I want to share a home together with you. You know I will take care of you while we live together, and I promise you that if anything happens between the two of us, I will give you $300 a week for at least two years following any separation, provided, of course, you don't remarry or live together with another person." I said, "That's okay with me, John, but I want it to come out now so that we understand each other and you know that I would not agree to living with you unless I had the assurance of this financial security."

In this example, there was no discussion regarding the division of property acquired during the parties' cohabitation, so there could not be any legal obligation for the couple to divide their property. Remember that only the express provisions made by the parties can be enforced—unless you live in a jurisdiction that permits contracts to be recognized by implication.

Become a Credible Witness

Becoming a credible witness is no easy job. It can only be accomplished through hard work, repetition, and the guidance of a competent trial attorney. A minimum of five hours, broken into 45-minute or one-hour segments, is the least amount of time that is necessary to properly prepare a witness to give testimony in a contested lawsuit. There is no way to cut corners and still make an effective presentation in the courtroom. Lawyers like to say that trial work is 90% preparation and 10% presentation. The successful litigant will have done his or her homework, will have spent the requisite hours necessary to properly prepare for trial, and will be adequately briefed in the techniques to withstand cross-examination. When answering questions put to you by your cohabitant's attorney under cross-examination, you should be instructed to never give more in your answer than is required by the question. For example, if you are asked "What color is your blouse?" the answer is "White," not "I am wearing a white blouse that has a puffed collar and grey pants." Obviously, such answer was not entirely responsive to the question. It gave more information than was required. Giving more information than is requested can only get a witness into trouble. If you are asked on cross-examination whether you visited your cohabitant's apartment on a specific date, such as April 8, 1990, and you reply, "No, I did not visit his apartment on that date, but I was there on April 15," you have again committed the cardinal sin of a witness who is subject to cross-examination, namely, establishing a fact through your own testimony that was not asked of you by the cross-examiner. Answers given during your cross-examination should be as brief as possible and entirely responsive to what is asked of you. Never answer a question upon cross-examination that you do not entirely understand. It is far better to ask the attorney to repeat the question until you are certain of the response that is required. Never engage in a verbal duel with the lawyer questioning you, because you will surely lose in a contest with an experienced trial attorney. Never lose your cool on the stand and engage in a verbal argument with your questioner, and, above all, never be disrespectful or belligerent while you are being cross-examined. In assessing your credibility, the court will consider your demeanor, the way in which you respond to questions, and whether you seek to be responsive or evasive. Remember, also, that you must wait until the question is completed; never blurt out an answer while the attorney continues to speak. Again, to do so can only lead you into trouble because you may, in fact, give out information that is otherwise uncalled for. The court (or a jury if one is involved in your case) will always seek to determine whether you are telling the truth. Resolving this issue can turn upon the most subjective criteria. If you fail to look directly at your questioner or hold your head down or speak very rapidly or haltingly, a judge or a juror might interpret such behavior as a sign that you are being less than truthful. You must attempt to answer questions in an unhurried, clear, and direct way and maintain eye contact with your examiner. You should never blurt out, "Must I answer that question?" since the job of your attorney is to make objections to questions that are improper. When the judge sustains the objection, you will not be required to answer the question, but if it is, in fact, overruled you will of course be required to respond. Never attempt to be an attorney while you are on the stand and wonder why a question is put to you. You are there to answer questions. If you attempt to do more, you will lose your spontaneity and get into trouble.

Becoming a good witness at trial is not an easy task and requires a great deal of hard work and preparation. You must understand that the courtroom is simply a place in which to tell your version of the facts to either a judge or a jury. Rarely, in cases involving personal relationships will there be witnesses to your conversation by third parties. It is the task of a judge or a jury to decide which testimony to believe when there are conflicting versions of what occurred between you and your partner. If you remain relaxed, speak in an even tone of voice, maintain eye contact, are responsive to the questions posed to you, and do not attempt to become embroiled in repartee or exchanges with the attorney who cross-examines you, you will have gone a long way in convincing a judge or jury that your testimony is entirely credible.

The way that you dress when you appear in court can also be important in a contested lawsuit. Whether you are male or female, it is best to wear conservative clothes and jewelry. If you are female, it would be wise to be moderate in your use of makeup. Your goal is to have the judge or jury focus on your testimony, not your physical appearance. Participating in a trial as a litigant is indeed a demanding task and will necessarily cause you great anxiety and emotional stress. It is like taking a ride on a roller coaster because there are so many rapid changes in the pulse of the trial, depending upon the witnesses who are called and the documentary evidence that may be introduced during your trial. It is not uncommon for a litigant to feel that the case is going the wrong way and that there is little chance for success at one moment and then in the next to feel exhilarated because victory seems within grasp.

When attempting to establish an expressed oral contract, you and your partner will play the major roles in the trial. Of course, there can be third party witnesses called in your behalf who can attest to the fact that they were present when there was conversation between you and your partner that was consistent with a promise to provide support; witnesses can also verify the standard of living that you enjoyed during the time of cohabitation. However, it is not required that your testimony be corroborated by an eye witness; most marital partners or unmarried persons who reside with one another normally do not have their most intimate thoughts or discussions in front of others. Success or failure in the courtroom will necessarily depend upon your own performance and your ability to communicate successfully with the judge or jury. That is why it has been stressed that preparation is 90% of the case and is the most important factor to ensure victory.

Defense of Common-Law Marriage Suits

Without knowledge such as that acquired through reading this book, it would be reasonable for you to assume that without a written agreement to support your live-in companion or share any of your property with him or her following a breakup you would be free to leave without any financial strings attached. You would receive the shock of your life when you are served with legal papers, normally a summons and complaint, that claim that you and your partner entered into a common-law marriage while spending an extended vacation at a hotel in the common-law state of Pennsylvania (for a list of the 13 states that, in addition to the District of Columbia, recognize common-law marriage, see Appendix A).

A major defense to the claim that a common-law marriage was made is that there was never a holding out by either party that they were husband and wife. If you can show that you and your partner maintained separate identities and that neither introduced the other as a spouse the court may reach the conclusion that a valid common-law marriage was never consummated. If, for example, you did not register as husband and wife at the aforementioned hotel, the hotel registry would be excellent proof to negate an intention that the two of you be regarded as a married couple. Any person with whom you may have had contact in a common-law state should be located and asked to appear as a witness in your behalf. To establish a common-law marriage, it is not sufficient to simply offer proof that the couple was merely present in a state that recognizes such marriages; thus, any proof you can offer in your defense of behavior that is inconsistent with a husband-wife relationship must be explored.

Let's say the complaint goes on to request that you be obligated to pay alimony to your former live-in companion and divide all property that was acquired during the time that you resided together. If you live in the state of New York, the complaint would be for equitable distribution of your "marital property." Although New York has not recognized common-law marriage since 1930, it is, nevertheless, obligated under the U.S. Constitution to give full faith and credit to the laws of sister states; since Pennsylvania recognizes common-law marriages, New York would have to consider you and your partner validly married if the elements of a common-law marriage can be proven under Pennsylvania law. Once that determination has been affirmatively made, New York would, for all purposes, treat you as a spouse under its Domestic Relations Law, which means that you could be obligated to pay alimony—or, on the other hand, have the legal right to obtain it— and that all marital property could be subject to equitable distribution (on the basis of factors that are discussed in chapter 8). Counsel and expert fees could be awarded to you (or you might be required to make payment of them), and you would be entitled to obtain all financial documents from your partner and to examine him or her under oath concerning income, assets, liabilities, and any other financial matters that may touch upon your relationship.

Obviously, the status afforded to a spouse is significant. There are no limitations other than the provisions of the law that exists in your state concerning whether property should be divided as community property or equitably distributed. By contrast, the agreement of cohabitants, if it can be enforced at all, is strictly limited to the precise terms of the agreement. For example, if there is no provision in the agreement made between the two of you for ongoing and continued support but only agreement to divide property that is acquired during your relationship, the court would have absolutely no power to impose an obligation of support. Likewise, if your agreement was simply for support to continue after a separation, then the court would be without power to divide any property that may have been obtained during your relationship.

The theory of implied contract is sparingly applied to cohabitants' relationships. Although the parties involved in a living-together relationship may have some expectation in their own minds that they will receive certain benefits during the relationship and even after the relationship is severed, these unilateral wishes cannot be legally enforced. However, there are instances where theories of recovery are used for what the law regards as an equitable remedy. *Quantum meruit*, or recovery for work performed at a reasonable rate, sometimes finds its way into court decisions regarding conflicts between separated cohabitants. In such a lawsuit the court recognizes that there was an implied promise to compensate another individual, on the basis of its reasonable value, for whatever work, labor, or services were performed. In order to prevail in such a lawsuit, there must be a finding by the judge hearing the case that the services were not rendered gratuitously but, rather, were performed with the expectation of receiving payment. A possible defense adopted by your ex-partner against an action by you to recover the reasonable value of services you performed would be a demonstration by your partner that whatever he or she contributed to the relationship was equal to or exceeded the compensation you seek.

When Children Are Involved

When the relationship involves children, there are additional legal problems that may be encountered. If you are the custodial parent (that is, the parent with whom the child resides), you will have a legal right to obtain from the noncustodial parent support based on a formula that has been adopted within your state. In New York, for example, the law known as the Child Support Standards Act requires, by and large, that the noncustodial parent contribute a certain fixed percentage from his or her gross income, after considering the income, if any, of the custodial parent, as well as furnish moneys for child care, health and life insurance, and educational expenses.[2] Gross income under the New York law is defined as income from all sources, that is, from employment, investment income, or tax-free income. The law will even compute a reasonable sum to be included in gross income to correspond to certain perks received on your job, such as travel and entertainment expenses. Under federal mandate almost every state has adopted a formula approach to child support, so the imposition of child support obligations has become fairly uniform throughout the country. Once paternity has been proven or admitted, there is really very little in the way of defense that can be offered against a lawsuit to obtain child support. However, in some states if it can be shown that it would be unfair or unjust because of the economic circumstances that exist in your case for the court to follow the formula approach adopted by your state, the court may be able to disregard the formula approach and fix a sum of money for child support that it believes to be fair and reasonable under the circumstances. The trend by the courts today is to impose the percentages set forth in state law, usually to the extent of the first $80,000 to $100,000 of gross income. Persons who enjoy salaries in excess of these amounts may find that the court is unwilling to make an additional discretionary award. Bear in mind, however, that it is the combined parental income that is subject to the formula approach, so that the court will have to consider the custodial parent's income as well as that of the noncustodial parent when applying the formula. Of course, only the noncustodial parent will be required to make the payment to the custodial parent, the law implying that the custodial parent is already contributing to the child's support. These concepts can be very difficult for a layperson to interpret or to present in a court of law, although the family courts throughout the country permit parents to appear before them without attorneys. Some states even provide for guardians to be appointed to protect the best interests of the child in support proceedings. Where finances will permit, there is no substitute for a trained attorney schooled in support matters to represent you before the court.

More difficulty arises when your ex-partner seeks to hold you responsible for the support of a child who lived with you during your relationship but whom you did not formally adopt. In some states there appears to be a doctrine of constructive adoption, a theory that would impose on you an obligation to support a child because of the past relationship that existed between you, the child, and your cohabitant and your acceptance of the obligation to support the child during that relationship. If this can be established, the court may impose a continuing obligation to support the child. Some courts have, instead, utilized the theory of express promise of support, similar to what was discussed earlier in this chapter pertaining to the cohabitants themselves. The courts stand ready to enforce express oral agreements between the parties, especially in cases where the welfare of a child is at stake and he or she is in danger of becoming a public charge without such support. Jurisdictions that recognize implied contracts between cohabitants may also recognize an implied contract to support a child.

Whatever legal theory can be asserted in your state must be explored if you intend to legally enforce an oral promise of support. If finances do not permit you to retain an attorney, it would be wise to bring such a support proceeding in the family court in your home state. All courts will lean over backward to attempt to do the right thing to protect a child; when a court can reasonably adopt a legal theory to ensure the continued support of a child, it will do so.

In fixing the proper amount of support, even where guidelines are applicable, it would be wise for you to spend time preparing a budget of weekly expenses for food, clothing, shelter, and entertainment, and including any other expenses that will be incurred by the child during his or her minority. Most courts require that when an application for child support is made, a weekly budget be completed and submitted at the time a hearing is scheduled. Appendix K contains a typical form that is utilized in the family courts in conjunction with a child support proceeding. You can see that the budget must be fully comprehensive and include all expenses, including extracurricular activities, vacations, entertainment, medical care, and summer camp.

If you are attempting to convince the court that it would be unjust to apply the percentage formula applicable in your state, then you must be certain to prepare an arithmetic, rather than an emotional, argument in order to have the court reach this conclusion. For example, if there are two children involved for whom you are seeking support and your gross income is $300 weekly, your obligation of child support, assuming the percentage to be applied to gross income is 25%, would be $37.50 per child, or $75 weekly. If your expenses on a weekly basis exceed $225 and the child's other parent is gainfully employed, you might find a court willing to reduce the child support payment by a sum that will permit you to meet your own living requirements. For example, if your weekly expenses include $75 for rent, $75 for food, and $25 for clothing and medical expenses, these three basic necessities of life will total $175 weekly, leaving you but $50 to apply toward child support. Under such circumstances, the arithmetic clearly evidences an inability to comply with the statutory formula, since $50 would be insufficient to provide for your own necessities of life. If you are able to demonstrate such circumstances to the court and your state law permits deviation, it is likely that the court will relieve you of the state's percentage and fix a sum it deems fair under the circumstances.

In the final analysis, the court will utilize reason and common sense in order to resolve litigation between cohabitants. You must always be prepared to take a reasonable approach to frame a complaint and commence a lawsuit. Asking for the moon and the stars might result in receiving only a rebuke from the court. Adjusting your ultimate goals to the financial realities of you and your former cohabitant's circumstances may be the best formula for success. Although law is premised upon prior precedents, that is, decisions that have considered facts that are similar to those in your case, in the field of matrimonial and family law this doctrine of *stare decisis* is not always strictly followed, as it is in commercial matters. The courts look to do the right thing and to adjust the parties' respective rights and obligations. Whether they are able to do so may sometimes depend upon a state law and sometimes on how they view the credibility of the parties concerning their claims. The course of litigation is never an easy one; it can prove to be extremely expensive as well as gut wrenching. Nonetheless, litigation may in some circumstances be the only course to pursue, since without such action your rights may never be upheld or your reasonable expectations satisfied.

More often than not, an agreement between cohabitants will be stricken by the court when it can be found that the "consideration" for the contract was the exchange of sexual favors. Those who would seek to strike down a cohabitants' agreement on such grounds would, of course, have to prove that there was no benefit to either party other than sexual favors.

Notes

1. *Unmarried Couples and Unjust Enrichment: From Status to Contract and Back Again. Casad*, 77 Michigan Law Review 47 (1978).
2. Seventeen percent of combined parental income for one child; 25% of combined parental income for two children; 29% of combined parental income for three children; 31% of combined parental income for four children; and no less than 35% of combined parental income for five or more children.

    The above percentages are computed into an amount that the noncustodial parent must pay to the custodial parent for child support after considering the gross income, if any, of the custodial parent. For example, the calculation for two children (25% required) would be as follows: noncustodial parent's gross annual income, $20,000; custodial parent's gross annual income, $40,000; combined parental gross annual income, $60,000; required support (25%), $15,000.

    To compute the noncustodial parent's share of the total support requirement ($15,000) simply determine the percentage that his or her gross income bears to the custodial parent's income; here 66.66% ($40,000 over $60,000). Then multiply this percentage by the total support requirement ($15,000) to arrive at the noncustodial parent's payment, which would be $10,000 ($15,000 × 66.66%).

Chapter 13

Selecting an Attorney or Health Care Professional

After reading the other chapters in this book and the repeated suggestion that you must consult with a competent attorney in order to obtain legal benefits or avoid liabilities, as the case may be, in your living-together circumstances, it is appropriate to explore the best ways to obtain meaningful representation and to find or select an attorney who will be able to assist you in these most delicate of matters. Preparing a prenuptial or living-together agreement, avoiding an adoption by implication, which could compel you to support a child who was neither legally adopted by you nor born of your relationship with your live-in companion, obtaining support, and preserving assets—these are but a few of the many legal needs you may have.

The most competent and qualified attorney may not be the right person for you to consult or retain unless you have established a rapport with that person and find that he or she is attentive to your needs, will be available to you by telephone or in person, as the occasion arises, and is willing to undertake your representation, for a reasonable fee, based upon all of the circumstances involved in your particular case. The process is much akin to finding a physician in whom you will place your care. A doctor may hold the highest credentials and qualifications but may seem aloof and indifferent to your medical problems. The search for an attorney is no different. You must, of course, find the most qualified attorney to represent you in a given matter, but you must also be able to feel a high degree of trust and confidence in that person. It is not uncommon today for a prospective client to interview several attorneys before making a choice to retain one, and you should be prepared to do so.

Many, but not all, attorneys will not charge a consultation fee when a client contacts them for the first time. Whether or not an attorney chooses to charge a fee for an initial consultation should not deter you from seeing a person who has been recommended to you or whose name you have found in a reference manual, since an attorney's time and advice, as Abraham Lincoln had once observed, are his stock-in-trade. There are a variety of ways to obtain the name of an attorney to interview when you are deciding whether to commence a lawsuit (or to defend one). Certainly, the word-of-mouth recommendation of a friend or relative who has gone through a proceeding similar to the one you are contemplating or have become involved in would be an excellent starting point. Of course, a word-of-mouth recommendation must be viewed with some caution, since the fact that an attorney obtained a successful result for one person does not mean that there is any guarantee that he or she will achieve a successful result for you. However, if others have been satisfied with the legal services they have obtained, which necessarily include the attorney's commitment, creativity, and diligence in his or her representation, this information can be a compelling factor in making your final selection.

One of the most frequent complaints made by a client of the attorney is that he or she has been unresponsive to the client's needs during the course of the lawsuit. In these cases, it is not unusual to hear that the lawyer did not return telephone calls, was unavailable for in-person conferences, and had associates fill in for him or her at times when the client felt the presence of the retained attorney was indeed appropriate, if not essential.

Once you have received a recommendation from another person who has completed a lawsuit similar to the one in which you have become involved and who was satisfactorily represented by an attorney, you should then attempt to ascertain the credentials, training, years of experience, and professional distinctions that have been accorded to that attorney before making your final decision. The single best source book available throughout the country can be found in any law library and is the *Martindale-Hubbell* Law Directory (Martindale-Hubbell 1992), which virtually lists by city and state almost every attorney admitted to practice throughout the United States. In addition to such a listing, the book includes a rating of each attorney listed. The highest rating given to an attorney is AV, which means that the attorney enjoys the highest reputation for excellence and professionalism in the practice of law. Martindale-Hubbell sends questionnaires throughout the community to lawyers who are familiar with the attorney being rated and then determines the proper ranking to accord to the attorney after considering all completed and returned questionnaires. This law digest is perhaps the single best source of background material available to the lay public and is frequently used by attorneys to refer matters to other attorneys.

Local bar associations may also provide lawyer referral services, but unfortunately these referrals do not normally rate the attorneys but, rather, list them in alphabetical order according to their areas of interest. A local bar association will normally recommend an attorney who is registered with it and who has paid a fee to be on the referral list, but it takes no steps to determine the effectiveness of a lawyer or his or her special qualifications.

In states that have legal certification statutes for practice in specialty areas, there will be standards promulgated by the state, which may include a certain minimum number of years of active practice, a requirement to be proficient in trial advocacy, a requirement to pass written or oral boards administered in the state, and a need to attend continuing legal education programs over a period of time, usually several times a year.

Obtaining the name of an attorney certified to practice in the field of matrimonial and family law will ordinarily assure you of competence and sufficient training. When a recommendation is obtained from a specialty bar group, such as the American Academy of Matrimonial Lawyers, which now certifies its members for proficiency and being current in continuing legal education programs, you can be assured of a highly qualified lawyer. The academy maintains chapters throughout most of the states and was formed in order to preserve the best interests of the family and 3of society, improve the practice, elevate the standards, and advance the cause of matrimonial law. In order to obtain membership in the academy, an attorney must have at least ten years experience and must have done in the field of matrimonial law substantial trial work and passed an oral or written examination concerning his or her area of expertise.

The local and state bar associations usually have, in addition to their referral services, domestic relations law or family law committees composed of some of the leading members of the local or state bar, who may or may not be on the referral list. Frequently, members of the American Academy of Matrimonial Lawyers are also members of the committees within the local and state bar associations. However, there are usually no formal requirements to obtain membership on a committee of a local or state bar association other than the payment of the requisite dues.

If you are fortunate enough to know a judge who sits on such cases, he or she would be an excellent source of a recommendation, since judges can observe firsthand the expertise of the attorneys appearing before them. There are private organizations that are beginning to conduct referral services to help the general public in the selection of an attorney. For example, the National Organization for Women interviews many lawyers who are involved in matrimonial or family law, obtains their curriculum vitae (professional qualifications) and their track records, and follows up on all of their referrals to clients who report to them following the conclusion of their cases.

Whatever the source of the initial recommendation for an attorney may be, it would be wise to acquire at least three names for your consideration and expend the time and, if required, the money to interview each of the attorneys to determine which one you would be comfortable with who would best meet your needs. When appearing for an interview, you should be willing to answer all questions put to you by the attorney and discuss them openly and frankly. There is a privilege of confidentiality that exists between a lawyer and a client, so you need have no fear that anything disclosed to the attorney during the initial interview will later be disclosed to a third person. It would be terribly unwise on your part to withhold any fact that will bear upon your particular case, since doing so is an invitation to disaster when the case is finally tried.

Once an attorney has completed his interview of you and you have given the information he or she requests, then it is your turn to ask any question you see fit in order to make a reasoned choice concerning your representation. The following areas should be explored with your attorney:

1. The fees he or she will charge and whether they will be billed to you as is most common today on an hourly basis, or as a fixed fee.
2. Whether other expenses, such as out-of-pocket disbursements for postage, process servers, court fees, and the like, will be billed to you.
3. Whether the attorney will personally handle your matter or whether he or she will work in conjunction with associates. (If associates are being used, you should explore the experience and background of the associates whom you will deal with.)
4. Whether you will receive a monthly statement that will itemize all services performed on your behalf.
5. Whether the attorney is responsive to telephone calls and what his or her practice in the office is concerning return

calls when he or she is on trial. (You should expect to receive a return call from an attorney, even if he or she is on trial, within 24 hours of having called his or her office.)

6. Whether the attorney you select will try the case in court or whether someone else in his or her office will do so. (It might also be prudent to discuss with the attorney the extent of his or her trial room experience, since this is an essential ingredient to effective representation. Lawyers who would prefer to settle your matter rather than go to trial may compromise your rights.)

7. Whether the attorney has written any learned articles that have appeared in professional journals concerning the area that you have consulted him or her about. (Although the writing of scholarly articles in and of itself may not indicate that an attorney is effective in day-to-day practice or in the courtroom, this information nevertheless indicates that the attorney is current with recent developments in his or her field.)

8. Whether the attorney will provide you with copies of all papers that are prepared during the course of your litigation. (This too is an important facet in selecting an attorney since it is more than likely that more care will be given to the final product if you are to be furnished with copies of all documents drawn.)

These are but some of the questions that should be explored at your first meeting in order to acquaint yourself with the practices of the attorney's office and his or her own philosophy and to determine whether you are comfortable working with the individual. If there is not the necessary chemistry between the two of you, chances are that you should select another person to represent you, even though the attorney may be highly qualified. The lawyer-client relationship is a very personal one, and you will be spending a great deal of time with each other. There must be a mutual respect exhibited by both of you in order for the relationship to be successful. If you do not feel comfortable with the lawyer, no matter what your personal reasons, it would be wise to eliminate that person from your consideration.

Entering into a Written Agreement

Once you have made your decision to hire an attorney to represent you, there should be a formal agreement drawn between the two of you so that you both know what is expected during the course of your representation. A written agreement that may take the form of a letter is a common way to affirm your understanding concerning the attorney's retention in your behalf. A retainer letter agreement should clearly define the services that will be performed on your behalf and the fees that will be charged, not only for your attorney's services but for his or her out-of-pocket disbursements as well, which may include the cost of a deposition before trial, court fees, photocopies, postage, process servers, long distance telephone calls, and the like. Nothing should be left to chance, and the letter agreement should contain all of the terms of your understanding. Appendix M contains a letter agreement that is typical of such retainer agreements between lawyer and client. If you have any questions concerning the contents of the retainer agreement, you should review them in their entirety with your attorney and obtain a fuller explanation if one is needed regarding any of its provisions. The retainer agreement should be in clear, understandable language, not peppered with legal jargon. If you do not fully understand the retainer letter, do not sign it. The agreement that the attorney proposes and requests that you sign is not etched in stone; if you feel that you desire any changes, you should request that they be made. If your requests are reasonable, they will be honored. An attorney who tells you that this is a "standard form," and one not normally changed, should be suspect. All agreements are subject to the approval of *both* parties.

Attorney's Fees

In discussing the fees of the attorney you visit on an initial consultation, you should be free to suggest that a lesser fee or hourly rate than has been proposed to you should be accepted in your case. An attorney is free to either accept your recommendation or tell you that he or she is unable or unwilling to do so. That is really the give-and-take of the marketplace. Most attorneys will be willing to have a full and frank discussion concerning their fees and any adjustments that they may be willing to make. In most major cities throughout the country hourly legal rates range anywhere from $150 to $400 an hour. Lawyers who bill at the high end of the fee spectrum may be willing to reduce their hourly rates to accommodate your financial needs. Some, of course, will not, but if you do not explore this area with the attorney, you will never receive any concession. An attorney's experience and reputation will pretty much dictate the hourly rate that he or she will charge. A seasoned attorney, one who has been in practice for more than 20 years, will normally be on the high end of the fee spectrum whereas an attorney who has limited experience, perhaps 5 years of practice, will normally charge fees at the low end. That is not to say that the attorney with less experience is not competent, but there is no substitute for experience. The larger fee charged by the more experienced attorney is normally worth the difference. All things being equal, if the difference between the hourly rate of two lawyers to whom you have narrowed the choice is $100 and it is anticipated by both attorneys that approximately 50 hours will be devoted toward your representation, the difference between the two attorneys would be $5,000. Whether you spend $15,000 or $10,000 (for an attorney who charges $300 an hour or one who charges $200) for your representation may be meaningful to you, but if the larger sum can provide a more experienced attorney, the additional cost may well be worth it, especially when you have the potential to recover (or successfully defend against the recovery of) a substantial sum of money in the lawsuit in which you are involved. The fee to be charged by an attorney is indeed a very important aspect of your consideration but should by no means be the sole criterion for your choice.

One other matter that must be assessed is the complexity or difficulty of your case. If the issues involved are rather simple and do not require extensive research or preparation, then it might be more cost effective to choose an attorney with less experience who charges a lesser rate.

Becoming a Good Client

Once you have selected the attorney of your choice to represent you, your focus should be on becoming a good client, one who is responsive to his or her attorney's directions and will accept the attorney's guidance and advice. Learning to be a good client is not always an easy job. It will be your attorney's objective to channel your thoughts and prepare you for the day that you must enter into the courtroom and give testimony in your own behalf. Learning to become a good witness will be one of the most important aspects of your case. In this respect, your attorney's ability to mold you into an effective courtroom weapon will be challenged. This process may even start at your initial consultation. It is far better to have an attorney ask you questions concerning your matter than for you to attempt, in explaining to him or her the facts involved in your case, to discern the important from the unimportant matters. What may seem very important to you may be trivia in the eyes of the law. For example, if during your relationship with your live-in partner you were not treated well and your relationship was beset with constant bickering and quarreling, you may be tempted to give to your attorney all of the details concerning such incompatibility during the entire course of your relationship. However, doing so would not be very productive since the law would not place much weight on such alleged misconduct but would be far more interested instead in any written or oral promises made by your live-in companion concerning support for you or your child or a division of any property that you acquired during the time that you lived together.

It is the job of a competent attorney to separate the wheat from the chaff, to know the important from the unimportant, and to make certain that, as you proceed with your litigation, you are learning the qualities of a good witness. A good witness must be a responsive one. For example, if you are on the stand and a question is put to you concerning a conversation that took place on a specific date preceding the time that you agreed to live with your partner, you must have the discipline to answer the question in kind and not to volunteer information concerning another conversation, even though in your own mind you may feel that to do so would be in your best interest. You must resist the temptation of thinking that you are able to determine which facts will be important for the judge or jury to consider. Volunteering information that is not requested of you is probably the worst blunder a witness can commit. No layperson is a match for a seasoned trial attorney. Once you slip, the cross-examining lawyer will descend upon you in an unrelenting barrage of additional questions, all calculated to destroy your credibility, confuse the issues, and detract from the points that your attorney may wish to emphasize. Once you commit the cardinal sin of failing to be responsive to the questions of the cross-examining attorney and supplying information that he or she did not ask for, it is much akin to jumping into a tank of sharks with mosquito repellant as your only defense.

You should discuss with the attorneys you interview during your initial consultations whether they are prepared to take the time to sit with you for many hours in trial preparation or whether they will relegate this task to an associate. If you are to be prepared for trial by an associate rather than by the attorney who will actually try the case, you may not be able to be as effective in the courtroom as you might like. It is really far better for the attorney who prepares you to try the case because he or she will be able to assess your weak points as a witness beforehand and work with you in order to present the facts of the case in their most favorable light. There is no substitute for trial preparation. The more you practice and rehearse your testimony—by answering questions posed by your own attorney and then having him cross-examine you—the better prepared you will be to undergo the rigors of trial. You must remember that in the courtroom you will be constantly scrutinized by the trier of the facts, whether it be a judge or a jury who will listen to your case.

It is very difficult to ever discern what will be perceived as offensive testimony in the courtroom. An inflection of the voice, a sharp response, a discourteous attitude to the cross-examiner, or any other untoward display or negative response may prove costly. In the hands of a competent trial attorney, all of these pitfalls can be avoided. Learning to give testimony that will be believed is a task that can be mastered under the tutelage of a seasoned trial lawyer. It should become apparent to the reader that the selection of such an attorney is a most serious concern since presenting your case in the most favorable light in order to receive acceptance by the trier of the facts is your goal.

Selecting a Health Care Professional

In litigation concerning custody of children or visitation rights it is frequently necessary to engage the services of a psychiatrist, psychologist, or perhaps a psychiatric social worker to offer testimony in your behalf regarding your ability to serve as a custodial parent (or perhaps to offer testimony regarding your partner's inability to do so). The courts rely most heavily on the opinions of medical experts in dealing with these problems affecting custody and visitation.

In chapter 6 of this book, "The Legal Rights of Gay Persons," we explored some of the prejudices that might be harbored by potential judges or jurors concerning a homosexual lifestyle. In any of these cases concerning children, it would be essential to call a psychiatrist as an expert witness to give testimony regarding the effect of this lifestyle on the raising of a child. As was pointed out in chapter 6, most medical evidence today indicates that a child raised in the home of a gay parent is no more likely to adopt a homosexual preference than a child raised in a heterosexual home. Such testimony would be essential to neutralize a prejudice toward a homosexual parent and might be the basis for an award of custody or visitation in a contested setting.

Often, claims are made that one ex-partner is an unfit parent, either emotionally, psychologically, or physically. Such claims can include charges of alcoholism, drug abuse, sexual promiscuity, gambling, child abuse, and other socially unacceptable behaviors. When unfitness is being charged, especially when a claim of mental instability is lodged, it is vital that one employ the services of a psychiatrist who has given testimony before the courts in the past in order to defend against these charges and rehabilitate oneself in the eyes of the court.

The search for a competent psychiatrist is quite similar to that employed in the search for an attorney. Certainly, a friend or relative who has been involved in a legal proceeding where the issue of mental competence was an issue would be an excellent referral source. Consulting the department of psychiatry in a teaching hospital for the names of practicing psychiatrists in your community would be another approach. In many instances, your attorney may be able to recommend a forensic psychiatrist, one who has appeared before the courts in this type of matter in the past and who enjoys a good reputation in the judicial community. The psychiatrist chosen will become part of your team and will work with you and your attorney toward your common goal. It would not be wise to isolate the professionals from each other, and an attorney who does not take part in your decision making regarding the choice of a psychiatrist, or who has not at least met with him or her to discuss your case prior to trial, is not acting in your best interest. At a minimum, a meeting should be scheduled at which you, your attorney, and your chosen psychiatrist have the opportunity to sit down and discuss your case at length in order to agree on a course of conduct to pursue and to determine what should be emphasized by the psychiatrist during the time of his or her examination and subsequently at the time of trial.

The psychiatrist selected will rely—or should rely—most heavily on the advice of your attorney in this regard because the latter is better able to predict what the courts will be looking for in deciding the issues in your case. If you are uncomfortable with the selection of the psychiatrist and feel that he or she is not working well with your attorney, another person should be considered for the task. Many of the standards that we discussed in selecting an attorney should be applied to the selection of a psychiatrist.

There are other areas that may also require the expert testimony of a psychiatrist or psychologist. When a prenuptial or living-together agreement is being attacked because of fraud, duress, or overreaching and the claim is being made that when you entered into the agreement you had severe emotional problems and could not discern the nature and quality of your own actions, a psychiatrist would certainly be the only person who could legally give evidence in your behalf in a courtroom. A layperson cannot address a medical malady; if you offer your own mental condition for the court's consideration, a psychiatrist is the only person competent to give testimony regarding your mental condition at the time you signed an agreement with your live-in partner involving either support or the division of property.

In order for you to succeed in your claim, the court must be convinced that you were incapable of making a reasoned decision regarding the terms of the agreement and incapable of fully comprehending the recommendations of an attorney who may have represented you during the course of the negotiations and the signing of the agreement. There is no way to be successful by giving such testimony without the benefit of an expert witness. Litigants who have attempted to convince the court of their past emotional difficulties without calling an expert, such as a psychiatrist or psychologist, who can give testimony regarding the client's state of mind at the time of the negotiations and signing of the agreement, have been uniformly unsuccessful. It is most difficult to win a lawsuit seeking to set aside an agreement because of mental duress perpetrated against you by the other signatory of your agreement.

Preparation with an expert witness, such as a psychiatrist, is also extremely important in order to have a reasonable chance of being successful at the conclusion of your case. It is usually not sufficient for a psychiatrist to make a medical evaluation on the basis of a single interview spanning a short duration of time. It is also difficult, if not impossible, for a psychiatrist to testify to your state of mind many years ago when you signed the agreement. Accordingly, unless you can produce a psychiatrist or psychologist who treated you at or about the time you signed the property agreement, it may be impossible to prove to the satisfaction of the court that you indeed suffered from a mental disability. These lawsuits are complex and certainly cannot be waged without an attorney who is highly skilled in these matters and a psychiatrist who will be able to give medical testimony concerning your mental disability.

While it is not essential that the psychiatrist you select to give testimony in your behalf be one who has testified in the past before courts in the state in which you live, certainly one who has done so and has been recognized as an expert witness in other cases in your community would be a better choice, all other qualifications being equal.

In custody litigation, or where visitation of a child is involved, the selection of a psychiatrist is also extremely important. One who has been trained in child psychiatry should be sought out. The psychiatrist should examine not only you but also the children, so that he or she can make a full evaluation concerning your ability to function as a custodial or a visiting parent. He or she should observe the interaction between you and the children. In states that permit it, the psychiatrist whom you retain to act in your behalf should also have the opportunity to evaluate your ex-partner. Otherwise, the psychiatrist cannot speculate on your ex-partner's parenting abilities, since his or her diagnosis would be based only on information supplied by you, which would normally be inadmissible in a court of law.

In the last analysis, in order to wage a successful lawsuit, you will be required to assemble a team that includes competent professionals who can guide you through the morass of legal and medical entanglements, identify the issues that must necessarily be resolved by the court, and present your case in an understandable and cogent manner. Whether you win or lose will depend upon your own performance as a witness in the courtroom and on the skills of the experts and attorneys who will represent you. Do not make the mistake of treating the selection of experts casually, and, above all, never be penny-wise and pound-foolish.

Chapter 14

Getting Help

Throughout this book, the reader has been referred to a number of state, local, and private agencies that can afford aid, in a variety of ways, to persons in need who have ceased living together. In addition to the needs of cohabitants and spouses involved in troubled interpersonal relationships for the services of an attorney or health care professional sensitive to their circumstances, discussed at length in chapter 13, other needs of formerly cohabiting gay persons, senior citizens, and individuals with emotional problems must also be addressed. This chapter sets forth many sources of help available throughout the country. The listing is by no means exhaustive of the available facilities but is certainly illustrative of the organizations that devote themselves to these needs.

Where can a person turn for help? Trying to face a problem without someone to talk to and share the pain is one of the most difficult tasks in life. Finding out that you are not alone and that there are many other persons who have overcome similar heartaches will offer you renewed strength to cope with almost any problem.

Crises come at various times in life. They may beset you in your youth, at midlife, or in the twilight years. When trouble strikes, the speed with which you obtain advice and counsel can soften the blow and enable you to make a swift decision that may ward off unwanted liabilities or enable you to obtain legal benefits and pursue life's challenges. The agencies listed below can provide the help you may need to get through a most difficult personal problem.

Separation and Divorce

Men's Rights Association
17854 Lyons
Forest Lake, MN 55025
(612) 464-7887

National Congress for Men
2020 Pennsylvania Ave. NW, Suite 277
Washington, DC 20006
(202) FATHERS

National Organization for Changing Men
794 Pennsylvania Ave.
Pittsburgh, PA 15221
(412) 371-8007

National Organization for Men
381 Park Ave. South
New York, NY 10016
(212) 686-MALE

ADAM
1008 White Oak
Arlington Heights, IL 60005
(312) 870-1040

America's Society of Separated and Divorced Men
575 Keep St.
Elgin, IL 60120
(312) 695-2200

Divorce After 60
% Turner Geriatric Clinic
1010 Wall St.
University of Michigan Medical Center
Ann Arbor, MI 48109
(313) 764-2556

Divorce Anonymous
P.O. Box 5313
Chicago, IL 60680

Ex-Partners of Servicemen (Women) for Equality
P.O. Box 11191
Alexandria, VA 22312
(703) 941-5844

Fathers For Equal Rights
P.O. Box 010847, Flagler Station
Miami, FL 33101
(305) 895-6351

Joint Custody Association
10606 Wilkins Ave.
Los Angeles, CA 90024
(213) 475-5352

Judean Society
1075 Space Pkwy., No. 336
Mountain View, CA 94043
(415) 964-8936

National Action for Former Military Wives
1700 Legion Dr.
Winter Park, FL 32789
(407) 628-2801

National Committee for Fair Divorce and Alimony Laws
11 Park Pl., Suite 1116
New York, NY 10007
(212) 766-4030

National Council for Children's Rights
721 Second St. NE
Washington, DC 20002
(202) 547-NCCR

National Institute for Child Support Enforcement
7200 Wisconsin Ave., Suite 500
Bethesda, MD 20814
(301) 654-8338

North American Conference of Separated and Divorced Catholics
1100 S. Goodman St.
Rochester, NY 14620
(716) 271-1320

PACE (Parents and Children's Equality)
1816 Florida Ave.
Palm Harbor, FL 34683
(813) 787-3875

Parents Sharing Custody
420 S. Beverly Dr., No. 100
Beverly Hills, CA 90212-4410
(213) 286-9171

Women Helping Women
% Ruth Kvalheim
525 N. Van Buren Ave.
Stoughton, WI 53589
(608) 873-3747

Single Parents and Child Care

SHARE
St. Elizabeth's Hospital
National Share Office
211 S. Third St.
Belleville, IL 62222
(618) 234-2415

Single Mothers by Choice
P.O. Box 1642
Gracie Square Station
New York, NY 10028
(212) 988-0993

Single Parent Resource Center
1165 Broadway, Room 504
New York, NY 10001
(212) 213-0047

Sisterhood of Black Single Mothers
1360 Fulton St., Suite 413
Brooklyn, NY 11216
(718) 638-0413

Women on Their Own
P.O. Box 0
Malaga, NJ 08328
(609) 728-4071

Committee for Mother and Child Rights
Rt. 1, Box 256A
Clear Brook, VA 22624
(703) 722-3652

Single Gourmet
133 E. 58th St.
New York, NY 10022
(212) 980-8788

National Association of Single Adult Leaders
3777 Holton Rd.
Muskegon, MI 49445
(616) 744-4844

Unmarried-Catholics Correspondence Club
P.O. Box 872
Troy, NY 12181

Parents' Choice Foundation (PCF)
P.O. Box 185
Waban, MA 02168
(617) 965-5913

Parents Helping Parents
535 Race St., Suite 220
San Jose, CA 95126
(408) 288-5010

Parents Without Partners
8807 Colesville Rd.
Silver Spring, MD 20910
(301) 588-9354

Remarried Parents, Inc. (RPI)
% Jack Pflaster
102-20 67th Dr.
Forest Hills, NY 11375
(718) 459-2011

Resolve Through Sharing
LaCrosse Lutheran Hospital
1910 South Ave.
LaCrosse, WI 54601
(608) 785-0530

Child Welfare League of America
440 First St. NW, Suite 310
Washington, DC 20001
(202) 638-2952

Child Care Action Campaign
330 7th Ave., 18th Floor
New York, NY 10001
(212) 239-0138

National Association for Family Day Care
815 15th St. NW, Suite 928
Washington, DC 20005
(202) 347-3356

National Child Day Care Association
1501 Benning Rd. NE
Washington, DC 20002
(202) 397-3800

National Coalition for Campus Child Care
P.O. Box 258
Cascade, WI 53011
(414) 528-7080

Comprehensive Day Care Programs
Stevens Administrative Center
Spring Garden at 13th St.
Philadelphia, PA 19123
(215) 351-7200

Fathers Are Forever
P.O. Box 4804
Panorama City, CA 91412
(818) 566-3368

Mothers at Home
P.O. Box 2208
Merrifield, VA 22116
(703) 352-2292

Mothers Matter
171 Wood St.
Rutherford, NJ 07070
(201) 933-8191

Mothers Without Custody
P.O. Box 56762
Houston, TX 77256
(713) 840-1622

National Foster Parent Association
Information and Services Office
226 Kilts Dr.
Houston, TX 77024
(713) 467-1850

National Singles Registry
17311 Dulles International Airport
Washington, DC 20041

Singles in Service
1201 Sycamore Terr., No. 40
Sunnyvale, CA 94086
(408) 248-8244

Concern for the Dying

Hemlock Society
P.O. Box 11830
Eugene, OR 97440
(503) 342-5748

Society for the Right to Die
250 W. 57th St.
New York, NY 10107
(212) 246-6973

Center for the Rights of the Terminally Ill
2319 18th Ave., S.
Fargo, ND 58103
(701) 237-5667

Concern for Dying
250 W. 57th St.
New York, NY 10107
(212) 246-6962

Association for Death Education and Counseling
638 Prospect Ave.
Hartford, CT 06105
(203) 232-4825

Center for Death Education and Research
1167 Social Science Bldg.
267 19th Ave. South
University of Minnesota
Minneapolis, MN 55455
(612) 624-1895

Foundation of Thanatology
630 W. 168th St.
New York, NY 10032
(212) 928-2066

International Institute for the Study of Death
P.O. Box 8565
Pembroke Pines, FL 33084
(305) 435-2730

Living/Dying Project
P.O. Box 357
Fairfax, CA 94930

St. Francis Center
5417 Sherier Pl. NW
Washington, DC 20016
(202) 363-8500

Senior Citizens and Aging

B'nai B'rith International Senior Citizens Housing Committee
1640 Rhode Island Ave. NW
Washington, DC 20036
(202) 857-6580

Aging in America
1500 Pelham Pkwy., S.
Bronx, NY 10461
(212) 824-4004

American Association of Homes for the Aging
1129 20th St. NW, Suite 400
Washington, DC 20036
(202) 296-5960

American Senior Citizens Association
P.O. Box 41
Fayetteville, NC 28302
(919) 323-3641

American Society for Aging
833 Market St., Suite 512
San Francisco, CA 94103
(415) 543-2617

Association of Informed Senior Citizens
560 Herndon Pkwy., Suite 110
Herndon, VA 22070
(703) 437-7600

Beverly Foundation
70 S. Lake Ave., Suite 750
Pasadena, CA 91101
(818) 792-2292

The Center for Social Gerontology
117 N. First St., Suite 204
Ann Arbor, MI 48104
(313) 665-1126

Center for Understanding Aging
Framingham State College
Framingham, MA 01701
(508) 626-4979

Children of Aging Parents
2761 Trenton Rd.
Levittown, PA 19056
(215) 946-6900

Daughters of the Elderly Bridging the Unknown Together
% Pat Meier
710 Concord St.
Ellettsville, IN 47429
(812) 876-5319

Ebenezer Society
2722 Park Ave., S.
Minneapolis, MN 55407
(612) 879-1467

Episcopal Society for Ministry of Aging
Sayre Hall
317 Wyandotte St.
Bethlehem, PA 18015
(215) 868-5400

Families U.S.A. Foundation
1334 G St. NW
Washington, DC 20005
(202) 628-3030

International Senior Citizens Association
1102 S. Crenshaw Blvd.
Los Angeles, CA 90019
(213) 857-6434

Jewish Association for Services for the Aged
40 W. 68th St.
New York, NY 10023
(212) 724-3200

Mature Outlook
Sears Tower, 23rd Floor
Chicago, IL 60684
(800) 336-6330

National Alliance of Senior Citizens
2525 Wilson Blvd.
Arlington, VA 22201
(703) 528-4380

National Association for the Advancement of the Black Aged
% Patricia Abston
18046 Dresden St.
Detroit, MI 48205

National Association of Human Development
P.O. Box 100
Washington, DC 20044
(202) 328-2191

National Caucus and Center on Black Aged
1424 K St. NW, Suite 500
Washington, DC 20005
(202) 637-8400

National Council on the Aging
600 Maryland Ave. SW
West Wing, Suite 100
Washington, DC 20024
(202) 479-1200

National Council of Senior Citizens
925 15th St. NW
Washington, DC 20005
(202) 347-8800

National Hispanic Council on Aging
2713 Ontario Rd. NW
Washington, DC 20009
(202) 265-1288

National Senior Citizens Law Center
1052 W. Sixth St., Suite 700
Los Angeles, CA 90017
(213) 482-3550

New Age
1212 Roosevelt
Ann Arbor, MI 48104
(313) 663-9891

Asociacion Nacional Por Personas Mayores
2727 W. Sixth St., Suite 270
Los Angeles, CA 90057
(213) 487-1922

American Association of Retired Persons
1909 K St. NW
Washington, DC 20049
(212) 872-4700

Association of Retired Americans
Lincoln Center
1660 Lincoln St., No. 2240
Denver, CO 80264
(800) 622-8040

International Society for Retirement Planning
% L. Malcolm Rodman, CAE
11312 Old Club Rd.
Rockville, MD 20852
(301) 881-4113

Gay and Lesbian Rights

Alliance for Gay and Lesbian Artists in the Entertainment
   Industry
P.O. Box 69A18
Los Angeles, CA 90069
(213) 273-7199

Association for Gay, Lesbian & Bisexual Issues in Counseling
Box 216
Jenkintown, PA 19046

Columbia Lesbian, Bisexual and Gay Coalition
303 Earl Hall
Columbia University
New York, NY 10027
(212) 854-1488

Committee of Black Gay Men
P.O. Box 7209
Chicago, IL 60680
(312) 248-5188

Custody Action for Lesbian Mothers
P.O. Box 281
Narberth, PA 19072
(215) 667-7508

Federation of Parents and Friends of Lesbians & Gays
P.O. Box 27605
Washington, DC 20038
(202) 638-4200

Fund for Human Dignity
666 Broadway, 4th Floor
New York, NY 10012
(212) 529-1600

Gay & Lesbian Parents Coalition International
Box 50360
Washington, DC 20004
(202) 583-8029

Homosexual Information Center
Box 8252
University City, CA 91608

Lesbian Feminist Liberation
Gay Community Center
208 W. 13th St.
New York, NY 10011
(212) 620-7310

Lesbian Mothers National Defense Fund
P.O. Box 21567
Seattle, WA 98111
(206) 325-2643

Media Fund for Human Rights
P.O. Box 8185
Universal City, CA 91608
(818) 902-1476

National Center for Lesbian Rights
1370 Mission St., 4th Floor
San Francisco, CA 94103

National Gay Alliance for Young Adults
P.O. Box 190426
Dallas, TX 75219
(214) 701-3455

National Gay and Lesbian Task Force
1517 U St. NW
Washington, DC 20009
(202) 332-6483

Senior Action in a Gay Environment
208 W. 13th St.
New York, NY 10011
(212) 741-2247

Spouses of Gays Association
1329 Levick St.
Philadelphia, PA 19111
(215) 288-6959

Trikone (Gay/Lesbian)
Box 21354
San Jose, CA 95151
(408) 270-8776

APPENDIXES

A. States That Recognize Common-Law Marriages

Alabama
Colorado
Georgia
Idaho
Iowa
Kansas
Montana

Ohio
Oklahoma
Pennsylvania
Rhode Island
South Carolina
Texas
District of Columbia

B. Sample Agreement of Living-Together Couple Concerning Paternity and Child Support

Waiver of Periodic Support or Property Division

AGREEMENT, made this   day of   , 1991, between [mother's name], residing at [address], hereinafter referred to as "[mother's first name]," and [father's name], residing at [address], hereinafter referred to as "[father's first name]."

WITNESSETH

WHEREAS, [mother's name] is the mother of [child's name] and [father's name] is the father; and

WHEREAS, it is the parties' intention that [father's name] formally acknowledges the paternity of such child; and

WHEREAS, the parties have not married and in the past, from time to time, resided with one another but no longer do so; and

WHEREAS, it is the desire of the parties to provide for the child's custody, support, education, and welfare.

NOW, THEREFORE, it is mutually agreed as follows:

1. The parties agree that they shall exercise joint custody [or sole custody] of [child's name] and provide specific visitation rights to the nonresidential parent as set forth in this agreement. [insert visitation schedule agreed to by the parties]

2. In the event [child's name] shall reside with [mother's name], and [mother's name] does not reside with another person, [father's name] agrees to contribute as his share for child support, which shall include amounts for [child's name]'s health, education, and welfare requirements, payments to [mother's name] for the benefit of the [child's name], as follows:

(a) the sum of $[ ] per week payable the first Friday following the execution of this Agreement and continuing weekly thereafter until the earliest happening of one of the following events:

(i) [child's name], attaining the age of twenty-one (21) years, or at an earlier age becomes self-supporting;

(ii) the death of [child's name];

(iii) [father's name] death.

3. In the event that [mother's name] shall reside with another person and [child's name], then [father's name] shall pay only fifty percent (50%) of the amount set forth herein.

4. In the event that [child's name] shall reside with [father's name], [father's name] shall have no obligations to make any child support payments to [mother's name] and will not seek any contribution from [mother's name].

5. [Optional clause]: [father's name] shall make a provision in his Last Will and Testament that if he shall predecease [child's name] during the period of time that he is obliged to make support payments pursuant to the terms of this Agreement, a trust will be created for the benefit of [child's name], naming [mother's name] as the Trustee thereof, consisting of money or property having a value to sufficiently fund the child support payments as required by the terms of this Agreement.

6. The parties acknowledge that they have lived together from time to time but in no way have held themselves out to be married, and they have always maintained their individual names and separate identities.

7. The parties expressly agree that they will not seek either a division of any property that may have been acquired by either of them during any time they lived together or support or maintenance from each other in any jurisdiction based upon a common-law marriage or an express or implied agreement, whether written or oral.

8. [mother's name] represents that she is financially self-sufficient and that the sums provided for the support of [child's name] are, together with her own income, sufficient to provide for all of the child's needs for health, education, and welfare during the times [he, she] may reside with her.

9. In addition to the sums for support for [child's name], as set forth in paragraph "2" herein, [father's name] agrees to pay all of the costs of [child's name] health care as incurred.

10. Unless [child's name] may be possessed of sufficient assets of [his, her] own, or shall be older than twenty-three (23) years of age, [father's name] agrees to pay for all costs to be incurred in the event that [child's name] shall attend college as a full-time matriculating student, which shall include, but not be limited to, tuition, room and board, books, lab and registration fees, and travel to and from the permanent residence of [child's name].

11. In the event that [father's name] shall make such expenditures for college expenses, as provided in paragraph "10" of this Agreement, he shall be relieved of the obligation to provide support to [mother's name] for the benefit of the child, as provided in paragraph "2(a)" of this Agreement.

12. [mother's name] presently resides in the State of [name of state] and [father's name] resides in the State of [name of state] and they share their time with [child's name] on a weekly basis. It is agreed that in the event that either parent shall change his or her present residence to one that will require an automobile ride of

more than two and one-half (2½) hours, or exceeding 125 miles, to the other parent's place of residence, the parent wishing to move his or her residence shall grant sole custody of the child to the parent who shall remain in his or her present residence. In such event, liberal visitation rights shall be afforded the parent removing his or her residence beyond such 2½-hour driving distance, or 125-mile radius, as may be in the best interest of [child's name].

13. This agreement shall be governed by the laws of the State of [name of state].

IN WITNESS WHEREOF, the parties hereto have hereunto set their respective hands and seals the day and year first above written, and they hereby acknowledge that the provisions of this Agreement shall be binding upon their respective heirs, assigns, executors, and administrators.

_____ L.S.
[Mother's name]

_____ L.S.
[Father's name]

STATE OF [name of state]   )
) ss.:
COUNTY OF [name of county])

On the   day of   , 1992, before me personally came [mother's name], to me known to be the individual described in and who executed the foregoing instrument and she did duly acknowledge to me that she executed the same.

_____

STATE OF [name of state]   )
) ss.:
COUNTY OF [name of county])

On the   day of   , 1992, before me personally came [father's name], to me known to be the individual described in and who executed the foregoing instrument and he did duly acknowledge to me that he executed the same.

_____

Note: The terms of this agreement can be modified to include property division or spousal support if the parties desire such provisions.

C. Agreement between Cohabitants (Letter Form)

Dear _____,

You and I have decided to live together in a common household and to divide our responsibilities to one another, as expressed in this letter. It is our intention not to live in a state of matrimony or to hold ourselves out as husband and wife or to enter a common-law marriage in any state that recognizes such marriages.

Inasmuch as you have [insert the reasons for your agreement, such as "given up your career as a _____ and have agreed to assist me in my career and to be responsible for the care of our household"], I agree that [set forth your understanding, e.g., "we will share equally in any and all property that we may acquire during the time we live together through investment earnings or otherwise, other than by gift or inheritance from a third party"] or ["you are only entitled to retain such property that may be placed in your own name during our relationship"] or ["we will divide any property we acquire during our relationship 75% for me and 25% for you (or any other terms to which you have agreed)"].

In the event that we cease living together or in the event of my

231

death, if we are still living together at such time, I agree that you will receive your share of the property, as set forth above, within thirty (30) days following our separation or my death. You understand that you will make no other claim against me, either by way of a division of property or against my estate, other than as provided for by the terms of this letter agreement, but I nevertheless may choose to provide for you in my Last Will and Testament.

In the event we separate ["I will pay to you $_____ a week for _____ weeks to enable you to return to work and establish a separate household"] or "there will be no periodic support payments made to you"]. In the event that we may marry in the future, the contents of this agreement, with respect to our cohabitation, [will "cease and terminate" or "will continue to be binding upon us"]. However, any property acquired by either of us ["shall remain the property of the person in title" or "shall be considered marital property"].

Although it is our intention that our relationship will continue indefinitely, we have both, in order to avoid disputes that may arise in the future and to avoid any animosity or acrimony, acknowledged the terms and conditions of this agreement by affixing our signatures to the foot of this letter.

It is my suggestion that you consult with an attorney of your own choosing concerning the contents of this letter agreement as I have done, before signing it. After such consultation if this letter expresses our entire understanding, please sign and date it where indicated below.

Sincerely yours,

Dated:_____   _____
                              (Signature of cohabitant)

Dated:_____   _____
                              (Signature of cohabitant)

D. Sample Prenuptial Agreement

AGREEMENT made this [month and year], by and between [man's full name], residing at [address], hereinafter "[man's first name]" and [woman's full name], residing at [address], hereinafter "[woman's first name]."

WHEREAS, [man's first name] and [woman's first name] intend to marry in the future and enter into this Agreement in contemplation of such marriage; and

WHEREAS, [man's first name] has fully disclosed to [woman's first name] his present assets and earnings; and

WHEREAS, [woman's first name] has fully disclosed to [man's first name] her present assets and earnings; and

WHEREAS, the parties acknowledge that despite their best intentions, the passage of time and changed circumstances may result in their marriage being terminated as a result of death, divorce, or dissolution during their lifetime, and they desire to make provision now for such a possibility as it relates to support and the ownership, possession, and control of certain property at

---

The terms of this prenuptial agreement can be utilized by living-together couples, where relevant and applicable, and incorporated into the letter agreement found in Appendix C. In essence, this agreement is conditioned on marriage whereas the living-together agreement is not.

the termination of their marriage; whether such termination occurs by death or divorce, and

WHEREAS, [woman's first name] acknowledges that by entering into this Agreement she may receive as a widow substantially less than the amount she might otherwise be entitled to
receive if [man's first name] died intestate, or if she elected to take
against his Last Will and Testament pursuant to statute, and may
receive substantially less support and property than she might
otherwise be entitled to receive in the event of the parties' divorce;
and

WHEREAS, the parties understand that nothing in this
Agreement shall preclude either or both of them from making a
voluntary provision for the other out of his or her separate estate
and income; and

WHEREAS, [woman's first name] acknowledges that by entering into this Agreement she may receive substantially less
maintenance and/or child support in the event that children are
born of their marriage and if [woman's first name] shall have
custody of said children than she might otherwise be entitled to
receive in the event of the parties' separation or divorce; and

WHEREAS, [woman's first name] has carefully weighed all of
these aforesaid facts and circumstances and desires to marry
[man's first name] regardless of any financial provisions made for
her benefit or those she may waive pursuant to the terms of this
Agreement.

NOW, THEREFORE, in consideration of the premises and of
the mutual covenants and conditions herein, the parties hereto
agree as follows:

Article I

Effective Date

The terms of this Agreement are intended to have effect only
in the event that the contemplated marriage shall be solemnized,

and in the event it is not, all obligations of the parties expressed in this Agreement shall be and become wholly null and void.

Article II

General Release to the Date of This Agreement

The parties agree, except as may otherwise be provided in this Agreement, that they have no claims of any kind, nature, or description against the other party, and each party hereby releases the other and his or her heirs, executors, administrators, successors, and assigns from all actions, causes of action, suits, debts, dues, sums of money, accounts, reckonings, bonds, bills, specialties, covenants, contracts, controversies, agreements, promises, variances, trespasses, damages, judgments, extents, executions, claims, and demands whatsoever, in law, admiralty or equity, against the other he or she or his or her heirs, executors, administrators, successors, and assigns ever had, now have, or hereafter can, shall, or may have for, upon, or by reason of any matter, cause, or thing whatsoever that may have accrued prior to the date of this Agreement.

Article III

Waiver of Property Interest on Divorce

The parties have entered into this Agreement with the full knowledge of their rights and with their express waiver of the provisions of [include applicable law in parties' state of residence; e.g., New York Domestic Relations Law §236 Part B], including but not limited to the distribution of marital property or a distributive award that might otherwise accrue by virtue of their proposed marriage. The respective rights to each other's property and their rights to receive property from the other upon divorce shall be fixed by this Agreement, which shall be binding upon their respective heirs and legal representatives.

Article IV

Division of Marital Assets

1. While the parties contemplate a long and lasting marriage, terminated only by the death of one of the parties, they also recognize the possibility that their marriage may be terminated by way of divorce, annulment, dissolution, or otherwise during the lifetime of both of the parties. In the event of a termination of their marriage, regardless of which party hereto shall initiate an action for divorce and regardless of the jurisdiction, venue, or location of such action and regardless of who shall desire or have caused such termination of the marriage, the parties agree that the monies provided for [woman's first name], as set forth in Schedule "A" ("Schedule A Property") below, shall be in lieu of any division of marital property or a distributive award to which [woman's first name] may be otherwise entitled, as defined or provided for by [applicable law in parties' state of residence, e.g., New York Domestic Relations Law §236 Part B].

2. Schedule A property, for purposes of this Agreement, shall be deemed to mean all property, real or personal, acquired by [man's first name] only during the marriage and owned by [man's first name] at the time of the initiation of the action for divorce. It is expressly understood, however, notwithstanding the foregoing sentence, that Schedule A Property shall not include:

(i) property, real or personal or the appreciated value thereof, owned by [man's first name] and acquired during the marriage by reason of gift, purchase, or otherwise from his mother, father, or other family members;

(ii) any "separate property," which is defined as all property owned prior to marriage by [man's first name] and any increased or appreciated value that occurs during marriage; and

(iii) any property acquired by [man's first name] during marriage with separate property.

3. [woman's first name] shall receive the greater of Column "1" or Column "2" of Schedule "A" during the indicated years of the marriage. [insert number of years, amounts, and percentages agreed to; e.g.]

Schedule "A"

Years of marriage	Column "1" Amount	or	Column "2" A sum equal to the product of the indicated percentage × the value of Schedule "A" property acquired during the marriage
1 to 3 years	$ 25,000.00		0%
4 to 5 years	50,000.00		5%
6 to 10 years	75,000.00		7%
11 to 15 years	100,000.00		9%
16 to 20 years	125,000.00		10%
21 years and over	250,000.00		12%

4. The payments provided for in Schedule "A" are conditioned upon:

(i) the entry of a divorce judgment between the parties;

(ii) [man's first name]'s net worth at the time a judgment of divorce is entered being at least $4.4 million, and in the event that his net worth is less than $4.4 million, the sums to be paid or computed pursuant to this schedule shall be reduced by the same proportion as $4.4 million bears to [man's first name]'s net worth at the time that a judgment of divorce is entered between the parties.

5. [woman's first name] acknowledges that by the terms of this Article she has waived any and all rights she may otherwise

have had pursuant to [applicable law in parties' state of residence; e.g., New York Domestic Relations Law §236 Part B] as to:

(i) any property from his mother, father, or other family members acquired by gift, inheritance, purchase, or otherwise held in [man's first name]'s name between the date of the marriage and the date of the commencement of an action for divorce;

(ii) any property owned by [man's first name] prior to marriage and any increase in value or appreciation of such property during marriage, or

(iii) any property acquired by [man's first name] with such separate property, it being the intention of the parties that the provisions contained hereinabove as computed pursuant to Schedule "A" shall be the only monies or property to which [woman's first name] shall be entitled in the event of divorce between the parties.

6. Any monies that may become due to [woman's first name] shall be paid by [man's first name] within thirty (30) days following the entry of a judgment of divorce.

7. All property that shall hereafter be acquired in the joint names of the parties (hereinafter referred to as "jointly owned property"), whether title thereto shall be held by the parties as tenants in common, tenants by the entireties, or joint tenants with right of survivorship, shall be deemed to be owned by the parties equally without regard to the source of funds utilized to effect the purchase thereof. Unless otherwise specifically provided in connection with the purchase of any such jointly owned property, the following provisions shall apply:

(i) In the event of the death of either party, the surviving party shall be deemed the sole owner of such jointly owned property, as if the property shall have been owned as joint tenants with right of survivorship, provided that no separation event, as defined in Article V hereof, shall have occurred as of the time of such death.

(ii) In the event that a separation event, as defined in Article V hereof shall occur, all jointly owned property shall be sold as soon as practicable after the occurrence of such separation event and the net proceeds derived from such sale shall be divided equally between the parties, unless otherwise agreed upon in writing by the parties, or in the event an agreement cannot be reached by the parties. In such event, the parties shall cooperate fully with one another to effectuate a prompt disposition of their jointly owned property.

8. All property heretofore or hereafter acquired solely in [woman's first name]'s name or in her name jointly with a person other than [man's first name] shall be and remain her separate property as to which [man's first name] shall make no claim of use, right, title, or ownership at any time.

Article V

Separation Event

1. A separation event shall be deemed to be (i) either party instituting suit for divorce, separation, or support or (ii) a physical separation by either of the parties by a removal from the parties' marital or other residence with or without the consent of the other party.

2. This Agreement shall be deemed to be and shall constitute either a separation agreement or a stipulation of settlement between the parties within the meaning of [applicable law in parties' state of residence; e.g., New York Domestic Relations Law §170(6)].

Article VI

Mutual Release and Discharge of Claims in Estates

1. Subject to the provisions of this Article, each party hereby waives, releases, relinquishes, renounces, and surrenders any and all rights that either might otherwise have in the estate, both real and personal and wheresoever situated, of the other upon his or

her death, including, but not limited to, any and all right or rights of dower, curtesy, homestead, exempt property, or family or spousal allowance, any and all right or rights that either hereafter has or may have, as surviving spouse, to take a share of the estate of the other in intestacy, and, without limiting the scope of the foregoing, each party also hereby specifically waives, releases, relinquishes, renounces, and surrenders:

(i) any right of election that he or she may have to take against any Last Will and Testament of the other, or against any testamentary substitute, under any law now or hereafter in force in any jurisdiction, or

(ii) any right to act as administrator or administratrix of the estate of the other. Nothing in this paragraph shall preclude either party from:

(a) naming the other to serve as personal representative or executor or executrix of his or her Last Will and Testament, or

(b) specifically waiving in writing the provisions of this paragraph pertaining to the other party serving as administrator or administratrix, except as provided in Schedule "B" on page 241.

2. Notwithstanding any provisions of [law applicable in parties' state of residence; e.g., Sections 4–1.1, 5–1.1, or any other provision of the Estates, Powers and Trusts Law of the State of New York, or any other law of the State of New York] concerning the distributive share of a surviving spouse or the right of election of a surviving spouse, [woman's first name], in the event of [man's first name]'s death, hereby waives any interest she may otherwise have acquired in property owned by [man's first name], either by way of intestacy or by right of election against the provisions of the terms of any Will made by [man's first name] and any right to serve as a fiduciary in the administration of [man's first name]'s estate, except as provided in Schedule "B" below. [insert number of years and amounts agreed to]

3. In addition to the sums specified in Schedule "B" below, if [man's first name] shall die prior to the twenty-first (21) year of the

Schedule "B"

Years of marriage	Amount without children	Amount with children
1 to 5 years	$ 100,000.00	$ 200,000.00
6 to 10 years	200,000.00	300,000.00
11 to 15 years	500,000.00	1,000,000.00
16 to 20 years	750,000.00	1,250,000.00
21 years and over	1,000,000.00	1,500,000.00

parties' marriage, and if at the time of his death the marital residence is not owned as tenants by the entirety by [man's first name] and [woman's first name], then in that event, [man's first name]'s estate shall purchase a residence ("New Residence") for [woman's first name] as fee owner of said New Residence. Should the New Residence be purchased pursuant to the terms of this provision, [woman's first name] shall select same in her sole discretion provided that (a) the purchase price of said New Residence is not more than $350,000; (b) such New Residence shall be in the same school district that any children of the parties may attend.

4. During the time that [woman's first name] shall reside in such New Residence, [man's first name]'s estate shall pay for all taxes and maintenance on the residence until the earliest happening of one of the following events:

(a) [woman's first name]'s death or remarriage

(b) [woman's first name]'s cohabiting with another man

(c) the youngest child of the parties attains the age of twenty-three (23) years

(d) [woman's first name] removing herself and/or the children from such residence

(e) [woman's first name]'s rental of the residence.

5. If the parties shall be married for twenty-one (21) years or more at the time of [man's first name]'s death, title to any residence then occupied by the parties shall be transferred to [woman's first name] free of any and all liens and encumbrances.

Article VII

Waiver of Child Support

1. The parties acknowledge and represent that they have read and are familiar with the provisions of [law applicable in parties' state of residence; e.g., Domestic Relations Law §248(1), commonly known as the Child Support Standards Act], and that their respective attorneys have advised them with respect to its legal effects upon them.

2. In the event that there are any children born of the marriage between [man's first name] and [woman's first name] and in the further event that [woman's first name] shall obtain legal custody of such children following a separation or divorce, the parties expressly waive the provisions of Domestic Relations Law §248(1), commonly known as the Child Support Standards Act, which they acknowledge contains, inter alia, provisions for the fixation of child support to a custodial parent based upon fixed percentages of gross income, and [man's first name] shall pay to [woman's first name], in equal weekly installments, the sums specified in Schedule "C" below, instead of any sums that may otherwise be specified in the Child Support Standards Act. [insert amount of child support agreed to; e.g.]

3. It is further agreed that in the event that [woman's first name] shall obtain sole custody of any child or children born of

Schedule "C"

Number of children	Amount of annual child support
1	$ 15,000.00
2	35,000.00
3	50,000.00
4	65,000.00
5 or more	100,000.00

the marriage that she will not remove them more than a thirty-five (35) mile radius from the marital residence the parties occupied prior to the commencement of a matrimonial action.

4. The sums provided in Schedule "C" above shall be paid to [woman's first name] regardless of any income received or earned by her from any other source.

Article VIII

Maintenance

1. In the event that a matrimonial action is commenced by either party against the other and a temporary or permanent award of maintenance is requested, [woman's first name] agrees to accept the sums as provided in Schedule "D" below in full satisfaction of any and all claims she may have against [man's first name] for support, maintenance, necessaries, and/or any other provisions for support contained in [law applicable in parties' state of residence; e.g., New York Domestic Relations Law §236B] or elsewhere: [insert number of years, amount, and period of maintenance; e.g.]

Schedule "D"

Number of years of marriage	Amount of annual maintenance	Period annual maintenance, in equal monthly installments, shall be paid
1 to 3 years	$ 25,000.00	½ of the months that the parties resided together between the date of marriage and the date of commencement of matrimonial proceeding
4 to 5 years	50,000.00	
6 to 10 years	75,000.00	
11 to 15 years	85,000.00	
16 years or over	100,000.00	

2. Said maintenance payments shall be conditioned upon [man's first name]'s net income, after payment of federal and state income taxes, being no less than the sum of $250,000 at the time a request is made to the court for support. In the event that [man's first name]'s net income is less than $250,000, then the sums of money provided for maintenance in Schedule "D" shall be reduced in the same proportion as the percentage decline of his net income below $250,000. For example, if [man's first name]'s net income at the time a motion for support is made by [woman's first name] is $200,000, the decrease of net income would be twenty (20%) percent and all amounts specified in Schedule "D" would be reduced by twenty (20%) percent.

3. The payment of maintenance to [woman's first name] pursuant to this Article shall terminate upon the earliest happening of one of the following events:

    (a) death of either of the parties

    (b) remarriage of [woman's first name]

    (c) [woman's first name] residing with an unrelated male.

Article IX

Disclosure of Assets

[man's first name] represents that his net assets, after deducting liabilities, is in the present sum of $, and that his annual income is approximately $, and that he has appended to this Agreement, and [woman's first name] acknowledges receiving a copy, and initialed same, a net worth statement as of   , 1992. [woman's first name] acknowledges and represents that she has fully considered [man's first name]'s financial prospects and circumstances in the negotiations and execution of this Agreement, and that her net worth is not meaningful.

Article X

Terms of Agreement are Fair and Reasonable

The parties acknowledge that they are entering into this Agreement voluntarily, that the terms hereof are fair and reasonable, and that they have weighed all of the facts and circumstances likely to influence their judgment, including but not limited to [man's first name]'s assets and earnings and [woman's first name]'s past, present, and future financial circumstances. The parties expressly waive the provisions of [law applicable in parties' state of residence; e.g., New York Domestic Relations Law §236B(3)] and any other law, statute, or judicial decision that may hereinafter be enacted or hold that the validity of the parties' agreement will be conditioned upon a finding that the terms of their agreement was fair when made and not unconscionable at the time that a judgment of divorce may be entered between the parties.

Article XI

Payment of Joint Debts

In the event of a separation event, any liabilities incurred by the parties jointly during the marriage shall be paid by the parties as provided in written agreements executed by the parties at the time such joint debts shall be incurred. If no written agreement pertaining to any joint debt shall be executed by the parties, such joint liability shall be defrayed equally by the parties so that each of them shall be responsible to pay 50% of such outstanding joint liability. Each party agrees to indemnify the other party against any liability and to hold the other party harmless from his or her share of the joint debt.

Article XII

Annuity and Retirement Benefits

1. [woman's first name] hereby consents to [man's first name]'s election to waive a qualified joint and survivor annuity form of benefit and a qualified preretirement survivor annuity form of benefit under any plan of deferred compensation to which Section 401(a)(11) of the Internal Revenue Code ("the Code") or Section 205(b)(1) of the Employee Retirement Income Security Act of 1974 ("ERISA") shall apply and in which [man's first name] currently is or hereafter may be deemed a vested participant within the meaning of Section 417(f)(1) of the Code and Section 205(h)(1) of ERISA. [woman's first name] further consents to [man's first name]'s current and future designation of benefici- aries other than herself under any of such plans (and to any revocation or modification of such designations), including any of such plans referred to in Section 401(a)(11) of the Code or Section 205(b)(1) of ERISA. [woman's first name] hereby acknowl- edges that she understands the effect of [man's first name]'s elections and her consents thereto. To the extent that the law shall require any additional documentation to confirm the consents set forth herein, [woman's first name] agrees to execute and deliver the same at [man's first name]'s request, and without charge therefor.

2. [man's first name] hereby consents to [woman's first name]'s election to waive a qualified joint and survivor annuity form of benefit and a qualified preretirement survivor annuity form of benefit under any plan of deferred compensation to which Section 401(a)(11) of the Code or Section 205(b)(1) of ERISA shall apply and in which [woman's first name] currently is or hereafter may be deemed a vested participant within the meaning of Sec- tion 417(f)(1) of the Code and Section 205(h)(1) of ERISA. [man's first name] further consents to [woman's first name]'s current and future designation of beneficiaries other than [man's first name] under any of such plans (and to any revocation or modification of

such designations), including any of such plans referred to in Section 401(a)(11) of the Code or Section 205(b)(1) of ERISA. [man's first name] hereby acknowledges that he understands the effect of [woman's first name]'s elections and his consents thereto. To the extent that the law shall require any additional documentation to confirm the consents set forth herein, [man's first name] agrees to execute and deliver the same at [woman's first name]'s request, and without charge therefor.

Article XIII

Entire Agreement

Each party acknowledges that no representations of any kind have been made to him or to her as an inducement to enter into this Agreement other than the representations specifically set forth herein, and that this Agreement contains the entire understanding of the parties with respect to each party's respective rights to receive dower, curtesy, homestead, exempt property, family or spousal allowance, community property or quasi-community property, equitable distribution of property acquired by either or both of them during their marriage, distributive awards, awards of support and maintenance, awards of counsel fees or costs, and rights of inheritance, whether in intestacy or pursuant to the Last Will and Testament of the other.

Article XIV

Representation by Counsel and Counsel Fees

1. The parties acknowledge that they have given due consideration and have reviewed with their respective attorneys the provisions of this Agreement and completely understand and assent to all of its terms and believe them to be entirely adequate for their financial needs and requirements and that the provisions

are fair and reasonable and entirely adequate now and for the future. The parties further acknowledge that they independently selected their own counsel who have reviewed the provisions of this agreement with them and have advised them as to the meaning, effect, and consequence of such provisions.

2. The parties will pay their own legal expenses in connection with legal representation for the negotiation, drafting, and execution of this Agreement from their own separate property.

3. [man's first name] acknowledges that he has been represented by [attorney's name and address], and [woman's first name] acknowledges that she has been represented by [attorney's name and address] with respect to the negotiation, drafting, and execution of this Agreement.

Article XV

General Provisions

1. This Agreement shall become effective only in the event that the contemplated marriage between the parties hereto is solemnized, except that the mutual releases contained herein in Article II shall be effective on the execution of this Agreement.

2. Each party will at all times, upon request by the other party or his or her legal representatives, execute and deliver all instruments that may be necessary or desirable for the purpose of effectuating the terms of this Agreement, without charge therefor.

3. This Agreement may not be amended, modified, or annulled by the parties except by written agreement signed by both parties. The failure of either party to insist upon a strict performance of any provision of the Agreement will not constitute a waiver of any of the provisions or of the right to insist upon strict performance.

4. This Agreement shall bind the parties, their heirs, executors, administrators, legal representatives, and assigns and shall

inure to the benefit of their respective heirs, executors, and assigns.

5. In case any provision of this Agreement should be held to be invalid, illegal, or unenforceable under or contrary to the law of any country, state, or other jurisdiction, this invalidity, illegality, or unenforceability will have no effect on any other provisions of this Agreement, all of which shall continue to be effective.

6. The provisions of this Agreement are to be incorporated in but not merged in any judgment or decree of divorce, separation, annulment and shall survive said decree or judgment.

7. This Agreement shall be governed by the laws of the State of _____ .

8. Each party hereby consents to the jurisdiction of the State of _____ in the event there is any dispute with respect to the terms of this Agreement.

9. This Agreement contains the entire understanding of the parties, who acknowledge that there are no representations or warranties other than those embodied in this Agreement.

10. Nothing in this Agreement shall be construed as a waiver or relinquishment by either party of any gift, bequest, or devise made to either [man's first name] or [woman's first name] in the Last Will and Testament of the other during their lifetime.

11. Nothing in this Agreement shall be deemed to constitute a waiver by either of the parties in any property jointly acquired by the parties, whether real or personal.

12. All notices required to be given hereunder shall be given and shall be deemed effective if sent by certified or registered mail, return receipt requested, as of the seventh day following such mailing or by hand delivery, in which case the notice shall be effective as of the date on which it shall be delivered, provided such notice is given as follows:

> If to [woman's first name], to her addressed "PERSONAL AND CONFIDENTIAL" at _____ with a copy to: [name of woman's attorney]

If to [man's first name], to him addressed "PERSONAL AND CONFIDENTIAL" at: _____ with a copy to: [name of man's attorney]

or to such other address as a party shall designate by notice given in accordance with the provisions hereof.

13. The parties agree that any income or other taxes they may pay pursuant to any joint return that they shall file shall be apportioned between them on a basis that they jointly in their sole discretion shall deem appropriate.

14. This Agreement shall not impair or prevent either party from making any voluntary disposition to or for the benefit of the other by gift, Will, beneficiary designation, testamentary substitute, or otherwise, and the waivers herein contained shall not apply to any such voluntary disposition.

15. Each party shall, upon the request of the other, and without requesting any charge therefor, take any and all steps and execute, acknowledge, and deliver to the other party any and all further documents necessary or expedient to effectuate the purpose and intent of this Agreement prior to, during, or after a termination event or the termination of their marital relationship.

16. This Agreement and its provisions shall not be amended, modified, or terminated, or be deemed to have been amended, modified, or terminated, unless such amendment, modification, or agreement to terminate is contained in writing, duly subscribed by both parties and acknowledged with the same formality as this Agreement. No oral statement or written matter concerning this Agreement or any of its provisions shall have any force or effect.

17. This Agreement may be signed in any number of counterparts, each one of which shall constitute an original.

Article XVI

Law Applicable

This Agreement shall be interpreted and enforced in accordance with the laws of the State of _____ in effect at the time of its execution, regardless of any other residence either of the parties may establish following the execution of this Agreement.

Article XVII

Supplementary Documentation

The parties agree to execute, acknowledge, and deliver, without charge therefor, from time to time such instruments as may be necessary or appropriate to release any rights of dower or curtesy or similar interests or other statutory rights that either might have in the property of the other but for this Agreement, so as to enable the other to make such transfer or other disposition of his or her property as he or she may from time to time desire, in the same manner as if their proposed marriage had never been solemnized.

IN WITNESS WHEREOF, the parties have executed this Agreement on [date and year].

_____
[Man's name]

_____
[Woman's name]

STATE OF   )
) ss.:
COUNTY OF)

On the [date and year], before me personally came [man's name], to me known to be the individual described in and who executed the foregoing instrument and acknowledged that he executed the same.

_____
Notary Public

STATE OF   )
) ss.:
COUNTY OF   )

On the [date and year], before me personally came [woman's name], to me known to be the individual described in and who executed the foregoing instrument and acknowledged that she executed the same.

_____
Notary Public

E. Representative Annual Term Life Insurance Rates for Nonsmokers

$500,000 and up
Currently Billed Rates* Per $1000

Issue age M	Issue age F	1	2	3	4	5	6	7	8	9	10	Attained age M	Attained age F	Policy year 11 and thereafter
	25	0.70	0.87	1.00	1.06	1.11	1.18	1.23	1.29	1.34	1.42		35	1.53
	26	0.70	0.87	1.00	1.07	1.12	1.19	1.24	1.30	1.35	1.44		36	1.54
	27	0.70	0.87	1.00	1.07	1.13	1.21	1.26	1.32	1.37	1.45		37	1.56
	28	0.70	0.87	1.00	1.08	1.15	1.22	1.27	1.33	1.38	1.47		38	1.58
	29	0.70	0.87	1.00	1.08	1.16	1.24	1.29	1.35	1.40	1.48		39	1.60
25	30	0.70	0.87	1.00	1.09	1.17	1.25	1.30	1.36	1.41	1.50	35	40	1.61
26	31	0.70	0.87	1.01	1.10	1.20	1.29	1.36	1.44	1.51	1.61	36	41	1.73
27	32	0.70	0.87	1.01	1.12	1.23	1.33	1.43	1.53	1.60	1.72	37	42	1.85
28	33	0.71	0.88	1.02	1.14	1.26	1.37	1.49	1.61	1.70	1.83	38	43	1.97
29	34	0.71	0.88	1.02	1.16	1.28	1.42	1.56	1.70	1.79	1.94	39	44	2.08
30	35	0.71	0.88	1.03	1.18	1.31	1.46	1.62	1.78	1.89	2.05	40	45	2.25
31	36	0.71	0.88	1.04	1.20	1.34	1.51	1.68	1.86	1.99	2.18	41	46	2.40
32	37	0.72	0.88	1.04	1.21	1.38	1.56	1.74	1.93	2.09	2.32	42	47	2.55
33	38	0.72	0.88	1.05	1.22	1.41	1.61	1.80	2.00	2.19	2.46	43	48	2.70
34	39	0.72	0.89	1.06	1.24	1.44	1.66	1.85	2.07	2.30	2.59	44	49	2.85
35	40	0.72	0.89	1.07	1.25	1.47	1.71	1.91	2.14	2.40	2.73	45	50	3.07
36	41	0.75	0.94	1.16	1.37	1.62	1.89	2.11	2.36	2.64	3.01	46	51	3.38
37	42	0.78	1.00	1.25	1.48	1.76	2.07	2.31	2.57	2.87	3.28	47	52	3.69
38	43	0.81	1.05	1.34	1.60	1.91	2.25	2.51	2.79	3.11	3.56	48	53	4.00
39	44	0.85	1.10	1.43	1.71	2.06	2.43	2.71	3.00	3.35	3.83	49	54	4.31

40	45	0.87	1.21	1.52	1.83	2.21	2.61	2.91	3.22	3.59	4.11	50	55	4.73
41	46	0.90	1.32	1.63	1.97	2.39	2.83	3.19	3.56	4.02	4.60	51	56	5.29
42	47	0.97	1.43	1.74	2.11	2.58	3.06	3.48	3.91	4.45	5.09	52	57	5.85
43	48	1.04	1.53	1.85	2.26	2.77	3.29	3.76	4.25	4.88	5.58	53	58	6.42
44	49	1.12	1.64	1.97	2.40	2.95	3.52	4.05	4.60	5.31	6.07	54	59	6.98
45	50	1.19	1.75	2.08	2.54	3.14	3.75	4.33	4.94	5.74	6.56	55	60	7.71
46	51	1.30	1.89	2.21	2.72	3.38	4.05	4.72	5.42	6.33	7.27	56	61	8.54
47	52	1.41	2.04	2.35	2.88	3.62	4.35	5.11	5.89	6.93	7.97	57	62	9.37
48	53	1.53	2.19	2.48	3.06	3.86	4.65	5.50	6.37	7.52	8.68	58	63	10.20
49	54	1.64	2.33	2.62	3.24	4.11	4.95	5.89	6.84	8.11	9.38	59	64	11.03
50	55	1.75	2.48	2.76	3.42	4.35	5.25	6.28	7.32	8.70	10.09	60	65	12.11
51	56	1.86	2.67	3.03	3.76	4.80	5.84	7.03	8.27	9.81	11.42	61	66	13.71
52	57	1.98	2.86	3.32	4.12	5.27	6.43	7.79	9.22	10.92	12.76	62	67	15.31
53	58	2.09	3.04	3.60	4.46	5.74	7.02	8.55	10.17	12.03	14.09	63	68	16.91
54	59	2.20	3.24	3.88	4.82	6.20	7.62	9.30	11.12	13.14	15.43	64	69	18.51
55	60	2.32	3.43	4.17	5.17	6.68	8.21	10.06	12.07	14.25	16.76	65	70	20.53
56	61	2.52	3.78	4.76	5.90	7.65	9.15	11.14	13.35	15.70	18.52	66	71	22.68
57	62	2.72	4.13	5.36	6.63	8.64	10.09	12.23	14.62	17.16	20.27	67	72	24.83
58	63	2.92	4.48	5.95	7.37	9.63	11.03	13.31	15.90	18.61	22.03	68	73	26.98
59	64	3.12	4.83	6.55	8.12	10.64	11.98	14.39	17.18	20.06	23.78	69	74	29.14
60	65	3.32	5.18	7.14	8.88	11.65	12.92	15.48	18.45	21.52	25.54	70	75	31.93
61	66	3.65	5.81	7.88	10.02	13.04	14.67	17.64	20.99	24.50	28.85	71	76	36.06
62	67	3.98	6.44	8.62	11.16	14.45	16.43	19.80	23.53	27.47	32.15	72	77	40.19
63	68	4.31	7.07	9.36	12.33	15.87	18.18	21.96	26.06	30.45	35.46	73	78	44.32
64	69	4.64	7.70	10.10	13.51	17.30	19.94	24.12	28.60	33.43	38.76	74	79	48.46

(Continued)

$500,000 and up (Continued)

Issue age M	F	1	2	3	4	5	6	7	8	9	10	Attained age M	F	Policy year 11 and thereafter
65	70	4.97	8.33	10.84	14.70	18.75	21.69	26.28	31.14	36.41	42.07	75	80	52.59
66		5.60	9.45	12.12	16.59	21.50	24.84	29.88	35.41	40.84	46.99	76	81	58.74
67		6.24	10.57	13.40	18.50	24.26	27.98	33.49	39.68	45.27	51.91	77	82	64.89
68		6.87	11.68	14.68	20.39	27.02	31.13	37.09	43.96	49.69	56.83	78	83	71.04
69		7.51	12.80	15.96	22.30	29.77	34.28	40.70	48.23	54.12	61.75	79	84	77.18
70		8.15	13.91	17.24	24.19	32.53	37.42	44.30	52.50	58.55	66.67	80	85	83.33
		—	—	—	—	—	—	—	—	—	—	81	86	92.13
		—	—	—	—	—	—	—	—	—	—	82	87	101.55
		—	—	—	—	—	—	—	—	—	—	83	88	111.78
		—	—	—	—	—	—	—	—	—	—	84	89	122.94
		—	—	—	—	—	—	—	—	—	—	85	90	135.23
		—	—	—	—	—	—	—	—	—	—	86	91	148.78
		—	—	—	—	—	—	—	—	—	—	87	92	163.48
		—	—	—	—	—	—	—	—	—	—	88	93	179.11
		—	—	—	—	—	—	—	—	—	—	89	94	195.46
		—	—	—	—	—	—	—	—	—	—	90		212.31
		—	—	—	—	—	—	—	—	—	—	91		229.80
		—	—	—	—	—	—	—	—	—	—	92		248.08
		—	—	—	—	—	—	—	—	—	—	93		266.93
		—	—	—	—	—	—	—	—	—	—	94		286.14

*The currently billed rates although not guaranteed after the fifth year cannot exceed the maximum rates.

F. Social Security Benefits

Approximate Monthly Social Security Benefits
Based on Your Earnings in 1990

Your age in 1991	Your family	$20,000	$30,000	$40,000	$50,000	$51,300 or more[1]
45	You	863	1,124	1,263	1,392	1,422
	You and spouse[2]	1,294	1,686	1,894	2,088	2,133
55	You	783	1,014	1,106	1,181	1,195
	You and spouse	1,174	1,521	1,659	1,771	1,792
65	You	725	926	982	1,021	1,022
	You and spouse	1,087	1,389	1,473	1,531	1,533

Note. The accuracy of these estimates depends on the pattern of your actual past earnings and on your earnings in the future.

[1] Use this column if you earn more than the maximum Social Security earnings base.

[2] Your spouse is assumed to be the same age as you. Your spouse may qualify for a higher retirement benefit based on his or her own work record.

Approximate Monthly Social Security Survivors Benefits Based on Deceased Worker's Earnings in 1990

Worker's age	Worker's family	$20,000	$30,000	$40,000	$50,000	$51,000 or more[1]
35	Spouse and 1 child[2]	1,090	1,430	1,610	1,784	1,790
	Spouse and 2 children[3]	1,338	1,668	1,879	2,082	2,088
	1 child only	545	725	805	892	895
	Spouse at age 60[4]	519	682	768	850	853
45	Spouse and 1 child[2]	1,082	1,422	1,566	1,668	1,670
	Spouse and 2 children[3]	1,330	1,658	1,828	1,945	1,948
	1 child only	541	711	783	834	835
	Spouse at age 60[4]	515	678	747	795	696
55	Spouse and 1 child[2]	1,086	1,402	1,496	1,560	1,562
	Spouse and 2 children[3]	1,334	1,635	1,745	1,820	1,822
	1 child only	543	701	748	780	781
	Spouse at age 60[4]	517	668	713	744	744

Source: Extracted from U.S. Department of Health and Human Services, Social Security Administration, SSA Publication No. 05-10024, January 1991.

Note: The accuracy of these estimates depends on the pattern of the worker's actual earnings in prior years.

[1]Use this column if the worker earned more than the maximum Social Security earnings base.

[2]Amounts shown also equal the benefits paid to two children, if no parent survives or surviving parent has substantial earnings.

[3]Equals the maximum family benefit.

[4]Amounts payable in 1991. Spouses turning 60 in the future would receive higher benefits.

G. State Provisions to Enact Living Wills

	Written declaration required	Oral declaration allowable	Declaration must be signed by two witnesses	Life support does not include nourishment	No presumption of intent if no declaration is made	Declarant must furnish copy to physician	Valid only for a certain length of time	Declaration may be signed by someone else if declarant can't
Alabama	×		×		×	×		×
Alaska	×		×		×	×		×
Arizona	×		×	×		×		
Arkansas	×		×					
California	×		×				×	
Colorado	×		×	×	×	×		×
Connecticut	×		×	×	×			
Delaware	×		×		×	×		×
Florida	×	×	×	×	×	×		×
Georgia	×		×	×	×			×
Hawaii	×		×	×	×	×		×
Idaho	×				×		×	
Illinois	×		×	×	×	×		
Iowa	×		×	×	×	×		×
Kansas	×		×	×	×	×		×
Kentucky	×		×			×		
Louisiana	×	×	×		×	×		

State	1	2	3	4	5	6	7
Maine	X		X		X		X
Maryland	X	X	X	X	X		X
Massachusetts*							
Michigan							
Minnesota					X		X
Mississippi	X	X			X		X
Missouri	X	X	X		X		X
Montana	X	X	X	X	X		X
Nebraska*							
Nevada							X
New Hampshire		X			X		X
New Jersey		X	X	X	X		X
New Mexico		X	X		X		X
New York*					X		X
North Carolina					X		X
North Dakota		X	X		X		X
Ohio		X	X	X	X		X
Oklahoma		X	X	X	X		X
Oregon				X	X		X
Pennsylvania*							
Rhode Island		X	X		X		X
South Carolina			X	X	X		X
South Dakota	X	X	X	X	X	X	X
Tennessee		X	X	X	X		X

(Continued)

	Written declaration required	Oral declaration allowable	Declaration must be signed by two witnesses	Life support does not include nourishment	No presumption of intent if no declaration is made	Declarant must furnish copy to physician	Valid only for a certain length of time	Declaration may be signed by someone else if declarant can't
Texas	×	×	×		×	×		
Utah	×		×		×	×		×
Vermont	×		×	×	×	×		
Virginia	×	×	×		×	×		
Washington	×		×					
West Virginia	×		×		×	×		×
Wisconsin	×		×	×	×	×		×
Wyoming	×		×	×	×			×
District of Columbia	×		×		×	×		×

*Legislation pending.

H. Sample Health Care Proxy

1. I, _____

   hereby appoint _____
   (name, home address, and telephone number)

   as my health care agent to make any and all health care decisions for me, except to the extent that I state otherwise. This proxy shall take effect when and if I become unable to make my own health care decisions.

2. Optional instructions: I direct my proxy to make health care decisions in accord with my wishes and limitations as stated below, or as she or he otherwise knows. (Attach additional pages if necessary).

   _____

   _____

   (Unless your agent knows your wishes about artificial nutrition and hydration [feeding tubes], your agent will not be allowed to make decisions about artificial nutrition and hydration.)

3. Name of substitute or fill-in proxy if the person I appoint above is unable, unwilling, or unavailable to act as my health care agent.

_____

(name, home address, and telephone number)

_____

4. Unless I revoke it, this proxy shall remain in effect indefinitely, or until the date or condition stated below. This proxy shall expire (specific date or conditions, if desired):

_____

5. Signature _____

   Address _____

   Date _____

   Statement by Witnesses (must be 18 or older)
   I declare that the person who signed this document is personally known to me and appears to be of sound mind and acting of his or her own free will. He or she signed (or asked another to sign for him or her) this document in my presence.

   Witness 1 _____

   Address _____

   Witness 2 _____

   Address _____

I. Sample Living Will

I, JOHN DOE, residing at [address] in the event that I become unable to make decisions regarding my medical care, make the following directions:

(1) My attending physician shall cease or withhold treatment that serves only to prolong the process of dying if I be in an incurable mental or physical condition without reasonable expectation of recovery. This instruction shall also apply if I am in a medically terminal condition, permanently unconscious or conscious but have irreversible brain damage and in my physician's opinion will never again be able to express my wishes.

(2) Any treatment to be administered to me shall be limited to measures to keep me free of pain and to make me comfortable during such period of incapacity.

(3) I do not wish the following treatment to be administered: (a) cardiac resuscitation, (b) mechanical respiration, or (c) tube feeding.

(4) [Insert any personal instructions you desire].

These instructions that I have set forth in this document shall not change unless I formally rescind this document and make a new writing.

Signed: _____ Dated: _____

Witness: _____

Address: _____ Dated: _____

Witness: _____

Address: _____ Dated: _____

J. States That Can Require Nonparents to Support a Child by Specific Law

	Support
Missouri	§568.040
Montana	§40-6-217
North Dakota	§14-09-09
Oklahoma	10§15
Utah	§78-45-4.1

K. Financial Disclosure Affidavit

FAMILY COURT OF THE STATE OF NEW YORK
COUNTY OF NASSAU

In the Matter of a Proceeding for
Support under Article 4 of the
Family Court Act

Index No.

_____

Petitioner,

—against—

_____

Respondent.

_____

STATE OF   )
)   ss.:
COUNTY OF   )

the (Petitioner) (Respondent) herein, being duly sworn, deposes and says that the following is an accurate statement of my net worth (assets of whatsoever kind and nature and wherever situated minus liabilities), statement of income from all sources and statement of assets transferred of whatsoever kind and nature and wherever situated:

That I reside at _____

I. INCOME
   (a) Employer (state if self-employed) _____
   (b) Employer's address _____
   (c) Social Security number _____
   (d) Number of Dependents Claimed   _____
   (e) Number of Members of Household   _____
   (f) Hours worked per week   _____
   (g) Weekly Gross Salary or Wages   _____
   (h) Weekly Deductions
       1. Social Security   _____
       2. New York State Tax   _____
       3. Federal Tax   _____
       4. Other Payroll
          Deductions   _____
          (specify)   _____
       5. Total Deduction   _____
   (i) Weekly Net Salary or Wages   _____
   (j) Income from other sources—(specify)   _____
       (For example: part-time job, tips, rents, _____
       pension, dividends, unemployment   _____
       insurance, disability, etc.)   _____
   (k) Total Gross Income last year   _____
   (l) Income of other Members of Household: (specify)
       1. Weekly Gross Salary or Wages   _____
       2. Weekly Net Salary or Wages   _____

II. ASSETS
   (a) Savings Account Balance   _____
       1. Name of Bank(s)   _____
          Account number   _____
   (b) Checking Account Balance   _____
       1. Name of Bank(s)   _____
          Account number

  (c) Automobile(s)
      1. Year and Make
      2. Value   _____
  (d) Residence Owned (address) _____
      1. Market Value   _____
      2. Mortgage Owed   _____
  (e) Other Real Estate Owned
      1. Market Value   _____
      2. Mortgage Owed   _____
  (f) Other Property (For example: stocks and bonds, trailer, boat, etc.)

_____ Value   _____
_____ Value   _____

LIST ALL ASSETS TRANSFERRED IN ANY MANNER DURING PRECEDING THREE YEARS, OR LENGTH OF MARRIAGE, WHICHEVER IS SHORTER:

Description of Property	To Whom Transferred	Date of Transfer	Value
_____	_____	_____	_____
_____	_____	_____	_____
_____	_____	_____	_____

III. EXPENSES (You may elect to list all expenses on a weekly basis or all expenses on a monthly basis; however, you must be consistent. If any items are paid on a monthly basis, divide by 4.3 to obtain weekly payment; if any items are paid on a weekly basis, multiply by 4.3 to obtain monthly payments)

                                            Amount

  (a) Rent or Mortgage Payment:
      House _____ Apt. _____
      Room _____   _____
  (b) Real Estate Taxes (if not included in mortgage)   _____

(c) Food:
   Self _____ Children _____ (include lunches, etc.) _____
(d) Utilities
   1. Gas   _____
   2. Electric   _____
   3. Telephone   _____
   4. Heating Fuel   _____
   5. Water and Garbage Removal   _____
   (e)   Clothing:
   Self _____ Children _____   _____
(f) Laundry and Dry Cleaning:
   Self _____ Children _____   _____
(g) Medical, Dental, and Medication:
   Self _____ Children _____   _____
(h) Insurance:
   Life _____ Auto _____ Fire _____   _____
(i) Other Insurance: (Health and Accident,
   Hospitalization) (if not deducted from pay)   _____
(j) Transportation:
   Carfare _____ Gas and Oil _____
   Auto Maintenance _____   _____
(k) Auto Payment:
   Total Balance due on loan _____   _____
(l) Union Dues (if not deducted from pay)   _____
(m) Tuition (specify) _____
(n) Other (For example: baby-sitters, recreation, etc.)
   (Specify) _____
         TOTAL (weekly) (monthly) EXPENSES   _____

IV. LIABILITIES, LOANS AND DEBTS, JUDGMENTS

                                                    Monthly
                                                    Payments
(a) Owed to whom _____   _____
   1. Purpose _____   _____
   2. Date incurred _____   _____
   3. Total Balance Due _____   _____

(b) Owed to whom _____ _____
   1. Purpose _____
   2. Date incurred _____
   3. Total Balance Due _____
(c) Owed to whom _____ _____
   1. Purpose _____
   2. Date incurred _____
   3. Total Balance Due _____
(d) Owed to whom _____ _____
   1. Purpose _____
   2. Date incurred _____
   3. Total Balance Due _____

TOTAL MONTHLY PAYMENTS _____

Other financial data that should be brought to attention of Court:

Do you own a safe deposit box?　Yes ( )　No ( )
Name of bank(s)

The foregoing statement has been carefully read by the undersigned who states that it is true and correct.

_____
(Petitioner)　　　(Respondent)

Sworn to before me this
   day of　　, 19　.

L. Eligibility for Medicare

If You Are 65 or Older

Most people 65 or older are eligible for Medicare hospital insurance based on their own—or their spouse's—employment. You are eligible at 65 if

1. you are getting Social Security or railroad retirement benefits or

2. you are not getting Social Security or railroad retirement benefits but you have worked long enough to be eligible for them or

3. you would be entitled to Social Security benefits based on your spouse's work record and your spouse is at least 62 (your spouse does not have to apply for benefits in order for you to be eligible based on your spouse's work) or

4. you have worked long enough for federal, state, or local government to be insured for Medicare.

If You Are under 65

Before age 65 you are eligible for Medicare hospital insurance if

1. you have been getting Social Security disability benefits for 24 months or

2. you have worked long enough in federal, state, or local government and you meet the requirements of the Social Security disability program.

If you receive a disability annuity from the railroad retirement board, you will be eligible for hospital insurance after you serve a waiting period (contact your railroad retirement office for further details).

Family Members Who Can Get Medicare

Under certain conditions, your spouse, divorced spouse, widow or widower, or a dependent parent may be eligible for hospital insurance when he or she turns 65, based on your work record.

Also, disabled widows and widowers under 65, disabled divorced widows or widowers under 65, and disabled children may be eligible for Medicare.

If You Have Kidney Failure

There are special rules for people with permanent kidney failure. Under these rules, you are eligible for hospital insurance at any age if you receive maintenance dialysis or a kidney transplant and

1. you are insured or are getting monthly benefits under Social Security or the railroad retirement system or

2. you have worked long enough in government to be insured for Medicare.

In addition, your spouse or child may be eligible for benefits, based on your work record, if she or he receives maintenance dialysis or a kidney transplant even if no one else in the family is getting Medicare.

M. Sample Retainer Letter

[law firm letterhead]

[client's name]
[client's address]

Dear [client's name]:

This letter will serve to confirm that you have retained this office to represent you with respect to certain marital difficulties existing between you and your [husband or wife].

You shall pay to us an advance retainer fee of $_____ . It is understood that this retainer shall be applied for your representation at the following rates: [senior partner's name], $_____ per hour; [junior partner's name], $_____ per hour; all associates, $_____ per hour.

In the event that our firm devotes more time than exceeds $_____ in charges for your representation, then you shall pay to the firm the sum of $_____ per hour as an additional fee for each hour that I devote to your matters, $_____ per hour

for [junior partner's name]'s time, or $_____ for associates'
time. You will be billed monthly for the additional fee as
incurred and you will be expected to make payments of any
monthly balance due upon receipt of a statement. If there is
any dispute concerning these additional fees, you will
communicate with this office during the month the statement is
rendered to review any time charges and/or to adjust any
errors in billing. Whether or not additional charges are made,
you will receive a monthly bill from the office indicating the
time remaining against the retainer fee paid.

It is understood that our retainer or overall fee does not include
out-of-pocket disbursements, which may include court costs,
service of process, photocopies, transcripts of examinations
before trial, the fees of expert witnesses and accountants and
the like, which will be billed directly to you as they are
incurred from month to month and which you agree to pay
upon receipt.

We have agreed that we will seek reimbursement from your
[husband or wife] of any attorneys' fees paid to this firm. Any
payment received, whether by court award or agreement, will
be applied to your overall bill.

You may feel free to discharge this firm at any time, with or
without cause, and have returned to you any unused portion
of the retainer paid to this office.

If the foregoing meets with your approval, would you kindly
affix your consent to the foot of this letter.

We look forward to serving you.

Very truly yours,
[full name of firm]

By: _____
[Senior partner's name]

ABC:de

The terms of the foregoing are hereby consented to:

_____
[Client's name]

Bibliography

Divorce

Ahrons, Constance R., *Divorced Families: A Multidisciplinary Developmental View*, Norton, New York, 1987.

Andrews, Stephen Pearl, *Love, Marriage and Divorce and the Sovereignty of the Individual*, Source Book Press, New York, 1972.

Arendell, Terry, *Mothers and Divorce: Legal, Economic and Social Dilemmas*, University of California Press. Berkeley, CA, 1986.

Atkin, Edith Lesser, *Divorced Fathers: Family Relationships*, Vanguard Press, New York, 1976.

Blume, Judy, *It's Not the End of the World*, Bantam Pathfinder Editions, Toronto, 1976.

Cantor, Donald J., *Escape from Marriage: How to Solve the Problems of Divorce*, Morrow, New York, 1971.

Goode, William Josiah, *After Divorce*, Free Press, Glencoe, IL, 1956.

Goode, William Josiah, *Women in Divorce*, Greenwood Press, Westport, CT, 1978.

Jacobson, Gerald F., *The Multiple Crises of Marital Separation and Divorce*, Grune & Stratton, New York, 1983.

Kressel, Kenneth, *The Process of Divorce: How Professionals and Couples Negotiate Settlements*, Basic Books, New York, 1985.

Bereavement

Barrentine, Faith N., *Bereavement: The Relationship of the Acuteness of Grief, Treatment Preferences and Stress*, Hofstra University Press, New York, 1986.

Bowlby, John, *Attachment and Loss*, Institute of Psycho-Analysis, Hogarth, London, 1980.

Bowling, Ann, *Life After Death: A Study of the Elderly Widowed*, Methuen, New York, 1982.

Doyle, Polly, *Grief Counseling and Sudden Death: A Manual and Guide*, Thomas, Springfield, IL, 1980

Glick, Ira Oscar, *The First Year of Bereavement*, Wiley, New York, 1974.

Johnson, Stephen M., *First Person Singular: Living the Good Life Alone*, Lippincott, Philadelphia, 1977.

Kalish, Richard A., *Caring Relationships: The Dying and the Bereaved*, Baywood, Farmingdale, NY, 1980.

Lukeman, Brenda, *Embarkations: A Guide to Dealing with Death and Parting*, Prentice-Hall, Englewood Cliffs, NJ, 1982.

Moriarty, David M., *The Loss of Loved Ones: The Effects of a Death in the Family*, Warren H. Green, St. Louis, MO, 1983.

Pincus, Lily, *Death and the Family: The Importance of Mourning*, Pantheon Books, New York, 1975.

Rando, Therese A., *Grieving: How to Go on Living When Someone You Love Dies*, Lexington Books, Lexington, MA, 1988.

Schneider, John, *Stress, Loss and Grief: Understanding Their Origins and Growth Potential*, University Park Press, Baltimore, 1984.

Schoenberg, Bernard, *Bereavement: Its Psychological Aspects*, Columbia University Press, New York, 1975.

Stroebe, Wolfgang, *Bereavement and Health: The Psychological and Physical Consequences of Parting*, Cambridge University Press, New York, 1987.

Homosexuality

Boggan, E. Carrington, *The Rights of Gay People: The Basic ACLU Guide to a Gay Person's Rights*, Discus Books, New York, 1985.

Clunis, D. MeriLee and Dorsey Green, G., *Lesbian Couples*, Seal Press, Seattle, WA, 1988.

Dynes, Wayne R., *Homosexuality: A Research Guide*, Garland, New York, 1987.

Gibson, Gifford Guy, with the colloration of Mary Jo Risher, *By Her Own Admission: A Lesbian Mother's Right to Keep Her Son*, Doubleday, Garden City, NY, 1977.

Mendola, Mary, *The Mendola Report: A New Look at Gay Couples*, Crown, New York, 1980.

Mitchell, Roger S., *Gays/Justice: A Study of Ethics, Society, and Law*, Columbia University Press, New York, 1988.

Mitchell, Roger S., *The Homosexual and the Law*, Arco Press, New York, 1969.

Parker, William, *Homosexuality: A Selective Bibliography of Over 3,000 Items*, Scarecrow Press, Metuchen, NJ, 1971.

Schulenberg, Joy A., *Gay Parenting*, Anchor Press/Doubleday, Garden City, NY, 1985.

Weinberg, Martin S., *Homosexuality: An Annotated Bibliography*, Harper & Row, New York, 1972.

Living Together

Danziger, Carl, *Unmarried Heterosexual Cohabitation*, R. & E. Research Associates, San Francisco, 1978.

Freeman, Michael D. A., *Cohabitation Without Marriage: An Essay in Law and Social Policy*, Aldershot, Hants., England: Gower, 1983.

Greenfader, Hal, *Living Together and Loving Every (Other) Minute of It: A Guide to Successful Cohabitation*, Roundtable, New York, 1986.

Hirsch, Barbara B., *Living Together: A Guide to the Law for Unmarried Couples*, Houghton Mifflin, Boston, 1976.

Kiley, Dan, *Living Together, Feeling Alone: Healing Your Hidden Loneliness*, Prentice-Hall, 1989.

Simons, Joseph, *Living Together: Communication in the Unmarried Relationship*, Nelson-Hall, Chicago, 1978.

Stinett, Nick and Birdson, Craig Wayne, *The Family and Alternative Life Styles*, Nelson Hall, Chicago, 1978.

Weitzman, Lenore J., *The Marriage Contract: Spouses, Lovers and the Law*, Free Press, NY, 1981.

Senior Citizens

Brown, Robert N., *The Rights of Older Persons*, Southern Illinois University Press, Carbondale, IL, 1989.

Chandler, Edna W., *Lifestyles for the Aging*, Elsevier-Nelson Books, New York, 1980.

Myers, Teresa Schwab, *How to Keep Control of Your Life After 60: A Guide for Your Legal, Medical and Financial Well-Being*, Lexington Books, Lexington, MA, 1989.

Watts, Tim, *Legal Rights of Older Americans: A Selected Bibliography*, Vance Bibliographies, Monticello, IL, 1988.

Index